Acknowledgments

Someone once said: "By the time a book, any book, gets to its third or fourth edition, it becomes a classic." I wonder about this, and I remain in debt to all those who assisted me in getting this book to its fourth edition. If it is a classic, it is because of them.

Acknowledgments to the Third Edition

I am grateful for Gourmet America President Ron Johnson's levelheaded and healthy enthusiasm about the specialty food trade. His observations have balanced well with some of the highly entrepreneurial processes we see among the new-to-market food processors. I am indebted also to the editors of *New Product News* for their insights into specialty food trends, and to my elder son, Tully, for his assistance in surfing the Internet to find and confirm extensive appendix information (and, to "cover the bases," hello to my younger son, Colin).

Acknowledgments to the Second Edition

In addition to the good souls listed on the next page, I acknowledge gladly the advice and valuable counsel I received from Karen Cantor, the driving spirit and publisher of *Food Entrepreneur* magazine, and the altogether exhaustive reference-building by my wife, Patricia Teagle.

Acknowledgments to the First Edition

First and foremost, I am grateful to my wife, Patricia Teagle, for her unending good humor and editorial counsel. Many thanks also to my colleagues in the specialty food business, particularly Ron Johnson, of Gourmet America, Inc., who provided important viewpoints in defining how specialty food marketing works; Elliot Johnson, of Mark T. Wendell Co., for the precision with which he assesses industry trends; Liz and Nick Thomas, of Chalif, Inc., who provided comprehensive and helpful reviews of the first draft of this guide; Barry Raskin, a specialty food broker largely responsible for guiding me during my early education in this field; Ernie Fisher, an international food consultant who brought a "real world" perspective to examining this industry; and to Lee Robinson, who, as President of The Ruffled Truffle, provided me the opportunity to learn about the gift segment of the specialty food business.

I am grateful, further, to Page Pratt, cofounder of Food Marketing International, with whom I shared many a rewarding marketing moment, and to my editor, Jean Kerr, whose unflappable disposition eased the burden of perfecting this book.

Finally, I would like to acknowledge my late colleague, classmate, and best friend, Rolff Johansen, for bringing civility and wit to our hectic earlier years in specialty food marketing.

How to Use This Guide

From Kitchen to Market helps you learn about marketing food, a process that generally entails everything from product concept to after-sales service. This edition addresses important, and developing, aspects of specialty food marketing not addressed in previous editions, and provides up-to-date information in the Appendixes.

In addition to packaging, labeling, pricing, storage, and shipping, the guide tells you how to advertise, promote, and sell your product. Flowcharts describe how to process the orders you generate. Major sections include "Guidelines for Success" that you may use as you prepare to take your product to market. New sections deal with how to exploit overseas opportunities, the impact of technology (the Internet), and how to grow your enterprise. In other words: How to professionalize your business.

"Cases in Point" are used throughout the book to highlight so-called "real-world" experiences. In this edition, those Cases in Point identify the successes—and failures—of many winners of Outstanding Product Awards, the purpose being to show you that it takes more than an award to ensure your success.

Although *From Kitchen to Market* is designed for small cottage industries new to the food business, it will also be of significant value to large food processors and overseas food companies interested in learning how the U.S. specialty food trade functions.

Specialty food marketing is addressed in a straightforward, logical manner. It begins with introductory comments, followed by a general discussion of the industry. It proceeds to discuss the issues relevant to getting your product ready to market, and to taking your product to market. The appendixes offer information about additional sources of assistance, along with useful data regarding trade shows, trade journals, professional associations, etc.

Other helpful resources from Dearborn Trade include *The Business Planning Guide: Creating a Plan for Success in Your Own Business* (8th edition by David H. Bangs available in CD-ROM format from Dearborn Multimedia). *The Business Planning Guide* leads business owners through the most important step in founding a new business: Putting together a complete and effective business plan and financing proposal.

You will probably not need this guide if your name is Paul Newman or Emeril Lagasse. Deep pockets can make the difference between success or failure for a high-quality product. However, if, like the rest of us, you have neither the funding level to support a major marketing effort, nor the clout to see it through, then this guide is for you.

Before you begin: Do you want your food operation to be a full time occupation or a sideline business?

One of the following scenarios may describe your circumstances, and could help you respond to the important issue of just how involved you would like to become in the business. All four of these scenarios have been played out, with varying degrees of success, in the gourmet food industry.

Scenario One

You have just returned from another successful holiday church bazaar where you sold out your homemade supply of apple-cranberry chutney. Your chutney is based on a family recipe handed down for generations. Your friends and neighbors urge you to sell your chutney to Bloomingdale's, where they think it will be a great hit. You think it's a wonderful idea, but you haven't the foggiest idea of where to begin.

In this scenario, the entrepreneur has to decide, after significant investigation, whether to continue in the "sideline" mode or to take the risk of turning the operation into a full-time business.

On the one hand, the owner has a product that has been tested, in a fashion, with positive reactions from customers, friends, and neighbors. There is reason to believe that success, at least initially, might be achieved with a reasonable expectation of profit. On the other hand, what is the required level of funding available for the venture? If the owner has an outside source of income, then the venture may be undertaken. Otherwise, the possibilities for negative cash flow (more money going out than coming in) are quite probable.

Scenario Two

Your gourmet food store is doing a lot of business. You are especially pleased with the success of your prepared foods section, one item of which is your home-baked, seasoned breadsticks.

> ### CASE IN POINT
>
> You will need more than an Outstanding Product Award to succeed.
>
> For example, even though the following firms won distinguished awards for their products, we were unable to locate them for an update on their situation.
>
> ✧ City Bites NASFT Outstanding Hors d'oeuvres Component for Broccoli Cheddar Coquilles. One review stated, "They're so original, yet I can think of lots of uses for them."
>
> ✧ Clark's Gourmet Coffee won the NASFT Outstanding Beverage for their coffee from Costa Rica.
>
> ✧ Flinko, Inc., winner of the NASFT Outstanding Beverage for Pommac, a Swedish beverage composed of the extracts of 25 all-natural fruits.

You note that there seems to be a growing interest in this product from a broad segment of your customer base. You wonder if it would be possible to sell the breadsticks to a wider audience in other markets in your region. Where to begin?

If the second scenario fits, then your food marketing venture could be supported by revenues from the existing retail operation. This makes market entry more attractive because many initial costs of operation could be absorbed by the retail store sales of other products. Nevertheless, you will have to devote substantial time to developing markets for the breadsticks, which will take away from time spent in the store. If this can be accommodated, then a full-time sales and marketing operation can be adopted.

Scenario Three

You have recently taken over a small, local, chocolate manufacturing concern. Until now, revenues have come from bulk sales to walk-in and mail-order customers. You think there are substantial opportunities for developing a retail packaged version, and you want to begin distributing it to stores all over the country. How do you proceed?

Scenario three offers some of the same challenges as scenario two. Both require substantial time at the existing business. Scenario three, however, offers a chance to expand an existing base of sales to customers located outside of the local area. It also provides an existing source of revenue (from retail packaged sales) on which to base some of the expansion costs. It would appear, then, that turning the chocolate operation into a full-time sales and marketing operation might be an appropriate alternative.

Scenario Four

Your family and friends love your honey-and-pecan mustard. You have been very successful in selling at the local Women's

Exchange, and at area school holiday fairs. You also ran an ad in a slick "upscale" magazine that cost you a fortune, but produced results in mail-order sales sufficient to cover the cost. Your life is too busy to contemplate going into the gourmet food business full-time. What do you need to know about this business in order to make a little money on the side?

The challenge in scenario four is to transform your hobby into a sideline business. You can take your talent, your recipes, your promotional genius, and your money, and have your product produced, packaged, warehoused, and marketed by another company. You will definitely need the supporting funds and the knowledge of how gourmet food marketing works.

Your situation may differ from these scenarios, but the opportunity to turn your food ideas into an endeavor for financial independence prevails. The gourmet food business is one way of obtaining a significant shot at achieving success and acquiring wealth.

Now that you are armed with a sense of which option best applies to your situation, read on to learn how to take the next step in the exciting and challenging world of gourmet food marketing.

A Note about the Illustrations

Product appearance is one of the most important components of success in the specialty food industry. In order to give you a flavor of this, and to stimulate your imagination, I have included a representative sampling of graphics used in a variety of specialty food labels, packages, and company logos. These have been placed throughout the book, in no particular order.

The illustrations selected were among those requested from more than 100 companies whose products have been exhibited in various National Association for the Specialty Food Trade Shows over the past ten years.

A number of these are designed for reproduction in color, but, because of cost constraints, they have been shown here in black-and-white. Many of them are effective attention-getters with the use of only two colors. The objective is to emphasize the importance of graphics, regardless of color, in label, package, and logo design.

The examples in this book are those deemed typical, both good and, perhaps, not so good for this industry. You be the judge. And please note that use of them does not constitute an endorsement.

Introduction

Retail sales of all specialty foods are generating revenues of almost $39 billion a year, and averaging annual growth of more than 7 percent. To some, this means great opportunity. To others, it represents a formidable challenge.

Your ability to grab a slice of this pie, and make your mark, establish your independence, achieve success, and acquire wealth will depend on how effectively you prepare—and prepare you must!

How to prepare for the opportunities and challenges of taking your food products to the appropriate store shelves is the subject of this guide. You need not know the basics of small business operations just yet. For now, success will depend on your personal and business vision, drive, talent, and the amount of capital you can raise.

Let's put the latter into perspective: The average cost of getting national grocery store shelf exposure for a new product by a branded manufacturer is $5.1 million.[1]

---

[1] This figure comes from a 1991 study by a Joint Industry Task Force consisting of the Grocery Manufacturers of America, Food Marketing Institute, National American Wholesale Grocers Association, National Association of Chain Drug Stores, National Food Brokers Association, and National Grocers Association.

> "You'll need more than a dream to carry you across the starting line," says Liz Thomas, former Executive Vice President, Chalif, Inc. (producers and marketers of specialty food condiments).

Still reading? Take heart, there is a proven alternative. It is the specialty food industry that has become the proven vehicle for entry-level food distribution in the United States. Different market segments and new products can be tested in the specialty food industry without the initial investment required of the major food producers. The secret has to do with superior execution of often ordinary ideas.

Having considered that, you must pay heed to a phenomenon called "slotting fees" (see Chapter Three for more details). The slotting fee has drastically altered the complexion of specialty food marketing in this country. The slotting fee is, for all intents and purposes, what used to be called "payola." It is upfront money paid to the chain or distributor in order to have your product carried. It severely limits consumer choice and producer competition. Unless your marketing plan is just plain brilliantly and flawlessly executed, it means that new and alternative distribution must be explored. It will have an impact on the role of the Internet.

How Much Will It Cost You?

Depending on your approach, you can expect to incur minimum start-up costs of approximately $40,000 to $100,000—and more for each of the first three to five years. This includes production, packaging, labeling, advertising, and promotion of one product. It does NOT include the cost of success. Many firms that won Outstanding Product Awards were ill-prepared for the next move. Not all of them succeeded in profiting from their good fortune. The estimated cost also is based on the assumption that you will be doing a lot of the legwork. (Example: You do all the administrative, invoicing, clerical paperwork, etc., and you make most of the sales calls.)

Our purpose is to explore the inner workings of *niche* marketing. Niche marketing entails finding the best combination of product packaging, pricing, positioning, and promotion that will encourage the consumer to purchase a product not otherwise offered by the major suppliers. Imagination is a key ingredient, but adequate funding is essential.

In addition to the above, a successful undertaking requires you to center your activities on your competitive strengths, control your costs, know your competition, and learn how to professionally manage the entire process effectively. As with most new food entrepreneurs, you will have to learn to deal with finding resources, motivating employees, developing a compelling vision, and even handling family issues.

We are not addressing what you can do with a several-million-dollar budget. Rather, this guide deals with the essence of entrepreneurship. There is a lot of "ready, fire, aim" in the gourmet food marketing process that can lead to occassional success and frequent failure. This guide helps you accomplish most of the "aiming" during the "ready" phase.

Specialty food marketing requires creative responses. As soon as you adopt a successful marketing strategy, you may learn of another entrepreneur who is just as successful, but who has implemented an entirely different marketing scheme!

✧   ✧   ✧

The 1970s: "The specialty food business is an odd little segment of the industry that is better left to people who understand it fully, who deeply care about it, and who are willing to have a less predictable bottom line than most corporations are willing to tolerate," says Ted Koryn, specialty food marketing professional, as quoted in *Fortune* magazine, October 1978.

The 2000s: "Specialty food has come a long way from its easy-to-understand description of . . . exotic, ethnic, imported, unusual, and sold in a department or gourmet store. Today, it is much more complex. Thousands of new domestically produced specialty items . . . fit in established and high-volume product categories [are] sold in all types of retail formats."

—John Roberts, President, National Association
for the Specialty Food Trade (NASFT)

CHAPTER ONE

Understanding the Food Industry

This chapter defines industry terms, examines the primary sales territories and segments of the market, and describes transition products—those that make the transition from gourmet to grocery (the "big time")—along with a discussion of a typical gourmet retail store operation.

Defining the Territory

The food industry, in general, and the specialty food industry, in particular, have yet to sanction specific guidelines for the use of many industry terms. As a result, the process of tracking and understanding the myriad elements of specialty food sales and marketing activity has yielded additional challenges to those trying to understand the industry. Because few industry terms have been standardized, here is a list of terms as defined in this book.

- ❖ *Gourmet*. This guide uses the term "gourmet" sparingly, and as a synonym for "specialty."
- ❖ *Specialty food*. The National Association for the Specialty Food Trade has adopted the following description of specialty foods:

1

Specialty food products . . . shall mean: foods, beverages, or confections meant for human use that are of the highest grade, style, and/or quality in their category. Their specialty nature derives from a combination of some or all of the following qualities: their uniqueness, exotic origin, particular processing, design, limited supply, unusual application or use, extraordinary packaging, or channel of distribution, the common denominator of which is their unusually high quality.

Specialty food is the traditionally accepted term meaning food products that fit the following criteria:

❖ *High quality*. Above all, the specialty food product must be of the highest quality, in both content and form. As a rule, only the best ingredients are used, whether the product is a premium ice cream or a mustard with peppercorns. Specialty food products sold at retail must also look the part—a high price demands that the product appear to be fancy and high-tone.

❖ *High price*. Most specialty foods are priced higher than staple food products because of costly ingredients and labor used in their preparation. Others are high in cost because of high demand and limited supply. Still others are sold at high prices because of the low turnover they generate in retail stores (the longer they remain on the shelf, the more they cost the retailer).

❖ *Limited availability*. Many specialty foods have appeal because they are not generally available. Such foods often gain a cult status—fresh caviar is an example—in that they offer the consumer a cachet not offered by products sold everywhere.

❖ *Imported or unique*. Imported specialty foods no longer maintain a strong hold on the market. Many high-quality products are now produced in this country and retain the "imported" distinction that first brought them to U.S. consumers' attention.

✧ *Food producer/processor*. The producer is usually the grower, and the processor is the one who adds value by processing the raw commodity into a table-ready food product.

✧ *Food broker*. A commissioned sales representative, usually with broad experience in the food industry, who generally calls mostly on distributors and large retail chains.

✧ *Specialty food distributor*. A company that buys in volume, for its own account, and sells to retailers (and to other distributors).

✧ *Store-door delivery*. Delivery made to stores by distributors.

✧ *Direct store distributor*. A distributor who performs many of the same services as a jobber (described in this section).

✧ *Wholesaler*. Companies that contract with, for example, a chain supermarket to warehouse and deliver a product that has been sold by the food producer to the supermarket. Wholesalers usually buy the product only when the producer has sold it to the supermarket chain. It is highly unlikely that you will have to deal with wholesalers because most of them are not equipped to handle the very detailed nature of specialty food merchandising.

✧ *Rack jobbers*. These are the people you see in supermarkets stocking shelves (they are the ones with the suits and ties, as opposed to supermarket employees). They price the incoming merchandise with price stickers (in those states where this is still required), fix shelf labels, follow schematic diagrams approved by the store, remove damaged and returned merchandise, and stock and dust the shelves.

✧ *Customers*. Retailers and distributors.

✧ *Consumers*. "Our reason for existing."

Identifying Your Primary Markets

Sales of specialty foods tend to be concentrated in the more affluent market areas, both in the United States and abroad because of the relatively high retail prices involved. There are about 40 primary U.S. trade areas of this type, and the majority of your prospective clients will fall within them (see Figure 1.1).

FIGURE 1.1: Primary U.S. Specialty Food Markets

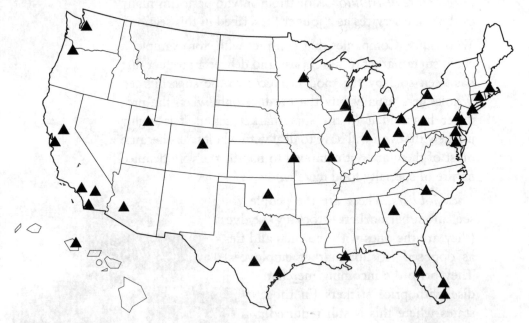

This map of primary U.S. specialty food markets provides a visual representation that will assist you in directing your marketing efforts. Note that entire states can be virtually ignored during your initial introductory efforts.

A variety of different retail outlets have the potential to handle specialty food products. So-called "gourmet shops" are the most obvious, but there are also cheese shops, delicatessens, gift stores, and, in increasing numbers, supermarkets and department stores. Supermarkets in the Midwest and Southwest tend to play a stronger role in the specialty food trade than have supermarkets in other parts of the country. Their imported, ethnic, or specialty foods sections are often quite large and offer a diverse selection of items. As a corollary, gourmet shops are fewer in that region.

Many more supermarkets, especially independent chains, in all major trading areas have taken on so-called gourmet products. Over the past 20 years, some of the nation's largest supermarket chains, such as Safeway (including Von's), Kroger (including Ralph's, King Soopers, City Market, Dillon's, Gerbes, Owen's, Smith's, QFC, and Fry's), and Giant Foods (now owned by Royal Ahold) have invested significantly in expanding their shelf space to carry specialty foods. Von's, and Giant have opened separate specialty food stores. Giant is called Someplace Special (in Northern Virginia), and Von's is called Von's Pavilions. Each offers a mix of high-quality staples, "picture perfect" fresh produce, frozen foods, and specialty items. Another example is Busch's, a 12-store supermarket chain in Michigan, which owns and manages specialty food stores called Vic's World Class Markets. The industry is watching these ventures with an eye to adopting new directions in distributing specialty foods.

There are approximately 155,000 food stores in the United States, and only 26,000 of them can be considered prime prospects for specialty food products. This figure results from careful, conservative paring down of the raw data presented in business directories. The total of prime prospects is composed

> **CASE IN POINT**
>
> *Dave's Gourmet—Started in 1993, Dave's sold nearly seven million bottles of sauce in more than 4,000 retail outlets, including supermarket chains. This is an example of a "transition product." Dave's also received eight NASFT awards, and numerous other honors including being named "Hottest Sauce" by Fancy Food magazine. Owner Dave Hirschkop started with less than $10,000 and defines his success as: "Full-time selling product, and making a good living at it."*

of approximately 4,800 gourmet shops, 7,300 cheese shops and health food stores, 7,500 delicatessens, and 6,400 chain supermarket outlets, warehouse clubs, gift shops, and major department stores. In 2003 sales of specialty food at retail (all stores) amounted to more than $22 billion, of which specialty-food retail stores accounted for more than $16 billion.

It would be unlikely for you to reach all these prime prospects without national distribution capability, either on your own or through a major specialty food distributor. In view of the "upscale" nature of specialty-food product lines, primary marketing targets can be identified by using weighted rankings of *The New Yorker* magazine's Selected Marketing System. This identifies and ranks markets for quality, premium-priced products, rather than simply ranking markets by total population and income data.

The 40 primary trade areas listed in Figure 1.2 are the most important United States markets for quality merchandise.

FIGURE 1.2: Primary Trade Areas (in order of primacy)

New York	San Diego	Hartford
Los Angeles	Denver	New Orleans
Chicago	Baltimore	Sacramento
San Francisco	Atlanta	Columbus
Detroit	Pittsburgh	Indianapolis
Washington, D.C.	St. Louis	Oklahoma City
Philadelphia	Phoenix	San Antonio
Houston	Milwaukee	Salt Lake City
Boston	Portland	Charlotte
Miami/Fort Lauderdale	Kansas City	Allentown/Bethlehem
Dallas/Fort Worth	Riverside/San Bernadino	Buffalo
Seattle-Tacoma	Cincinnati	West Palm Beach
Cleveland-Akron	Honolulu	
Minneapolis-St. Paul	Tampa/St. Petersburg	

About 15,000 of the 25,000 prime prospects are located in these areas. The listing is an accurate reflection of the trade in general. Although a strictly specialty-food ranking would include all of those listed, the order in which they are listed would be somewhat different.

Segmenting Your Markets

Our identification of geographic/demographic markets for specialty food represents one of the first elements of the marketing process. Matters of consumer preference, ethnic concentration, population movement, taste and historical trends further segment these markets.

> **CASE IN POINT**
>
> *Terra Chips—1992 Outstanding Snack Food (a mix of root vegetable chips). Started by Dana Sinkler and Alex Dzieduszycki in 1990, Terra pioneered new varieties of potato and vegetable chips that carved a new niche in the natural snacks market. Terra chips was acquired in 1998 by The Hain Celestial Group.*

An overall understanding of these differing market segments and varying distribution requirements will be helpful to you as you plan your marketing and distribution strategy.

To illustrate, hot and spicy foods have long been accepted in the Southwest, and they have gained a strong foothold in New England markets as well. In Southern California, everybody eats outdoors where the barbecue and barbecue products reign! And it is difficult to introduce a new product to Floridians in the summer when specialty food business tends to fall off drastically.

Health Food Stores

The mounting importance of health food stores should be taken into account. Annual sales of natural and health food products are approximately $10 billion. Distribution channels for health

foods differ in some cases. Some distributors carry only health food lines, while others service only the more upscale channels of distribution (e.g., fancy gourmet food stores). There are profitable opportunities to be explored in this segment of the industry if your product meets its criteria.

The Gift Trade

The gift trade is also playing a greater part in specialty food marketing, partly due to the widespread use of slotting fees in regular food-distribution channels. There are more than 70,000 gift or gift-type stores in the entire country. This figure includes both upscale and standard outlets. As with health food stores, distribution channels can differ in that segment. Food reps (brokers) who maintain a showroom, attend and exhibit at gift shows, and call extensively on retail accounts serve much of the gift trade. Such brokers are paid a 15 percent commission of the invoice value of all sales to retailers made in accordance with the broker contract.

Military Exchanges

If you can make the right connection, the Army and Air Force Exchange System, the Navy Exchange, and the commissaries (military supermarkets) offer interesting possibilities for substantial sales. These stores serve military families located in many parts of the world. Such families have many of the same needs and wants as do families in any of the major continental U.S. trade areas. I have seen a wide assortment of fancy and specialty foods available at these outlets.

Ethnic Foods

For our purposes, ethnic foods means retail and food-service packaged food products that can be described generally as either Italian, Hispanic, Kosher, Asian, or Greek. A variation of this is the so-called "fusion" style. A key fusion-style trend exists in Asian and Pan-Asian foods wherein one might encounter dishes made of combined food and flavor types from Thailand, Japan, China, Vietnam, and Indonesia.

Italian-style foods continue to comprise one of the largest categories, and Italian ingredients have joined the staples of our everyday cuisine. Because of this, there is an enormous market for Italian foods. But, is there room for another olive oil?

The United States is said to be the fifth largest Spanish-speaking country in the world. Our Hispanic population exceeds 37 million and is the fastest-growing consumer market. The best products for growth will be staples advertised and promoted in Spanish by the major food producer/processors. Your opportunity will lie in the growing interest in Hispanic and Hispanic-style foods and cooking.

The Kosher food market exceeds $7 million, and is expected to continue its 10 percent-plus annual growth. The broad appeal of Kosher foods beyond that which is mandated by Jewish dietary practice is based on the quality associated with such foods. More than 75 percent of Kosher food consumers are non-Jewish. In order to be certified Kosher, a food product must pass an exacting inspection by an authorized rabbinical agency.

American consumer interest in health and fitness has spurred growth of foods that are unprocessed and fresh. This includes a great number of Asian foods. The market for this category exceeds $62 billion at retail. Among the leading Asian food products are vegetables, sauces, and dry mixes. Increasing home use of stir-fry is also encouraging Asian food consumption. Today, once

Timing Is Everything?

NatureStar Foods—1993 Outstanding Snack Food Award for their Plocky's 100 percent Natural Popcorn with real, fresh, aged white cheddar cheese. The challenge? The product had what some thought were too many grams of fat, a fact that was pointed out in certain media during the no-fat, low-fat, craze. The company was forced to take its product off the shelves and has since developed a successful line of potato sticks, sweet potato sticks, and sweet potato nut mixes. NatureStar's founder offers the suggestion that a "from market to kitchen" approach is more realistic because it focuses on the market requirements, not the product features.

exotic foods such as ginger root, Asian vegetables, tempura sauce, and bean sprouts are readily available.

Greek foods, also referred to as "Mediterranean" cuisine, are growing in popularity because of their traditional reliance on freshness. Some examples include olive oil, cheese, honey, dressings, and baked goods.

Your opportunity with the ethnic food category may be twofold: (1) produce and market traditional ethnic food products not otherwise available to consumers, and/or (2) market new "ethnic-style" products to both ethnic and "nonethnic" consumers.

Taking Advantage of Export Markets

The following quotation comes from a guide to commercial food production: "The last thing you should consider . . . is the potential for overseas marketing of your product." That kind of thinking shows why the United States has failed so miserably in capturing profitable food marketing opportunities overseas. Aside from the product-oriented nature of U.S. food marketing, this kind of narrow minded approach simply opens the door to foreign competition.

Instead of just looking in your own backyard, try, instead, to identify the world markets where your product would have the greatest comparative advantage. It may be that, indeed, your region in the States is the best place for you to start. There are, however, lots of reasons to consider nontraditional markets. There is a commonality in food marketing, regardless of the market. Despite language and taste differences, you can profit from exploring markets abroad. Ask your State Department of Agriculture and the U.S. Foreign Agricultural

Service for information about current promotional support. This includes trade shows and other overseas market development services.

Initially, your primary overseas markets will be the major trade areas in Canada, Europe, and Japan, with potential in Latin America and the Middle East. (See Chapter Three: Exporting.)

Going for the Big Win with Transition Products

Many specialty food producers are attracted to the idea that their product will capture public imagination and sell like crazy. They envision the day when everyone will beat a path to their doors, demanding their products! When, and if, this happens (and it can happen), the product will reach a transition stage from up-market specialty food distribution to down-market grocery trade.

In some markets, your product will continue to be merchandised as a specialty item, while in others, it will be sold solely on grocery/supermarket shelves. Recent examples of transition products include Dave's Gourmet Sauces, Perrier water, Grey Poupon mustard, Red Oval Stoned Wheat Thins, Cadbury chocolate bars, and Häagen-Dazs ice cream.

Understanding Gourmet Store Concerns

Your understanding of how your product is merchandised (placed before the consumer in the retail store) will influence the direction of all

> **CASE IN POINT**
>
> *On the costs, perils, and pitfalls of specialty food marketing, Barbara Henry, President of Bogland (producers of a full line of Cranberry-based chutney, mustard, grill sauce, vinaigrette, marmalade, and blueberry preserves) has this to say: "Before you begin, don't quit your day job, don't quit your night job. Think about it . . . think about it again . . . then, wait six months and think about it once more." Sound advice from an entrepreneur whose company started selling BJ's Colonial mustard in 1987 and now has a full line of gourmet condiments with a growing national distribution.*

FIGURE 1.3: Specialty Food Store Classifications

Type	Classification
Upscale deli	Delicatessen foods and associated condiments.
Specialty	Gourmet foods, sometimes with specific upscale product lines (coffee, for example).
Cheese	All kinds of cheese and related items.
Gift	Gift baskets.
Housewares	Gourmet pots and pans and other cookware, with some impulse and companion food items.
Department	Upscale, with heavy emphasis on cookware and some confectionery. (Demonstrations play a key role in cookware sales.)
General	Combination of all of the above, including some traditional staples.

your marketing efforts. Figure 1.3 shows some of the types of classifications of specialty food stores. Having some knowledge of how a typical retail gourmet food store operates will enable you to work more effectively with your distributors, brokers, and with the store manager. Figure 1.4 illustrates the product mix an average store may carry.

CASE IN POINT

Mr. and Mrs. "T" Bloody Mary Mix—introduced by Taylor Foods in 1960. A big hit, now the brand is owned by Mott's (a U.S. division of Cadbury Schweppes) and marketed everywhere. This is a successful example of a "transition" product.

Product selection will depend on store type and on a variety of demographic conditions. In the past, certain food products have been in higher demand in certain regions. If you were selling your version of a hot salsa, you probably had better luck by introducing it to New England fancy-food stores than to those in the Southwest, where a "million" such products have been well established in grocery distribution. Today, almost any food type is available in

FIGURE 1.4: Product Mix in a Gourmet Store

The average gourmet store generally sells a mix of products along the following lines:

Product Line	Approximate Percentage of Sales
Condiments	35
Beverages (including bottled water)	5
Coffee and tea	5
Cheese	5
Pâtés and meats	10
Prepared foods	20
Confection	10
Other	10
	100%

each of the 40 primary trade areas, though one still finds more tortillas in the Southwest than in other parts of the country.

As a rule, the manager of a small specialty food store will work very long hours, in effect "marrying" the store. Many of the most successful retail specialty food enterprises are operated by families—for obvious reasons. You may be interested in knowing how the "average" manager spends her/his time:

8 AM to Noon	Opening/ordering/training food preparation
Noon to 2 PM	Luncheon sales
2 PM to 7 PM	General administration/ baking supplier meetings (this is you)

Average Opening Costs for a 1,000-Square-Foot Store

Leasehold, improvements	$55,000
Equipment	40,000
Start-up	17,000
Inventory	17,000
Total	$129,000

Your role is to operate for the convenience of the retailer, who, in turn, operates for the convenience of the consumer.

Your Role as Supplier

The Boston Consulting Group, a company involved in the purchase, sale, and management of restaurants and retail gourmet food stores suggests the following guidelines:

✧ *Become involved.* Get to know the particular challenges confronting each key retailer.

✧ *Educate the buyer.* Provide point-of-purchase materials. Arrange to spend some time with the sales staff.

✧ *Follow-up on deliveries.* Determine if all went well.

✧ *Follow-up on shortages.* Ascertain if still needed, and fill orders.

✧ *Develop seasonal guidelines.* Find out what works best and where.

✧ *Agree to minimum orders.* Be prepared to "break" cases.

✧ *Try to allow exclusivity.* Try not to sell the same product as your competitor across the street.

Understanding the Specialty Food Consumer

A good resource for learning more about the specialty food consumer is the National Association for the Specialty Food Trade (NASFT). Its 2004 report, "The State of the Specialty Food Industry," provides useful demographics about the size, magnitude, and trends in the specialty food industry. NASFT also has gathered data from market research sources and compiled some 20 specialty food brands onto one list, and then compared them with the demographics of consumers who purchased those products.

Topics about specialty food consumers covered in the research included the following (as an example, I have appended results to each category that show the demographic segment most likely to purchase specialty foods):

Demographic	Most Likely to Purchase
With whom they live	Two persons
How much they earn	$60,000–$75,999
How old they are	35–44
Their racial background	White
Age of children	No children
Homeowners or renters	Owners
Level of formal education	College graduate
Where they live (census division)	Pacific and South Atlantic

The report continues with an in-depth discussion of the specialty food consumer lifestyles and provides data about the specialty cookie consumer, specialty tea consumer, and specialty chocolate consumer.

taste:
inviting!

FRONTIER
SOUPS™

preparation: simple!

the finest all natural
soups, stews, chilis
and chowders
with no added salt
and no preservatives

Florida Sunshine CORN & PEPPER Chowder™

CHAPTER TWO

Getting Ready to Market

This chapter considers the importance of vision, understanding your business as part of a system, customer needs, start-up costs, consumer demand, and the market research required before you undertake a large production run for your product. The chapter also examines product categories in demand, and the issues of producing, packaging, labeling, and pricing your product. A description of warehousing, inventory, and shipping is included.

The Importance of Vision

Long-term success boils down to how we can better relate to one another. This is a way of doing business that is customer directed, and process-oriented, and in which decisions are based on facts. Long-term success is not assured by wholly intuitive, seatofthepants marketing.

Of course, there have been, and always will be, exceptions to this rule. In the food business, these will be based usually on products that are in high demand—ones that consumers will do or pay anything to get—or those that are associated with, and introduced by, marketers with deep pockets. Even then, if the product does not meet a specific consumer need at the right quality and right price, it will be short-lived.

We can no longer simply afford to think up a new food product, prepare it, and try to market it. Instead, use the information from Figure 2.1 to focus your efforts.

How does all this connect to the food entrepreneur? How does the entrepreneur, wearing all the hats at once, maintain focus? The answer is VISION. Simply put, your vision is what you envision yourself being (as food entrepreneur, professional, spouse, parent, neighbor, citizen, etc.) in about five to ten years. It is your dream. As a food entrepreneur, your vision should be a positive and inspiring statement of where your business will be at that time. A clearly articulated vision will help you and all your stakeholders (anyone with an interest in your venture) to keep on track. Important elements of your organizational vision might include: reputation, products to offer, values, types of customer, working environment, manner in which your people would work together, and how you and your team would handle both good and bad times.

You will want to share your dream with, and solicit input from, these stakeholders if you are to develop the appropriate response. Revisit your vision from time to time. See how it can be constantly refined. Your vision will help you determine if the task or activity you are doing now is adding value to getting from where you are, to where you ENVISION yourself being in five or ten years.

FIGURE 2.1: Checklist to Refine Your Focus

What to Do	How to Do It
1. Identify your prospective customers (retailers, distributors, etc.).	Visit stores where like products are sold; attend food-related trade shows; contact NASFT and regional food trade associations; contact state associations/agencies.
2. Determine customer needs (distinguish between customer and consumer needs).	Consumers are the ultimate users of your product. They will determine the quality of your product; retailers and distributors will determine the quality of your service. Each category has specific needs. Survey them to determine the quality characteristics of their specific needs.
3. Prepare a product in response to those needs.	Many of you most likely already have a product in mind. Make sure it conforms with your findings in number 2, above.
4. Test the product (trade shows are good vehicles for this).	This is extremely important. Test for taste acceptance, label and packaging effect, etc. Make sure your product meets, or exceeds, your customers' needs.
5. Refine the product based on data from the tests (change flavor, size, container, labels, etc.).	There will ALWAYS be room for improvement.
6. Return to number 2, repeat the cycle.	This process is the basis of what we call the PDCA cycle: Plan, Do, Check, and Act.

What you are doing, or are about to do in food marketing, is part of a system. This system consists of inputs, actions, and outputs. If you can develop the right supplier partnering (inputs), understand variation in your process (actions), and be able to set measurable quality standards (outputs), you have a substantially greater chance of delighting your customer.

To delight your customers, everyone involved must devote sufficient time to education and training in developing a quality philosophy. This is probably the most difficult part of this process . . . taking assets away from what we do best—firefighting—and focusing them on long-term thinking.

The point.—Food marketing, and the business supporting it, cannot continue in the same vein as it has in the past. The food industry is notoriously product-driven. We are being snookered out of profit-generating opportunities because we lack vision—a vision based on perceived customer quality standards. Make the bold move. Cut the waste. Set aside a half-hour or more each week to think about your vision. See if the path you have selected is headed in the desired direction.

Your vision is just one of the important elements to consider in your continuous improvement effort. Another way to put it: Think of your vision as you dream about the future. Other elements include the mission (what you do to realize your vision), guiding principles (standards of how you do business, your values and goals), and strategic objectives.

Assumption.—You want to develop, produce, administer, market, and sell food that is valued and wanted by customers. As the quality of your work improves, so does your productivity. And, costs go down. Knowing how to effect this requires knowing something about continuous process improvement. The term is self-explanatory. All processes you want to improve all the time are part of a system. What you do as a food entrepreneur should be understood in the context of this system.

Your system consists of:

✧ *Inputs*. Customer needs/feedback, ingredients, packaging materials, trained employees, etc.

✧ *Food processes*. What you do to formulate and prepare your food product (your response to the customer need).

✧ *Outputs*. The packaged, labeled, priced, and positioned product.

✧ *Outcomes*. Many satisfied repeat customers (or the opposite).

Managing your system and putting this all into perspective necessitates developing your company's vision, mission, guiding principles, and strategic goals and objectives.

Vision helps the food entrepreneur maintain focus and inspire employee loyalty and dedication.

A Vision Example: [by the year 2020] "Our company is internationally recognized as the premier supplier of [your food products]. We regularly exceed customer expectations by providing innovative and valuable [your food products]."

Why Do I Need to Think about a Mission?

Once you have articulated and shared your Vision with everyone in your firm, you will need to figure out what you are going to do to realize it. The result is called your Mission.

How to Develop a Mission Statement

The first and last rule is to know your customer. This presumes that you have people who want to buy and consume your food. It also presumes that you know something about your customers' needs. This information is then compared with your "bag of tricks"—your distinctive creative and production capabilities—that you use to formulate a response to the perceived customer needs. This process can be accomplished by brainstorming ideas.

Brainstorming Is a Useful Tool

Organize your *mission team*. This should consist of five to seven members from various departments in your company. As a small business, this might be everyone. Gather them for a brainstorming session. Brainstorming involves each member and encourages open thinking. There are a variety of brainstorming types. We suggest the following (from *The Team Handbook*, pp. 2–38 to 2–39, published by Joiner Associates, Inc.):

Rules for conducting a brainstorming session are:

- ❖ Encourage everyone to freewheel; don't hold back on any ideas, even if they seem silly at the time; the more ideas the better.
- ❖ No discussion during brainstorm. That will come later.
- ❖ Let people hitchhike—build upon ideas generated by others in the group.
- ❖ Write ALL ideas on a flipchart so the whole group can easily scan them.

The general sequence of events in a brainstorm is to:

✧ review the topic, defining the subject of the brainstorm. Often this is done best as a "why" or "what" question. ("What are possible ways to inform and train supervisors and hourly workers on all three shifts?" "How can we get all the information we need on a regular basis to complete these forms on time?")

✧ give everyone a minute or two of silence to think about the question.

✧ invite everyone to call out their ideas. The meeting facilitator should enforce the ground rules ("No discussion! Next idea…").

✧ have one team member write down all ideas on a flipchart, pausing only to check accuracy.

> **CASE IN POINT**
>
> *Beth's Fine Desserts—For the past 15 years, this company's principal—a Stanford alumna—has considered herself a baker and an artist. She feels all food entrepreneurs need to "Fix their vision," which in her case means to be on the shelf next to Pepperidge Farm and Sara Lee. Beyond that, she feels that success is a combination of inner peace and happiness. It took about six years for the company to be successful. Beth suggests seed money of at least $50K, better at $100K.*

Feel free to modify this procedure to fit the group and the topic. For instance, you could have everyone write down their thoughts, then go around the group and have each person say one of their ideas, continuing in this way until everyone's list is complete. Or you could do the entire sequence in stages: first, have everyone think of the minimal or partial solutions to a problem; then, the most outrageous, unconventional, or expensive solutions; then try to meld the two together into reasonable alternatives. Be particularly alert for ways to combine suggestions.

Brainstorming will help you define your mission and will clarify how you will go about meeting, even exceeding, perceived customer needs and expectations. This is your mission. It's what you do, the nature of your business.

A mission example.—My company produces the best [your food products] that offer outstanding value and result in regular and repeat sales. We do this in a working environment that is customer-oriented and in which our employees are fully involved team members. We make decisions based on facts. We continually plan, track, and measure performance. Our mission success is every employee's business. Management relies on team members—who know the work better than anyone else—to tell management how to help do the job better. We strive to produce the right product, the first time and every time, at a price both we and our customer can afford.

A clearly defined organizational mission will go a long way in building your employees' pride, dedication, and team effort. The key to this is to organize for quality.

Determining Start-Up Costs

Here's an important piece of advice that is based on over 25 years of gourmet food sales and marketing experience: You must have an independent source of income to successfully start your own gourmet food marketing business! You should have sufficient capital available to cover all your costs for the first three to five years. This includes all normal living expenses.

Your start-up costs will depend on your circumstances and on the type of product you plan to market. And even in light of such information, your specific start-up costs will be difficult to peg. As you will see in the following pages, our estimate ranges from $40,000 to $100,000 per year for the first three years.

If you will be using your own kitchen facility, you can save money until your production requirements outstrip your kitchen's capability. After that, you will want to negotiate with a food packer/processor to have your product produced to meet the increased

---

CASE IN POINT

Notes from a specialty food importer/distributor: "We do not have an 800 number and customers do not miss it at all. Phone calls are so cheap these days that no one complains about the lack of an 800 number, and no one (certainly at the distributor level of the industry) hesitates to place a lil 'ole long distance call to make an order. Though most orders are placed by fax.

"E-mail is the free method for reaching us. Faxing is still in vogue. Furthermore we set-up three personal phone numbers to take advantage of unlimited long distance in the U.S. and Canada for $58 a month. For all the talking we do, we now pay about $200 a month, including calls to Europe at $.07 a minute. Before this, our bills averaged $1,500 a month."

demand. The same goes for other overhead and administrative costs. You should take advantage of existing office space and equipment, and you might be able to use friends to help out part-time.

The people referred to in scenarios two and three, at the beginning of this book, had offices, production facilities, and administrative capability. They were also operating an existing business.

Start-up costs encompass production, packaging, warehousing, administration, and product advertising and promotion costs. The specific cost categories include those listed in the accompanying "Guidelines for Success."

The data in the table on this page give you an idea of cost elements used by the major leaguers. They cover costs of obtaining nationwide grocery distribution of warehouse-sourced products, and they do not include costs of direct-store delivered items. Your cost percentages will be lower in advertising and consumer promotion, while higher by about 15 percent in the trade deals and allowances segment. In the end, trade advertising, promotion, and deals will constitute the major portion of your costs.

> **CASE IN POINT**
>
> *Coach Dairy Goat Farm—1991 Outstanding Cheese (aged goat cheese brick with green peppercorns). The company was started 20-plus years ago by a successful manufacturer of handbags (yes, Coach handbags) who wanted to make goat cheese, even though such a product was not in any notable demand in the marketplace. He persevered, and succeeded. Visit them at http://coachfarm.com.*

Cost Elements of New Product Introduction by a Major Producer

Element	Percent of Costs
Advertising and consumer promotion*	46
Trade deals and allowances	16
Market research and product development	18
Other	20

*This means mostly promotions, such as mailing, trade show exhibition, in-store tastings, etc.

Source: "Managing the Process of Introducing and Deleting Products in the Grocery and Drug Industry," *Joint Industry Task Force*, 1990. Grocery Manufacturers of America, Inc.

GUIDELINES FOR SUCCESS

Start-Up Cost Analysis

Use these guides to determine your start-up costs.

Item	Cost Savings Considerations	Monthly Cost Estimate
Postage	Almost all your mail will be first class. If you plan to do a lot of mail-order selling, then ask the post office for information about postage-paid and bulk-mail privileges.	$100
Travel	You can reduce your travel costs by carefully planning your itinerary. Expect to make no more than four sales calls per day. Use a phone and e-mail whenever possible.	$600
Office supplies	You will need a computer (Pentium IV) with a minimum of 10 GB hard drive and 528 MB RAM, plus word processing, spreadsheet, database and accounting, and account management software, color laser printer, forms, bond paper, file cabinets, etc.	$300
Promotion	Business cards, catalog sheets, price lists, neck tags, point-of-purchase materials (possibly). Prepare your own press releases (at first). Do not advertise to the consumer unless you do mail order. Restrict trade ads to a complete—well-managed—promo campaign. Otherwise, save your money to make sales calls.	$600
Telephone	If you do any trade advertising, for example, the telephone company will require you to install a business, instead of personal, line. Look into the cost of an 800-number (for your fax, too). Also, if you are on the road a lot, a cell phone will be invaluable.	$120

Guidelines for Success, continued

Item	Cost Savings Considerations	Monthly Cost Estimate
Fax	Add a fax/voice-mail modem (internal or external) with the appropriate software to your computer, and buy a regular fax machine.	$20
Cable service	Broadband service for Internet hook-up.	$80
Utilities	Prorate your current utility cost (in your home) to cover that used by the business (if office is at home).	$75
Web site development	Costs for developing a good Web site have come down significantly in the past decade.	$75
Rent	If your office is to be in your home, take a percentage of your monthly mortgage equal to the space occupied by your office. That will be your monthly rent.	$900
Product ingredients	Try to arrange minimum bulk shipments. Ask your supplier(s) to store the ingredients and to invoice you only when you draw down supply.	Product dependent
Product packaging	Find other companies that are producing a product in a container similar to yours. Try to realize economies of scale by ordering a large quantity and splitting the shipment between, or among, the other companies.	Product dependent
Labels	Labeling by hand during your initial stage will save you money. It will also allow you to experiment with different labels without having to order 10,000 of one kind, only to find out they won't work. You will require the talents of a good graphic artist.	Product dependent
Miscellaneous	All the rest. Figure about 10 percent of total costs.	Product dependent

Guidelines for Success, continued

Notes to Start-Up Cost Analysis

These costs do not include labor, most of which will be borne by you. Other costs of production, including inventory management, site selection, and quality control should be considered if you will be establishing your own production facility. Also, the rent figure ($900 per month) can be deferred, since it will be you paying yourself. The same goes for utilities.

The office supplies include initial purchase of a computer, word processing and related software, telephone answering machine (or voice messaging service, which is preferred), printer, adding machine, etc. The conservative, annualized figure is $3,600. You may be able to do better with used or something other than top-of-the-line equipment.

The grand total, not including production (ingredients, packaging, labeling, and labor) or miscellaneous, comes to just over $32,400. This allows approximately $8,000 to $75,000 to cover the production element, bringing the estimated total dollar requirements in the range of $24,800, and $100,000 for each of the first three years.

How Long Does It Take and How Much Does It Cost?
Producers Respond

Some of the following companies have gone on to other pursuits, but their responses remain valid:

Sisters' Gourmet, started in 1996, offers its best-selling "Million Dollar Cookies." These are cookie mixes packaged in glass jars and now sold nationwide. Cost to start: Only the ingredients and some packaging. Profitable from year one, Sisters' Gourmet has been growing by approximately 24 percent per year but is not yet using the Internet extensively (so as not to compete with their wholesale customers). Owner's advice: "Start by getting your feet wet and see what you think. Go to some local stores and see if they are even interested. See if they can sell a few cases of the product not once, but several times. Is there staying power? Would the same customer pick it up again, knowing that it tasted good or it worked or whatever the case may be for that particular product?" She has seen no drop in sales due to what she calls the "low-carb phase."

***Blue Crab Bay Company's** most successful product is its Sting Ray Bloody Mary Mixer with Clam Juice (it saved the life of the business). The company started in 1985 on a farmhouse kitchen table with a $1,000 loan from a friend who the owner had met six weeks earlier. The firm is profitable, has 30 employees, and has expanded from 12,000 to 24,000 square feet. Its owner is "still scared" and suggests success is "enough profit to stay in business, pay competitively, have happy committed employees, be proud of our products, have satisfied customers, and challenging work in a rural location—a "lifestyle" job." They use the Internet with a retail consumer site as well as a wholesale Web site. Comments for "newbees": "Learn something new every day; never stop growing your mind and level of experience; trust your instincts; and take bold risks. It stays scary no matter how big you get."*

***The Herb Patch Ltd.** has spent the past 23 years producing instant cocoa mixes, flavored honeys, salt-free culinary blends, herbal teas, and vinegars. It names the following as examples of successful specialty food products: Honey Acres (honey and honey mustard), Jardines Foods (full line of Texas foods), and Maple Grove (pure maple syrup and maple syrup products).*

***Pelican Bay Ltd.** says it could not afford the start-up costs if it were to start today. The company produces and markets unique blends of all-natural herbs and spices for dips, seasonings, drink mixes,*

CASE IN POINT

Earth & Vine Provisions reports that its best seller is #1 Red Bell Pepper & Ancho Chili Jam. They started "very small" in 1997 with roughly $10,000 to $15,000. Company reps consider their enterprise successful and define it on many levels: Brandname recognition; key accounts; ability to pay vendors and keep debt to a minimum; and great relationships with stores and representatives. "I'm happy with the career path I have chosen. I can bring high-quality, all-natural products to market that consumers are passionate about and I can work with my husband, who is a great business partner. I'm meeting new friends through business relationships and growing personally from creating and growing a business." Earth & Vine uses the Internet as a marketing tool to service retail consumers who are unable to buy their products where they live. They do not use the Internet to sell wholesale, though they use it to communicate with customers. Comments for "newbees": "If you are considering marketing a food product, be willing to work long hard hours with no financial gain for at least three years. Be willing to invest a lot of your own money to grow your business. Be willing to take on some financial debt, be very passionate about your decision, and make a commitment to see it through the tough times."

and mixes for children. Principals at Pelican Bay advise that it would take upwards of five years for a new entrant to succeed. The company has grown from a kitchen-table business to a 30,000-square-foot warehouse.

North Aire Market *won the NASFT Outstanding Pasta, Beans, and Rice Award for their "Prairie Blaze Popcorn." Started in 1987, the people at North Aire consider themselves successful. In response to how much this cost, a partner responded: "It is not success in terms of money expanded, but in terms of close relationships held fast." She and her partner have remained on good terms throughout.*

John Wm. Macy's CheeseSticks *produces hand-rolled sourdough cheesesticks. In business for 20 years and in the black for the past seven years, owners recommend that beginning firms invest approximately $50,000 per year for the first three to four years.*

Goldwater's Foods of Arizona, Inc., markets Goldwater's "Taste of the Southwest," Sedona Red Salsas, Paradise Pineapple Salsa, and Rio Verde Tomatillo Salsa. Goldwater's principals recommend that beginners invest $250,000 over a seven-year period to succeed. They cite the following as a successful specialty food product line: Peggy-Jane's Salad Dressing (now marketed by Knotts Berry Farm).

Grace Tea Company, Ltd., founded in 1959, distributes Grace Rare Teas. The company principal says: "About money, it is best to try to use someone else's." He advises entrants to raise $100,000 to $150,000 per year for the first six years to succeed.

Golden Walnut Specialty Food has been marketing specialty foods for ten years. Operating in the black, it sells Golden Walnut Cookies, Golden Walnut Shortbread Cookies, Buckley's Original Cakes, and Monica's Cookies. The company principal comments that he was "very surprised at how complex and competitive" is the specialty food market.

Harney & Sons, Ltd., distributes Connoisseur fine teas. This company is a focused, niche player. It began by selling only to institutional accounts (mostly hotels and private clubs) through personal networking and is now expanding into gourmet and specialty food retail shops. The owner points out that the amount of money needed to succeed depends on too many variables to pin down, and suggests that success for a beginner will take at least three years.

Researching the Market to Identify Consumer Demand

One of your first and most important forays into the marketplace will be to determine the strength of demand for your product. You will also want to see who else is marketing a similar product (the competition), and at what price, in what packaging, and with what sort of promotional support.

Weigh the following market research considerations, and keep your findings in mind as you make your production, packaging, labeling, pricing, inventory, and shipping arrangements. Explore the issues of how the industry works, and acquire information that will provide you with a solid foundation about:

✧ major participants,

✧ recent trends,

✧ prospects for a product such as yours,

✧ technical and production requirements,

✧ regulatory influence (food and drug laws),

✧ competitive situation, and

✧ industry advertising and promotion methods.

Be prepared to gather as much information and data as possible about the potential for your product. Do not underestimate the value of networking. A lot of specialty food producers and marketers will be happy to share their experiences and insights with you. If they can't answer your question, ask them for the names of three other participants who might be able to respond.

Developing Your Product

Marketing strategies will differ depending on whether your product is fresh, refrigerated, or frozen. Also, matters of shelf life—the time it takes for your product to deteriorate—will have to be considered. For example, chocolate products are traditionally sold and shipped during cooler seasons. Otherwise, the cost of shipping can escalate and place your chocolate product out of the competition. A product with a short shelf life will have to move off the shelf faster. To ensure this happens may require a considerable promotional expenditure.

✦ GUIDELINES FOR SUCCESS ✦

Market Research

What to Do	How to Do It
Define and analyze the specialty foods industry.	Visit major specialty food-industry trade shows, especially those sponsored by NASFT.
Identify industry participants: producers, distributors, brokers, retailers, and consumers.	Visit shows and review this guide. Gather information from NASFT.
Develop an overview of major trends. Understand current changes in consumer requirements for specialty foods, in general, and for the food category you have in mind, in particular.	Review industry trade journals (see Appendix A).
Describe important suppliers, especially those with whom you will be competing. Understand the various sales, marketing, and distribution strategies they employ.	Visit food shows. Ask questions. Take notes.
Review the impact of technology on the entire marketing process, including production, packaging, and order processing. What are the technological implications for your application?	For example, will your ingredients require special machinery to process them? Will the package you have selected require special orders from high-tech packaging companies? Contact the Institute of Food Technologies, 525 West Van Buren St., Ste. 1000, Chicago, Illinois 60607 312-782-8424, http://www.ift.org.
Describe regulatory influence on the production, packaging, labeling, and marketing of your intended product.	Check your state's regulations and the FDA for sanitary certification. Check Title 21 of the Code of Federal Regulations (CFR) for labeling and ingredient statements. Most states prohibit the use of your own kitchen; a separate facility is required.

A comprehensive market profile appears in Appendix K. The profile discusses major specialty food product categories in terms of configuration, types, recent trends, size, market share, and other considerations. You will find it useful to review the category in which you hold an interest in order to become better informed about your prospects for success.

An ever-changing listing of upscale products rated with the highest growth potential appears as Figure 2.2. The products with the least potential for growth are in Figure 2.3. Those products with the greatest growth potential tend to be high-quality,

FIGURE 2.2: Upscale Products with the Greatest Growth Potential

Appetizers/hors d'oeuvres	Pasta
Candy	Oils/vinegars
Chutney	Cereals
Seafood	Nuts and nut butters
Coffee	Salsa/hot sauces
Chocolate	Pâté
Crackers	Goat cheese (chèvre)
Beverages	Salad dressings
Value-added meat/poultry	Sauces/bases (roasted red pepper, pesto, and sun-dried tomato)
Bottled water	Juices
Fruit	Seasonings/spices/herbs
Fancy mustards	Tea
Exotic mushrooms	Breads
Ice cream/sorbet	Cakes/pastry
Nonalcoholic beverages	Vegetables (and beans)

FIGURE 2.3: Upscale Products with the Least Growth Potential

Alcoholic beverages	Rice
Condiments (except certain sauces, mustards, and salsas)	Soups
Desert toppings	Syrups/honey
Jams/jellies and preserves	

---

convenience foods. They are foods that are perceived, for the most part, as being healthy, or healthier than others, while offering the benefit of a special treat.

There are all kinds of exceptions to the above listings. For example, almost any food that claims it is organic is probably carving out a profitable niche. Other "hot" aspects include genetically modified organisms, soy, organic and natural foods, orange, smoky, and sweet potatoes. Also, even though alcoholic beverages appear to be on the wane, there has been a mushrooming of so-called micro-breweries. Ommegang Brewery's Rare VOS Belgian-style beer is just one such exception. The Stonewall Kitchen line of jams and preserves is another exception, in this case to the slower growing jams/jellies and preserves category, and Peace Works "Meditalia" All Natural Pesto Sauces and Spreads seems to be in high demand.

Positioning Your Product

The term *product positioning* covers the overall concept of how your product will be marketed. It includes pricing, packaging, labeling, and advertising and promotion considerations. For example, a Cajun-style food might be better positioned as a gift/souvenir, when sold in New Orleans, than merely as a food product. It would be positioned in such a way as to attract the attention of tourists. Successful positioning has to do with your best assessment of what benefit you will be providing to your prospective consumer. How to appeal to this consumer is the point of product positioning.

There are many examples. Who knew that bottled water would make such a splash in the United States? Our tap water is supposed to be perfectly safe and wholly acceptable for all of our water needs. Then, in the 1970s, Source Perrier invested an estimated $3 million to position its bottled water as an alternative to tap water, and, even more important, as an alternative to alcohol in bars and restaurants. Perrier is bottled in a unique container, imported from France, and it commands a higher price than its competition. Yet it has developed a commanding lead in its market . . . all by effective product positioning. The point of positioning is to differentiate your product.

Everyone knows about the apple. Yes, it is healthy. Yes, it is inexpensive. Yes, it is available at every grocery in the nation. So, if you have a new "apple," then you will have to differentiate it from the others. Doing this is called product positioning. Think hard about novel means of packaging and promoting it. Remember the "Pet Rock?" Read "Pliskin's Phables," which follows, for an effective and amusing description of product positioning.

Pliskin's Phables
How Positioning Began

(With thanks to Mr. Pliskin)

In the beginning, the woman Eve was shopping in the Garden of Eden. As she was browsing through the fresh produce section, a serpent appeared unto her. "Psst, woman!" said the Serpent, "Try this." "What is it, O Serpent?" asked Eve. And the Serpent spake unto her, "It is a fruit, as yet unnamed. It grows on the tree of paradise, and it's mostly roughage, so it's good for what aileth you. And, it's a product of nature: 85 percent water, vitamins A and C, calcium, thiamin, riboflavin, iron, and niacin." "I've never heard of vitamins," said Eve, "and I don't aileth. I feel great." "Try a bite. Just a bite," urged the Serpent, holding an apple before her. "It's just what you needeth." "Who needeth anything that's good for them?" retorted Eve, as she headed for the heavenly hash ice cream. "Curses!" spake the Serpent unto himself. "I was sure she'd fall for it." And he slithered away to thinketh. "I know I've got a great product here. Yea, verily, the projected sales figures are out of this world. Maybe my segmentation aileth. Maybe I bar-keth up the wrong tree. Hmmmeth. Hallelujah! The woman Eve is also a mother. Maybe this product is for kids!"

And so the Serpent hired unto him a $100,000-a-year copywriter. And this copywriter delivered unto the Serpent a terrific advertising slogan: "An apple a day keepeth the doctor away.". . . . And the Serpent saw that it was good. The next day, when Eve was shopping, the Serpent appeared unto her again. "Psst, Mom!" hissed the Serpent. "Try this!" "What is it?" asked Eve. "It's a fruit named apple," said the Serpent. "Your kids are gonna love it. It's a sweet, crunchy fun food. Great for after-school quicketh energy!" "Forget it," said Eve. "Cain and Abel have enough energy as it is. They're killing each other already!" "But," said the Serpent, "'tis written: An apple a day keepeth the doctor away." "Who needeth a doctor in paradise?" laughed Eve. "Besides, my kids eateth only peanut butter and jelly." "Double curses!" hissed the Serpent, as he slithered off to thinketh

> **CASE IN POINT**
>
> The Infamous Cookie was exhibited by Duchess Farms Company at the 1977 National Fancy Food and Confection Show in New Orleans. Its packaging featured the comment "sinfully good," with the likeness of the late actor Vincent Price. This was a potentially winning combination. Where are the cookies today? The excellent product positioning apparently was not backed up by the required funding.

again. He thought and he thought and he thought. And his thinking begat an idea. He decided to undertaketh giant systematic research.

First he spake unto consumers in Kansas City, Rochester, and Des Moines. And they spake unto him of their desires. Then he called in Yankelovich to checketh the demographics. And Yankelovich spake unto the truth of the Serpent's findings in a 16-volume report. Then he handed the word of Yankelovich over to a new-product consulting firm, and he awaited their suggestions. And those of the firm spake unto him of the target market and communications thereto, and the Serpent did as he was told. He painted the apple bright red. He polished it until it shone even as the sun. He garnished it with a stem and a little green leaf . . . . And he saw that it was good. Then he placed it in the center of the fruit section and crawled off to waiteth.

The next day, the woman Eve came byeth pushing her shopping cart. The beautiful apple caught her eye, and she spake. "O Serpent," she asked, "What's this?" And the Serpent knew great joy, and he spake unto her, "It's something new. It's a tempting dessert. It's a little sinful, and all natural, and very, very indulgent, and loweth in calories, and it's called "Fatal Apple." You probably can't afford it." "Sayeth who?" snapped Eve. "I'll take a bushel." And lo, the Serpent and Eve begat positioning, which dwelleth among us, even unto this day.

Carving Out Your Share of Market

Market share is the percentage of a given market that a food producer is said to control. For example, XYZ Tea Company may claim a 75 percent share of the market for "imported retail packaged British tea." This means that of all the retail packaged British Tea sold in the United States, 75 percent is sold by XYZ Tea Company.

It will be unlikely for you to start out as the product leader in your category; therefore, you should think seriously about not being number two, but rather, becoming a market niche competitor. This is precisely why the specialty food industry works. Why is this? The leading seller of mustard, for example, may have a 30 percent share of the total mustard market, with a 10 percent net profit margin.

You, on the other hand, could carve out a 1 to 2 percent share of the mustard market, with a 20 percent net profit margin. The idea is to focus on overall profitability rather than beating the product leader in the market-share race.

Market share is generally of little consequence to the entry level marketeer; however, you should know that major food processors seem to "allow" small companies about 1 percent share of a given market before launching a competitive campaign.

General Foods, for example, claimed a 38 percent share of the estimated $440 million specialty coffee market. If your new specialty-coffee roasting business can sell up to $4 million per year, then you can expect some attention from General Foods. Otherwise, you will face most of your competition from other coffee roasters looking for a niche.

Actually, if you can sell $4 million of roasted coffee, then you might want to consider a "buyout" by a larger company. It has been one way to make a lot of money.

> **CASE IN POINT**
>
> Ciao Bella Gelato Company— 1994 Outstanding Foodservice Product (high-quality ice cream in such varieties as: chocolate jalapeño, avocado, and sweet potato). Since 1983, the Ciao Bella Gelato Company has created fine frozen desserts. They began as a neighborhood gelateria in Little Italy in New York City, producing gelato, sorbetto, and frozen yogurt. Soon, chefs from top restaurants and hotels requested that the company supply them with desserts. From their kitchen on 40th Street, trucks now deliver Ciao Bella throughout New York, New Jersey, Boston, and Washington, D.C.

Tapping Into Consumer Attitudes

Purchases of specialty foods have grown to more than $35 billion per year because of consumer demand for quality. Specialty foods represent affordable luxury. Even in recessions, purchases of many fancy foods tend to remain constant.

In the late 1970s, the United States experienced a consumer backlash to mediocrity. Notably, people had begun to take an interest in products with natural ingredients, no preservatives, and no artificial coloring. Purchases of fancy foods were based on considerations of quality and health.

The consumer backlash occasioned the remarkable growth of fine foods throughout the 1980s and 1990s. All of a sudden, everyone knew about brie. As more products were introduced, and new entrees proliferated, consumers developed a preference for a particular product brand or make. In the specialty food industry, the concept of brand preference was just becoming a factor in understanding consumer behavior. There is still plenty of room for experimentation, and, fortunately for new entrepreneurs, consumers appear disposed to continue in that vein.

With the exception of a handful of transition products, very few specialty food brand preferences have emerged. Those brands that are requested by name include: Heublein's Grey Poupon mustard, Celestial Seasonings herbal beverages, Godiva chocolates, Häagen-Dazs ice cream, high-end natural cheeses, sports drinks, bottled waters, and many more.

The specialty food retail business thrives on appealing to the senses. This makes for considerable impulse buying. Some of the most successful

CASE IN POINT

Almondina Biscuits (now sold by World Pantry) was started with $5,000 by a former conductor of the Ohio Symphony and his wife (a former member of the London Ballet). They were successful in five years and have been in business for 15 years. In 2000, they reported selling at nearly the $2 million-dollar level and won four NASFT Awards. Big help came from mention in Prevention *and* Women's Day *magazines. They use the Internet for direct sales to consumers and are getting more than 25 hits a day. Their Internet experience has been "like going from three cable channels to 700 channels."*

products are those sold in retail outlets, where shopping can be an exciting adventure. There, consumers are surrounded by new aromas and different tastes from sampled products. Products with eye-catching displays and packaging further enhance this experience.

Once consumers become familiar with a specific product, they will experiment with other products from the same line. For example, one company's strawberry preserve will be tried. If it is liked, consumers will feel more disposed to try other types of preserves offered by the same company. Other producers' products will be tried only if unavailable from the preferred brand. If the company does not have a blueberry preserve, then consumers may try one from another firm.

Finally, consumer attitudes toward specialty foods are influenced by what appears to be exclusive, new, and different. Products offering something unique will attract consumer interest. As long as consumers want newer and better foods, there will be continuing growth potential for new products.

Specialty foods that make the transition often fail in the mass market, and are eliminated by the chains. In turn, the eliminated lines, once the bulwark of gourmet food outlets, attempt to regain their foothold in those outlets, causing even further fallout in this widely over-assorted industry. Consider olive oil, which remains over-distributed and is carried in too many versions by too many supermarkets. The specialty food market, acting like a contracting accordion, has insufficient room to accommodate these and many other products currently in distribution.

Meeting the Competition

With whom will you compete? Aside from every other food producer, you will find your direct competition from others with similar products. Competition from other makers of condiments, for example, will occur when the consumer chooses their product instead of yours.

You will be competing for shelf space, too. There is a finite amount of shelving, and a growing number of products for the retailer to select. Fortunately, there is a lot of product movement. Product life cycles end, and products move to larger, down-market (grocery) distribution. As this occurs, specialty food stores demand products that will replace those that moved to supermarket shelves.

Consumer attitudes toward specialty foods are influenced by that which is exclusive, new, and different.—You will be competing for the "scarce dollar." Consumers must want to spend more for your fancy sauce, instead of a less expensive grocery-grade catsup. Consumers have differing perceptions of different products. Many are impulsive—they like the packaging, for example. Choices as to how to spend limited discretionary income are difficult to make. Products that impart the most "sizzle" will attract the most scarce dollars (see Figure 2.4).

In his book, *The Business Planning Guide* (8th edition, and available from Dearborn Trade in English and Spanish), David Bangs considers the following questions in analyzing competition: Who are your five major competitors? How is their business—steady, increasing, or decreasing? How are their products similar and dissimilar to yours? What have you learned about their operation? How will your product be better than theirs?

FIGURE 2.4: "Sizzle" Considerations for Your Product

Packaging . . . . upscale

Labeling . . . . upscale, refined

Ingredients . . . . the best

Size . . . . appropriate (no giant or economy size)

Price . . . . on the high side (cost of production)

Shape . . . . upscale, but practical

High Volume versus Lower Volume-High Margin

A margin is the amount of money (profit) charged above the actual cost of the product. The specialty food trade consists of products that are characterized by low sales volumes and high profit margins. Profit percentages are higher in the specialty food industry than they are in the grocery industry.

The specialty food retailer will normally take a 40 to 50 percent profit margin; whereas, the grocery store/supermarket uses markups of 3 to 20 percent on most staple groceries. In some cases, supermarkets will use 20 to 40 percent profit margins for certain fast-turnover items, such as bottled water, delicatessen products, and other products requiring service personnel.

The reasoning behind this difference in profits is twofold:

1. Industry tradition suggests that specialty food marketers determine their profits by computing them as a percentage of product sales, rather than adding a percentage to product cost.

2. Product turnover. Retailers need to achieve a targeted contribution (sales x margins) from space used. The specialty food retailer is likely to move ten jars of fancy preserves in a day. By comparison, the grocer may move several dozen jars of jam in the same period. Therefore, because it costs more to carry the fancy preserves, the specialty food retailer

must sell the product at a higher profit margin. A further explanation of the difference between "markups" and "margins" will appear later in this chapter on page 63 under the heading, "Pricing Your Product."

✦ GUIDELINES FOR SUCCESS ✦

Product Development

(With thanks to Daniel Best, Technical Director, *Prepared Foods* magazine)

Network

Contact others in the supplier community. Also, contact independent labs, universities, and reputable freelance product developers.

Know your customer

Be "market-oriented" rather than "product-oriented." Region, ethnicity, and eating occasion can all affect perceptions of quality. Don't equate your taste preferences with those of your customers.

Identify product traits

Begin by defining all consumer-relevant product features in advance of development. Engineer the desirable attributes into the product (packaging, color, flavor, etc.), rather than defining product attributes after product design. Consumer-test to determine how closely product variables match consumer needs and perception. Refine to reflect consumer reaction.

Manage your resources

You must manage by focus and flexibility. New products require time, labor, and capital. Investing in highly specialized processing systems closely married to a single product or product line is risky and expensive. Think long term. Apply processing systems that will be applicable beyond the immediate project requirements. However, by spreading your labor resources over a wide range of product development, you minimize the risk of generating both failures and superstars.

Guidelines for Success, continued

Maintain product quality
A long series of minute cost reductions will not reduce perceptions of quality in consumer testing. But the end result will be compounded, and the overall quality of the product will suffer.

Control your costs
If your costs come in too high, then reexamine the basic factors. Are your ingredients priced too high, and are lower-cost sources available? Are alternative processing methods available? Can you find other market segments to capitalize on, and consequently increase volume projections? Was the projected price for the product too low?

Commit for the long term
Failure to commit can result in constantly changing signals and erratic funding. Focus on your strategic objectives and tenaciously commit to their long-term achievement. However, know when to cut your losses and pursue alternatives.

Pay heed to the time factor
Timing is critical. Too soon, and your product may not be ready. Too late, and someone else will be in the market with the same product.

Tactics and strategy
Do not mistake tactics for strategy. Excessive focus on tactics can leave you struggling for strategies to fit. Tactics are the processes employed to achieve your objectives. Your objectives are your marketing and financial goals. Strategies combine tactics to achieve objectives.

Manage by confrontation
Risk avoidance can become the path of least resistance when there is no freedom to fail. In your case, management by avoidance will stop you dead in your tracks. You simply cannot avoid making the complex and success-threatening decisions associated with specialty food marketing.

Producing Your Product

Because this is a marketing guide, little attempt is made to tell you how to produce your product. Your options are to produce it yourself—in an approved facility—or have it either co-packed or licensed to some other food production company.

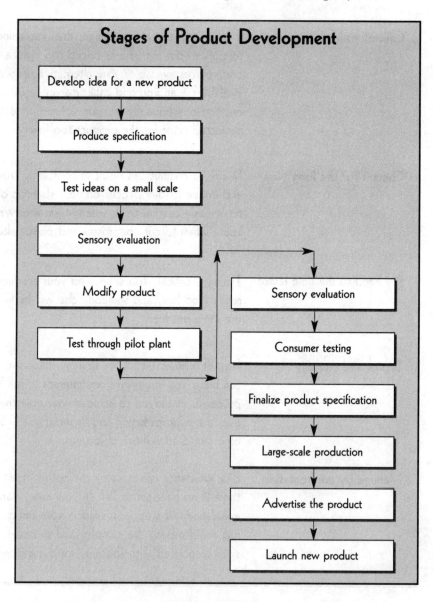

Stages of Product Development

Develop idea for a new product

Produce specification

Test ideas on a small scale

Sensory evaluation

Modify product

Test through pilot plant

Sensory evaluation

Consumer testing

Finalize product specification

Large-scale production

Advertise the product

Launch new product

Some attention will be devoted to product selection, packaging, and labeling, and you are encouraged to contact the NASFT for their listing of companies (co-packers) that can package and help you produce your product. (See Appendix D.)

The food industry is notoriously "product-driven." You must make a clear connection between your product development efforts on the one hand, and the market and consumer demand on the other. Just because you are convinced that your new product will take over the market is no assurance of success. You must keep listening to your customers in order to exceed their expectations.

Contract Packaging

Co-packers are food processing companies that either have excess packing capacity, or are specifically devoted to packing other people's products. Their capabilities vary and some can only pack tinned (canned) products, while others can only package dry, nonperishable products.

You may want to seek assistance in formulating and packing your product. See the comments that follow and check with industry sources in your state, especially your state's business development agency, for assistance.

The complexities of moving a product from conception to market can be overwhelming even to experienced entrepreneurs. Developing networking relationships with reliable co-packers will permit the small businessperson to achieve maximum utilization of physical and financial resources—and save time.

GUIDELINES FOR SUCCESS ✧

Co-Packing Drawbacks

Watch out for large run requirements (perhaps several thousand) where you may outstrip your assets through the preparation of the packages. Also beware of the "true" versus "fake" co-packing where your label ends up on their salsa, for example. Check the integrity of the co-packer.

Working with co-packers allows the business owner to call the shots while drawing on various team members to perform, when needed, on a fee-for-service basis.

When you approach co-packers, be prepared to present your product and your needs clearly and concisely. You will be received best if you deal efficiently without wasting their time or yours. Be open in discussing your needs and their costs.

The major areas of co-packer operation include basic product development services, food processing services, and food packaging services. Each is described below (with thanks to John Darack, formerly with the Dirigo Spice Corporation—now Newly Weds Food).

Basic product development services.—These are often available from ingredient suppliers, such as seasoning manufacturers. Such service providers perform an important function by helping you convert at-home or menu recipes to a manufacturable form. Then, dry ingredients, and often several "wet" ones such as fresh vegetables, liquid sauces, condiments, meats, fats, and so forth, can be formulated into one specialized ingredient package. The resulting product can either be sold as an easy prep-as-is item, or sent to a processor to be converted into a canned or jarred finished product.

Using basic product development services brings several benefits:

✧ *Quality control*. The blender guarantees that agreed-upon specifications for the product will be met.

✧ *Inventory control*. Only one item needs to be tracked, rather than several.

✧ *Recipe protection*. The blender signs a contract in which your recipe is kept confidential. Finished-product producers know only to add the simple liquids to a pre-weighed unit of ingredients.

✧ *Uniformity of finished product*. All ingredients are preweighed and batched. Opportunities for errors in production are eliminated.

✧ *Price stabilization and purchasing power*. The blender has the ability to purchase in large quantities from reliable and established sources. Cost averaging and unitized pricing eliminate being at the mercy of market fluctuations. You will know your costs over longer price periods.

✧ *Networking*. You will be "plugged in" to an existing array of related services, such as analytical laboratories, packagers, processors, marketers, and distributors that may not be otherwise available to the public.

Food processing services.—After having your recipe converted into manufacturable form, you can bring your ingredient package and conversion recipe to a food processor. Be prepared to discuss the preparation of your finished product to your specifications. Liquid ingredients, process parameters, packaging, labeling, shelf-life testing, and possibly even distribution are topics you should address.

Be ready to deal with some practical limitations such as larger or smaller batch proportions, limited size or shaped containers, production scheduling, and availability of ingredients (seasonally or otherwise).

Find the best fit—don't go to a large producer for small batch production. Conversely, be sure the processor has the capacity to accommodate your growth.

Food packaging services.—If yours is a dry product, find a packaging company that has the right equipment to make your ideal package. As with a processor, the right fit must be found. There are companies that specialize only in contract packaging.

Opportunities may also be found at plants that package products in similar-type materials to yours, and that would like to utilize downtime profitably. Good deals can be made here.

Co-Packer Benefits

Successful co-packing can provide you with significant benefits and cost savings, among which are:

✦ *Elimination of capital costs.* No plant to build or equipment to purchase.

✦ *Utilization of well-seasoned experts.* Solving problems that overwhelm you are a part of their daily routine.

✦ *Compliance.* Undergo the amazingly complex process of meeting federal, state, and local regulations.

✦ *Product uniformity.*

✦ *Purchasing power.*

✦ *Networking.*

✦ *Technical services.* Often at cost, or low cost.

✦ *Marketing assistance.*

✦ *Distribution.*

A Word about Licensing

Many food entrepreneurs do not want to get actively involved in the production and marketing of their product. They think that since their idea alone has merit that they can find a big food producer to whom they can license the formula and technology for their new product. Once again, this is an example of the product-oriented nature of the food industry. Not much attempt is made to find out what the customer needs.

There is very little to protect your formulation. If the big company sees your product as competitive, they will either copy (clone) it or make you an offer. Often times, such offers can be in the form of licensing or co-packing agreements. If you are fortunate enough to receive such an offer, consult your attorney for advice about the nature of such contracts.

> **CASE IN POINT**
>
> *The Republic of Tea—1995 Outstanding Beverage (Ginger Peach Tea). Started in 1992 and still in business, this company uses the Internet and considers itself successful. Company personnel would not divulge how much it cost to start the business, nor what they think success means.*

Food Safety and Sanitation Requirements

The U.S. Food, Drug, and Cosmetic Act is very specific as to sanitation requirements. You should ask the Food and Drug Administration to provide you with a copy of the Current Good Manufacturing Practice Regulations. These regulations set forth the requirements for establishing and maintaining sanitary conditions.

Food and Drug Administration regulations are contained in the *Code of Federal Regulations*. You can review these at a Government Printing Office in your area, or from the Superintendent of Documents, GPO, Washington, DC 20402. There are nine volumes of Title 21, but only Chapters 1 through 3 will apply to you. They cover general regulations, color regulations, food standards, good manufacturing practices, and food additives, among other subjects.

In addition to federal regulations, each state has special requirements for inspecting and certifying food-producing facilities. If your initial production effort will occur in your own kitchen facility (separate from your home kitchen), then have it inspected and certified by your local food-regulating agency.

Product Liability

Many distributors will ask you to provide them with a current certificate of product liability insurance coverage. They will request that the certificate name them as an additional insured, to be included under "Broad Form Vendor's" coverage.

Be prepared to pay a hefty premium. Lately, when courts in the United States have found in favor of plaintiffs, they have

✧ GUIDELINES FOR SUCCESS ✧

Government Regulations

Process	Responsible Agency
Business organization	State and local departments of economic affairs. Application depends on the type of organization (corporation, proprietorship, etc.) you elect.
Production	State health agencies. Sanitary certification, inspection laws.
Labeling	U.S. Food and Drug Administration. U.S. Customs (if you are marketing an imported product). Chapter 21 of U.S. Code of Federal Regulations includes the labeling laws.
Labor	Internal Revenue Service and state and local revenue agencies. Payment of FICA, withholding tax, and workers' compensation.
Tax	Internal Revenue Service and state and local revenue agencies for quarterly and annual income tax payments and procedures.
Distribution	Some states require registration of certain products before they can be sold in that state.

awarded sums that have exceeded existing levels of defendants' liability coverage. As a result, coverage can be difficult to find and expensive to maintain.

If you are setting up your own manufacturing facility, you will have to pay for workers' compensation insurance, as well as offer some sort of group medical insurance to your employees. Check with your insurance agent for guidance about the types of insurance coverage best suited to your operation.

Packaging Your Product

Packaging is the single most important element in the consumer's decision to purchase a new specialty food product. Attractive packaging type and design are paramount to success in the specialty food trade. Appealing packaging is just one factor that prompts people to try new products. Other factors include:

- ✦ Coupons
- ✦ Price
- ✦ Reputation (the brand name is accepted widely)
- ✦ Convenience
- ✦ New
- ✦ Recipes included
- ✦ Influence of advertising
- ✦ Recyclable packaging

Ultimately, the purchasing decision is rarely based solely on packaging (except for gifts), but on a combination of the above factors.

Types of Packaging

The packaging you select will depend on the product. For example, different merchandising is required for bulk fancy foods, such as snacks and

---

CASE IN POINT

Market Square Food Company developed a beautifully designed line of specialty foods, all packaged in containers depicting wildlife and water fowl paintings by noted artist James Lockhart. The company initially centered on sales to specialty food and department stores. Competition, especially with its lines of wild rice, vinegar, and olive oils, caused it to eventually refocus its efforts by targeting the gift trade. Today, it sells snack mixes, confections, and candy exclusively through "food reps" to the gift trade.

CASE IN POINT

Truzzolino Food Products, a longtime mainstay of canned foods in Montana, retained the Chicago-based design firm Power Packaging to redesign its line of canned Mexican-style tamales (almost a cult food in certain parts of Montana), and its gourmet chili. The result was a very fancy-looking canned tamale. Despite making many of the right moves, the line never caught on nationally, and Truzzolino returned to its co-packing and regional food-marketing activities.

confections. However, if you have alternative packaging types to consider, then you should be aware of the impact some packages have over others. Witness the shape of the Perrier bottle. Packaging encompasses consumer perceptions, as well as practical considerations.

Glass containers are used because the product can be seen and there is no tin taste; whereas, canned (tinned) products are generally restricted to soups, pâtés, caviar, and most loose teas. Most consumers tend to prefer products in jars, rather than cans, despite a can's practicality. Also, cans are slowly being overtaken by a new technology called *aseptic packaging*. This type of packaging is widely used by fruit juice producers, but it can be used wherever a carton, plastic cup or metal can might be required. These include fruit juices, coffee creamers, puddings, and yogurt. Aseptic packaging saves shelf space and is less expensive to transport because it weighs less than other types of packaging. You may find using this a challenge because of the equipment costs, but its use is growing, and the market for aseptic packaging has exceeded $3 billion.

Some of the fanciest packaging available is also the most expensive. At first, you will probably have minimum production "runs," so you will not want to purchase thousands of empty jars, boxes, or other containers. The objective is to limit your initial costs, regardless of the economies of scale associated with large volume purchases.

There is little point in ordering a thousand jars and a thousand labels if you are not sure of selling a thousand units of your product.

Packaging types for specialty food products are many and varied. You can select from among readily obtainable containers made of cardboard, plastic, wood, cellophane, glass, and metal. Try to find a good-looking and reasonably priced container. Try not to pack your product in an odd-shaped container. As a rule, your product must be able to fit and stack on standard store shelves. It is wise to start with stock items (such as jars and lids) rather than design special molds, etc.

Competitors' Packaging

It will serve your purpose to review products now on the shelves of specialty food stores. It stands to reason that, generally, you should package your product in a container type that is similar to those on the shelves. This comes under the heading of "you can't knock success."

It does not mean that your creative urges should be constrained, just that the consequent costs and requirements for educating consumers about your unique package may not be worth the expense.

Elements of Great Packaging

Aside from clearly conveying its contents, great packaging will cause your product to stand out from the others. It will command consumer attention and create interest in the product.

Visit several of your local gourmet food stores, and attend the next International Fancy Food and Confection Show to see examples of great packaging. The Fancy Food Show has a special display called Focused Exhibits. It offers you the opportunity to see hundreds of new products, gift products, and food service products away from the producer's show booth. And it will provide you with a terrific chance to compare differing packaging styles. Some products with great packaging are shown in Figure 2.5.

Cost-Saving Hints

Negotiate small initial production runs. Your unit costs might be higher, but you won't be saddled with a slow-moving inventory of thousands of units. Limit initial production costs by using readily available stock items.

FIGURE 2.5: Examples of Products with Great Packaging

Category	Product(s)	Producer(s)	
Condiment/dip	Cuban Black Bean Dip	El Paso Chili Co.	
Confection	Hazelnut Chocolate Dessert Pudding	King's Cupboard	
Sauce	Raspberry Chipotle Sauce Key Lime Ginger Wasabi	Delicae Gourmet	
Bagged Snack	Soy Thin Crisps	Stacy's Pita Chip Co., Inc.	
Tea	Darjeeling Nouveau	The Republic of Tea	

Packaging for Warehouse Clubs

A growing market for specialty foods is the warehouse or club store. Such chains include Costco and Sam's Club. They like to have the product delivered from truck to the shelf location all in one step. They don't require slotting fees (see "Arranging the Deals" in Chapter Three). They do require, however, that you package your product either in large, nearly institutional size, or that you bind your products together in a three- or six-pack package.

Packaging Considerations

In selecting the container and the means of packaging, review government regulations that may apply. For example, the state of California has required that honey be sold in 8-ounce and 16-ounce containers. Any other size is viewed as potentially misleading to consumers.

Most big cities have glass suppliers, and it is worthwhile to visit their showrooms, obtain their catalogs, and try your product in sample containers before making any final decision.

Increasing use of tamper-resistant seals suggests that you should consider employing such a device on your product's container. Also, if you want to add a consumer information neck tag to help educate the specialty food consumer about the benefits of your product, then this should be planned before you make your final packaging decision.

If you plan to sell to supermarkets, consider such elements as supermarket shelf depth and height. If your product is packaged in a container that exceeds the shelf height, then it will be placed on the top shelf, out of direct eye range. This applies to the number of facings that can be accommodated. If the product is too wide, it will take up more than one facing per product. This may limit the amount of space that the store will authorize for your product or product line.

Size Points

Cost: select best for your budget.

Selling price: cost to consumer can influence container size selected.

Usage (repeat sales): a 16-ounce jar may move once a month; whereas an 8-ounce jar may move three or more times a week!

Shipping containers: should hold no more than one dozen units.

Outer Containers

The outer container is the shipping container. The most common outer container is a strong cardboard carton capable of holding one dozen units of your product. Because you will be making use of such pickup and delivery services as United Parcel Service, make certain that the outer container can withstand the rather substantial punishment shipments often encounter. A master pack capable of withstanding a 200 pound test, with a size of 18 inches square will fit nicely on a pallet, for example, and make for easier and more cost-effective shipping.

Retailers are asking for products in smaller outer packages. Generally, one dozen products per outer package is sufficient; however, if you can break down the pack to two packs of six, for example, you will find retailers more willing to try your product. Also, your suppliers can provide glass jars in 12-pack cartons that you can reuse once the jars have been filled. Often these outer packs can be put into master cartons containing two-by-twelve by unit (one master carton with two inner cartons of 12 jars each), or four-by-six units (master carton with four inner cartons of six jars each).

You may want to purchase mailing containers that can be used for individual direct sales and for shipping samples to prospective buyers. These can be sold to retailers when your product has a gift potential, allowing the consumer to have the retailer mail it to the gift recipient.

Other packaging considerations include the use of corrugated cartons, bubble wrap, filler materials, and associated equipment such as wrapping tape and tape guns. There are numerous sources for these, and almost any manufacturer or co-packer will be able to provide you with the name of a packing materials supplier.

✧ GUIDELINES FOR SUCCESS ✧

Packaging

✧ Describe packaging type used by your competition (jar, can, plastic container, etc.).

✧ Describe your anticipated product package type (should be similar type to competition).

✧ Is the proposed package a stock item, or does it require special order? (Check with suppliers.)

✧ What is the minimum order for stock item (supplier requirements)?

✧ What is the minimum production run for special order (supplier requirements)?

✧ Is special handling required (e.g., cardboard to be lithographed or sticker labeled)?

✧ Are special shipping containers required (box, glass, etc.)?

✧ Are co-packers available to package for you? (See Appendix D.)

✧ Does your package design conform to federal and local regulations? To reiterate, honey in California cannot be put into 12-ounce jars; you need to use 8- or 16-ounce jars.

✧ Is your package size consistent with consumer demand? (Price will have an impact.)

✧ Does the outer container hold no more than one dozen (unofficial industry standard) of your product?

Labeling Your Product

All labels must conform to government regulations. Even so, you will have a wide choice. Remember, your label is a crucial element in attracting consumers. It must convey the nature of your product, as well as the "sense" of affordable luxury.

At first, you should consider some type of pressure-sensitive adhesive label that can be designed and printed in small batches. Compare the costs of applying labels by hand and by machine. After you get the product up-and-running, you can have your labels printed in quantity. As with packaging, the color and style of your label will be important in attracting consumers.

Avoid the "supermarket look" with its reliance on bold lettering and lots of primary colors. The same company that packs your product will be able to help you have it labeled. Otherwise, you can hire labor to hand-label the product until your volume warrants automated labeling.

Uniform Product Code

This is an optic-readable symbol that can be affixed to your product label. The UPC symbol allows use of automated checkout machines and conforms more readily to other products on the shelves. As items are presented to the checker, they are passed over an optical scanner that decodes the UPC symbol and transmits this information to a computer. The computer stores price and other information on all items carried in the store. It transmits back to the check stand the item's price and description, which are then displayed to the customer and printed on the customer receipt.

The UPC code is made up of of 12 numbers called GTIN— Global Trade Item Number. The code consists of a manufacturer identification number and an item code number. The last digit is a scanner-readable check digit. UPC codes are not required by all distributors; however, they are becoming more prevalent as food producers and distributors recognize the increasing influence of large grocery chains in specialty food distribution. These chains almost universally tend to require UPC coding to save the cost at checkout.

If you anticipate ever having your product on a supermarket shelf, it is less expensive and more efficient to have your initial label carry the UPC. In this manner, you will save labor by not having to affix it separately. UPC bar code software is available to assist you. Information regarding UPC allocation may be obtained from the Uniform Product Code Council (reference Appendix P).

FDA Labeling Requirements

Aside from your desire to impart ingredient information to the consumer, the U.S. Food and Drug Administration enforces label ingredient legislation. The laws require that ingredients be displayed clearly, and in accordance with the regulation. A net weight statement is also required.

> ### CASE IN POINT
>
> *Timpone's Fresh Food—1995 Outstanding Hors D'oeuvre (Salsa Muy Rica). Timpone's Fresh Foods was founded in Austin, Texas, on June 21, 1988, with the goal of creating high-quality food items that are nutritious as well as delicious. Today, Fischer & Wieser Specialty Foods, Inc., founded on June 18, 1969, in Fredericksburg, Texas, carries on Patrick Timpone's quality-first tradition in its production of Timpone's Fresh Foods.*

In this connection, the American Technology Pre-eminence Act, that amends the Fair Packaging and Labeling Act, will require all packaging and labeling to use metric measurements of net quantity. The use of ounces and pounds would become optional. The law is very specific about the nutritional claims that can be made for any food product. Claims as to health, purity, low-sodium, and the like must be made in no uncertain terms. The code specifies what wording is permitted, and what wording is proscribed.

The FDA promulgated new labeling regulations in 1990 (Public Law 101–535) that require practically every food to have nutritional labeling. Regulations as to cholesterol content and serving sizes have also been issued. Finally, there is some confusion as to which laws will take precedence when federal and state requirements differ. It will be necessary for you to check Title 21 of the Code of Federal Regulations, available from your local Government Printing Office (or from the Superintendent of Documents, Government Printing Office,

The Nutritional Labeling and Education Act

Exceptions to the requirement for nutritional labeling include coffee, tea, and spice; containers too small to carry a nutritional label; and producers whose total annual revenues are less than $500,000. The Nutritional Labeling and Education Act (NLEA) of 1990 took effect in May 1994. A total workup on a single sample to determine compliance with the NLEA by a food laboratory can cost more than $600. For more information, see: http://www.fda.gov/ora/inspect_ref/default.htm.

Washington, D.C.), to determine the requirements as they pertain to your ingredient statements. More information is available at http://www.gpoaccess.gov/cfr/.

There are regulations governing the physical aspects of labeling as well. Certain information has to be placed on certain parts of the label, and the lettering size has to be in specific relation to the overall size of the label, or "principal display panel."

What if you goof? The Food and Drug Administration will not officially approve your label; however, your local compliance branch will provide comment on the manner in which the label conforms to regulations. If you sell the product with incorrect labeling, expect the FDA to enforce the law at the store level. It can cause all the product to be removed from the store shelves.

Labeling Considerations

One of your greater setbacks can occur when you recognize that your beautiful labels might be "ruined" by the label requirements. You must have a net weight statement placed in the lower third of the principal display panel, for example. If you know of this requirement beforehand, then you can save time and money by designing your original labels to allow for the legal statements. There are many ways of retaining your artistic statement while complying with the law. Your labels should have eye appeal, be informative and legal. Remember that one of the key elements of a specialty food product is its presentation.

Labels offer more than practical and aesthetic forms of expression. They should be used to convey your sales message. Consider including usage instructions, cooking directions, recipe tips, and the like.

Labeling the Product

✦ Will you do the labeling yourself?

✦ Can labeling be completed by a contract labeler?

✦ Can your initial label be produced in a limited quantity?

✦ Does your label conform to local and federal regulations (Code of Federal Regulations, Title 21)?

✦ Will your label contain a nutritional statement? (Not required if total annual sales will be under $500,000, or less than $50,000 of gross annual food sales to consumers.)

✦ Is your label consistent with that of an upscale product? Does it impart a sense of high quality?

✦ Does your label stand out from your competition? Or, is it the same old, same old?

✦ Does your label give history of company, recipe tips, or other selling information?

✦ Describe how your label attracts consumer interest.

The front label (or principal display panel) is used for a different purpose than the side and rear labels. The front is the "tickler" that attracts consumer attention. The side and rear may include additional messages regarding product use, such as those mentioned above, or convey a message about other elements of your product. Remember the success of the "notes to consumers" on the boxes of Celestial Seasonings Herbal Tea?

Pricing Your Product

Earlier in this chapter I addressed the desirability of finding a market niche. Rather than concentrating on beating the product leader for market share, I suggested a goal of 1 to 2 percent market share, with a 10 percent net profit margin. In

Nutrition Facts	
Serving Size: 2 Tbsp (36g)	
Servings Per Container: 14	
Amount Per Serving	
Calories 20	Calories from fat 0
	% Daily Value*
Total Fat 0g	0 %
Saturated Fat 0g	0 %
Cholesterol 0mg	0 %
Sodium 150mg	6 %
Total Carbohydrate 3g	1 %
Dietary less than 1g	2 %
Sugars 2g	
Protein 1g	
Vitamin A 6 % • Vitamin C 0 %	
Calcium 2 % • Iron 0 %	
* Percent Daily Values are based on a 2,000 calorie diet. Your daily values may be higher or lower depending on your calorie needs.	

striving for this goal, I underscored the use of margins instead of markups (cost plus profit). When using margins, profit is calculated on selling price. The specialty food industry uses margins instead of markups to develop prices. The following examples will illustrate the difference.

Markup

The unit cost of your peppercorn breadsticks is $1.00. If you were to use a 40 percent markup, your selling price would be $1.40. To determine your selling price, multiply the $1.00 by 1.40.

$$\$1.00 \times 1.40 = \$1.40$$

Margin

The unit cost of your peppercorn breadsticks is $1.00 and you decide to use a 40 percent gross profit margin. Your selling price will be $1.67. To determine your selling price, subtract .40 from 1.00 and divide the $1.00 cost by .60.

$$\$1.00 - .40 = \$.60$$
$$\$1.00 \div .60 = \$1.67$$

The different selling prices of $1.40 and $1.67 occur when you use a mark up versus a margin. The markup is cost plus profit, whereas the margin is calculated on selling price less profit. Another example: Your honey mustard cost is $1.63. A 40 percent markup = $2.28 selling price. A 40 percent margin = $2.72 selling price.

Cost Accounting

This involves computing all your costs, adding your profit, and the profit margins taken by distributors and retailers, to reach a consumer price (see Figure 2.6). No matter what the costs, if your price to the consumer is greater than that of the competition, you will face substantial consumer resistance. It is for this reason that I recommend starting at your competitor's price and working backwards through the various profit margins to your product costs (unless you have that "one-in-a-million" product

FIGURE 2.6: **Selected Cost Factors**

Ingredients	Cost of Contents of Your Product
Packaging	Cost of outer package, the reinforced cardboard carton.
Production	Labor and materials used in getting the ingredients into the containers.
Containers	The jars, boxes, or cans used to hold your product.
Labeling	Design, artwork, electronic preparation, printing, and affixing costs.
Selling	Cost of making sales calls.
Promotion	Special events, trade shows, and in-store demonstrations.
Advertising	Sales literature, trade journals, and related media costs.
Administration	Cost of running your office—includes legal, accounting, etc.
Overhead	Regular costs of running the business that you will incur whether anything is produced or sold. Some include rent, utilities, upkeep, and taxes.
Draw	Your salary. Divide your annual gross salary requirements by 260 (average number of workdays per year) to get a realistic assessment of your daily pay. Divide that by eight for the hourly figure. Even though you probably will not take a draw, knowing this amount will be helpful in your breakeven analysis.

for which the world has been waiting; in that case, demand will be considered "elastic" and you will have more leeway).

You may use either a cost-plus or market-set pricing method. The former begins from the bottom up, while the latter works backwards from the consumer price to your product cost. My recommendation is to use the latter.

First, establish a consumer price (use your competitor's price as a reference). That will enable you to determine your gross profit after the retailer and distributor margins are deducted. Then determine if your costs and profit margin yield a price significantly different from your competition. Some of your strategic thinking can be assisted by applying a breakeven analysis that will help you determine the price range available for your product. A breakeven analysis will let you know at what point your dollar or unit sales will meet your total dollar or unit costs. Any revenue generated above the breakeven point is profit—below it is loss.

Delivered Price versus Ex-Warehouse Cost

Depending on the circumstances, some transactions will require that you include freight charges in your pricing for a "delivered price." Others will allow you to ship freight collect, or with the freight charges added to the invoice.

Ex-warehouse cost is the cost of the product (plus freight-in if you are importing) plus the cost of storage and handling. Your ex-warehouse cost plus profit margin yields your price to the retailer (see Figure 2.7). In these examples, we will use a gross profit margin of 40 percent, which is consistent with profit margins used by many food processors. In our examples, prices do not include freight, and they are called FOB (Free On Board). Freight will be "collect," or added to your invoice to be paid by the buyer.

Your gross profit margin will include administration costs, and sales and marketing costs (broker commissions, promotion, reserve for bad debts, advertising, and the like). Your gross profit margin will have to cover all of these costs. You should aim for a net profit of at least 10 percent. (See the suggested pricing formulas that follow in Figure 2.7.)

FIGURE 2.7: **Pricing Flow Example**

Following is a pricing flow example, from consumer price back through retailer, through the distributor, and your ex-warehouse cost.

Price to consumer		$6.25
Less 40%	x	60
Equals cost to retailer		$3.75
Price to retailer		$3.75
Less 25%	x	75
Equals cost to distributor		$2.81
Price to distributor		$2.81
Less 20%	x	80
Equals your ex-warehouse cost		$2.25

Customary broker commissions for sales direct to retailer = 10% ($.38 in the above example). For sales to a distributor, the commission = 5% ($.14 in the above example). You will use the same price to the retailer, regardless of whether you sell to a distributor. Sales to retailers will entail less volume, but you will make more in profit (40% gross profit before broker commission).

Suggested Pricing Formula for Sales to Distributors

Formula: D = E ÷ (100% – P)

where,

D = Price to distributor

E = Ex-warehouse cost per unit

P = Gross profit margin

Example: E = $2.25 (product cost of $2.20 plus $.05 for storage and handling)

P = 20%

Process: D = E ÷ (100% – 20%).

Then $2.25 ÷ 80% = $2.81 per unit. Your gross profit would be $.56 ($2.81 less $2.25) for a 20% profit margin. Broker commission is 5% ($.14) and will be deducted from the profit margin.

Most retailers in the specialty food industry work on at least a 40 percent margin. They will divide the cost to them from the distributor (or from you for a direct sale) by 60 to arrive at their price to the consumer.

Suggested Pricing Formula for Sales to Retailers

Formula: $R = E \div (100\% - P)$

where,

R = Price to retailer

E = Ex-warehouse cost per unit

P = Gross profit margin

Example: E = $2.25 (product cost of $2.20 plus $.05 for storage and handling)

P = 40%

Process: $R = E \div (100\% - 40\%)$.

Then $2.25 ÷ 60% = $3.75 per unit. Your gross profit would be $1.50 ($3.75 less $2.25), for a 40% profit margin.

This is before broker commission (10%). In this example, the price to the consumer will be $6.25

Retailer price of $3.75 ÷ 60% = $6.25

✧ GUIDELINES FOR SUCCESS ✧

Price Flow Worksheet

	Competitor's Product	Your Product
1. Price to consumer	$_____	_____
2. Less 40% (retailer profit margin)	x 60%	x 60%
3. Equals cost to retailer	$_____	_____
4. Price to retailer (same as 3)	$_____	_____
5. Less 25% (distributor profit margin)	x 75%	x 75%
6. Equals cost to distributor	$_____	_____
7. Price to distributor (same as 6)	$_____	_____
8. Less 20% (your profit margin)	x 80%	x 80%
9. Equals ex-warehouse cost	$_____	_____

Key question: How do the ex-warehouse costs compare?

You may find that the resulting consumer price of $6.25, in the example, is competitive for your eight-ounce jar of cooking sauce.

But, if you are selling a one-ounce packet of dill dip mix, then the product will be above the "price point" for its category, and you will probably encounter stiff consumer resistance.

Broker Commissions

Your gross profit margin should include, right from the beginning, the broker commission percentage. This will range from 5 to 15 percent, depending on the type of broker used. Brokers who sell to chain stores, independent wholesalers, and distributors will require a 5 percent commission. Sales via brokers to department stores, retailers, and gift shops will be commissioned at 10 percent. Brokers who have their own showrooms, and who call on retail gift and food stores, will require a 15 percent commission. A good policy is not to pay any commission to any broker until the referring order has been paid.

Distributor Margins

The distributor will add a profit margin to your distributor price, usually a minimum of 25 percent (divide the distributor cost by 75), to arrive at the distributor's price to the retailer.

Bear in mind the concept of price points, or thresholds, beyond which it would be imprudent to price your product. These price points are found usually just under the two, three, four, five, and up to ten-dollar figures. If your price is $4.09, for example, you may want to consider lowering it to $3.99 or $3.95 in order to overcome buyer objections.

The margins and discounts in the above examples are representative of specialty food trade margins and discounts. There are many variations to these, depending on the product, market, season, and so forth.

You should prepare two separate price sheets, one for the retailer and one for the distributor.

Breakeven Analysis

Applying a breakeven analysis that will help you determine the price range available for your product can assist some of your strategic thinking. A breakeven analysis will let you know at what point your dollar or unit sales will meet your total dollar or unit costs. Any revenue generated above the breakeven point is profit—below it is loss.

Detailed discussions of breakeven analyses appear in almost all of the business management books on the market. David Bangs' *The Business Planning Guide* (8th edition, Dearborn Trade) is the source of the following explanation on the topic:

The breakeven point can be calculated by the following formula:

S   = FC + VC

where

S   = Breakeven level of sales in dollars

FC = Fixed costs in dollars

VC = Variable costs in dollars

Fixed costs remain constant regardless of sales volume (at least until your sales volume grows so much as to require capital improvements, such as new buildings, etc.). They are the costs that must be met even if you make no sales. Fixed costs include overhead (rent, administration, salaries, taxes, benefits, etc.) and depreciation, amortization, and interest.

Variable costs are connected to sales volume. They include cost of goods sold (beginning inventory plus freight-in, warehousing, variable labor, broker commissions, etc., less ending inventory).

To calculate the breakeven point *in the absence of your total variable costs*, use the following variation:

S   = FC/GM

where

GM = Gross margin (profit) expressed as a percentage of sales, and determined by adding gross sales to total costs (variable and fixed) and dividing the resulting total by gross sales.

Replace the dollar figures with unit figures if you want to determine the breakeven point in units produced instead of dollars earned.

Sample Breakeven Analysis

Total sales = \$216,000

Cost of goods sold = \$158,320

Gross margin = \$57,680

Gross margin ÷ Total sales = GM%

Fixed costs FC = \$60,570

Gross margin GM = (\$57,680 ÷ \$216,000) = 26.7%

Thus, breakeven sales = S = FC ÷ GM

= (\$60,570 ÷ .267)

= \$226,854 per year

On a monthly basis, S = \$18,905

If sales are projected at a total of \$216,000 for the first year, you will not make a profit—but because you know what you are apt to face, you will be able to plan ahead to finance your business properly.

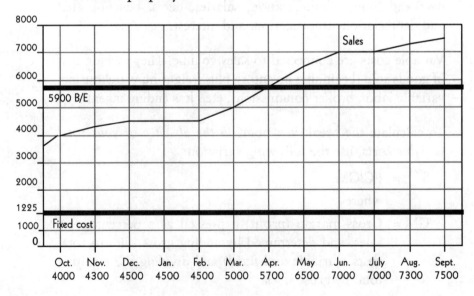

You can also use breakeven charts to measure progress toward annual profit goals. Suppose a $12,000 profit the first year. What sales would be needed?

$$S = (FC + Profit) \div GM$$

where Profit = $12,000;

$$S = (\$60,570 + 12,000) \div .267 = \$271,797 \text{ per year}$$
or $22,650 per month.

Graphically:

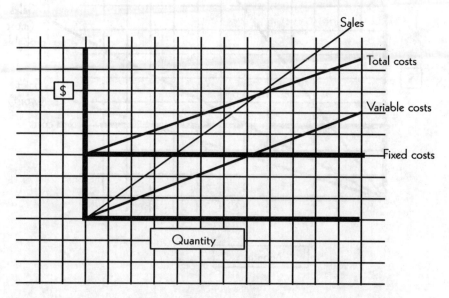

Any time you can help your employees visualize progress toward a goal, you benefit. Breakeven charts are useful for more than financial planning purposes. Once you have calculated breakeven sales, you may find it very helpful to break the sales down in terms of customers needed. As a reality check, this can keep you from making overly optimistic projections.

Breakeven analysis may also be represented pictorially. The diagramming helps establish forecasts, budgets, and projections. Using a chart lets you substitute different combinations of numbers to obtain a rough estimate of their effect on your business.

A helpful technique is to make Worst-Case, Best-Case, and Most-Probable-Case Assumptions, chart them to see how soon they cover fixed costs, and then derive more accurate figures by applying the various formulas and kinds of thinking displayed below. This is of particular value if you are thinking of making a capital investment and want a quick picture of the relative merits of buying or leasing.

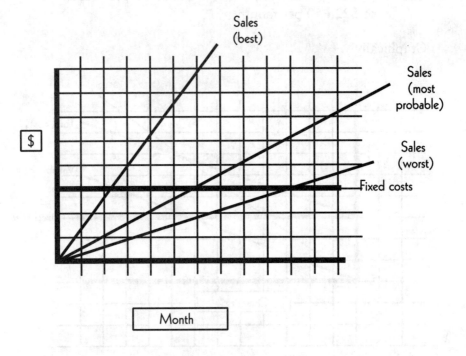

Understanding Terms

Terms are the arrangements for shipping and payment that you establish with your customer. Include your terms on your price lists. An important element of your statement of terms is the establishment of a clear credit policy, from which you should try not to deviate. Among the forms of such a policy are the following:

❖ *Terms of payment*. Either FOB your warehouse, or delivered, with entire invoice amount due in 30 days.

✧ *Early payment discount.* Offer either a 1 or 2 percent discount for payment made within ten days.

✧ *Line of credit.* Inquire into customer's credit references to determine just how much you should allow. Consider withholding shipment if there is an open invoice, or no more than two open invoices within the credit limit.

✧ *FOB (free on board).* FOB warehouse, or delivered, establishes who pays the freight, and when title passes to the customer. If your terms are FOB, your warehouse, then the customer pays the freight and takes title to the merchandise when it leaves your warehouse. This means that the customer will be responsible for taking up the issue of any damaged or missing cases with the shipping company. He/she cannot deduct the missing or lost merchandise from your invoice.

If your terms are FOB customer location, or prepaid, then you must seek recourse with the shipping company in the event that merchandise is missing on delivery or is damaged en route. Title passes to the customer when merchandise is delivered, signed for, and in good condition.

✧ *Suggested terms.* To distributors and large-volume purchasers: COD (cash on delivery), until credit is approved, then 2%/10 days, net 30 days, delivered. (This means that the purchaser may deduct 2 percent from the net invoice amount if paid in full within 10 days. Otherwise, the total is due within 30 days.)

When selling to retailers use COD, until credit is approved, then Net 30 days, FOB warehouse.

Include the comment: "Prices subject to change without notice," on price lists and invoices.

Invoicing Hints
Do not print up thousands of invoice forms! In fact, with the use of a computer, you can generate a different invoice each time you make a sale. Use your invoices as sales tools. From time to time, add a special deal on your invoices to retailers. Many of the retail buyers are also the payers. Offer them a special "reorder deal" that they can send in with their payments, with the deal to be billed later.

Credit

Your ability to assess effectively your buyers' integrity will influence the procedures you undertake to evaluate "creditworthiness." Do not become overly impressed by buyers from high visibility/high prestige outlets. Rarely do these companies pay according to your terms.

The process.—Request prospective buyers to provide you with three trade references and one bank reference. Ask for contact names and telephone numbers because some references will release this type of credit information over the telephone, and this will save time. You can expect that the credit-checking process will take about three to four weeks, which is why I recommend shipping COD for the first order.

In the specialty food industry, most credit arrangements consist of the following:

✧ *Open account.* This means that you are satisfied with the creditworthiness of your customer, and that you ship on receipt of orders on your usual terms, wherein payment is due at the end of the 30-day period. Note that the specialty food industry tends to interpret payment terms of net 30 days, for example, as starting on the day the merchandise is received, rather than on the date of the invoice, or ship date.

✧ *COD.* Cash on delivery is generally used with first-time customers, until their credit is approved. COD terms may also be used on request by some small retailers who prefer it to the requirements for accounts payable bookkeeping.

You request the trucking company to collect a specified amount, usually the FOB invoice amount, plus freight, plus any special COD charges. Note: This procedure will work only if you use specialized delivery services, such as U.S. Postal Service, United Parcel Service, Federal Express, etc.

✧ *Pro forma.* Used for prepayment. You prepare a standard invoice covering all costs agreed to (e.g., product and freight) and type on the front of the invoice the word "pro forma." Send the pro forma invoice to your customer, and ship product on receipt of payment. Pro forma invoices are rarely used for domestic shipments (and then only in circumstances in which credit cannot be established, or customer refuses COD). They are employed generally in those cases where buyer access to funds requires supporting papers, such as certificates of origin, etc.

✧ *Guarantees.* The only guarantee you will make will be against defects. If damage occurs during shipping, the buyer is usually called upon to pursue a claim with the freight company; however, it will be in your best interest to assist by offering to replace the damaged merchandise. Otherwise, some buyers will withhold payment of your invoice until the freight claim is resolved.

> **CASE IN POINT**
>
> *Moon Shine Trading Co.—1992 Outstanding Jam, Preserve, Spread or Topping (Apricot Honey). The company began in 1979 with 180 pounds of pure Yellow Star Thistle, Northern California's finest honey. The honey was carefully warmed, gently strained through a fine screen, and then bottled. With this tiny beginning, the seed of an extensive honey collection was planted. The firm has added butters and spreads to its line of honey.*

Warehousing and Shipping Your Products

Public Warehouses

These are companies that provide storage and warehouse services. Some offer cooled and refrigerated environments. They charge either flat rates by the month, or rates based on product stored, as well as in-and-out charges, charges for preparing shipping documents (bills of lading), charges for repacking damaged or broken products (coopering), and other related services. If you require public warehousing, you should shop around to find the best combination of location, services, and costs.

Many warehouses will take your orders over the telephone and ship according to your instructions. This is where a fax machine can come in handy.

Storage and warehousing will be an important factor in determining your ex-warehouse costs.

Common Carriers

Common carriers are trucking companies other than the United Parcel Service (UPS), Federal Express Ground, DHL-Airborne, and Parcel Post, that offer pickup and delivery service. You will have to use common carriers for shipping large orders. UPS, FedEx, and DHL will take any size order, but no one container can weigh over 150 pounds (70 pounds for home delivery) (you can save money sometimes by delivering large orders in two or more shipments). Note that most common-carrier charges are based on a minimum shipment rate of 500 pounds.

Your customer may request that you ship via a certain carrier. Most common carriers offer discount rates that are based on total shipment weight. UPS, FedEx, and DHL rates are based on the gross weight per case. Gross weight includes the product, outer carton, and shipping materials.

Rates are keyed to hundredweight, or per CWT (cost per hundred pounds). For example, if the quote is $4 CWT, you will pay $.04 per pound. Ask your warehouse to find the least expensive and most reliable carrier to fill your requirements.

If your production facility and warehouse are in your home, then you may have trouble working with a common carrier. They will be pleased to pick up and deliver your product, but you will have to arrange for the sometimes difficult process of working without a standard loading dock. Getting the product from your basement, or kitchen, out the front door and onto the truck can be a trial.

Private Pickup and Delivery Services

The United Parcel Service is one of the largest and best known of the pickup and delivery services. It has been joined in this by competitors FedEx and DHL. Call your local UPS, FedEx, or DHL office and request an information kit (or request one online). They will set up an account for you. They may require you to remit a deposit against which charges for shipping will be made. Generally, they charge a weekly fee for making daily calls at your pickup point. Shipments are charged by the pound, based on destination, and they offer redelivery, next-day, second-day air, and COD services. You can arrange for the shipment online and print complete shipping documents. Most carriers can also advise the shipper via e-mail of when the shipment arrives at its destination

✧ GUIDELINES FOR SUCCESS ✧
Warehousing and Shipping

✧ *Establish warehouse arrangements*. Shop around for the best deal. A nonunion warehouse offers greater leeway to remove samples, take inventory, etc., and is less expensive than union or "covered" warehouses.

✧ *Inbound*. Your product is shipped from your production facility, or pier, to the public warehouse.

✧ *Stocked*. It is inventoried and stocked in the warehouse.

✧ *Paperwork/records*. You will receive a monthly inventory statement and invoice for services provided, preparation of bills of lading (the shipping documents), storage, etc.

✧ *Select a carrier*. You may request the warehouse to select a common carrier to ship your products to your customers. If you have frequent shipments, you can also arrange for carriers to make daily calls on the warehouse to pick up and deliver the shipments to your customer.

✧ *Take inventory*. Once a quarter, or more frequently, you should personally supervise a physical inventory in the warehouse. This gives you a good inventory figure to use in preparing your accounts and in controlling your business, and it helps resolve any issues of missing or damaged merchandise.

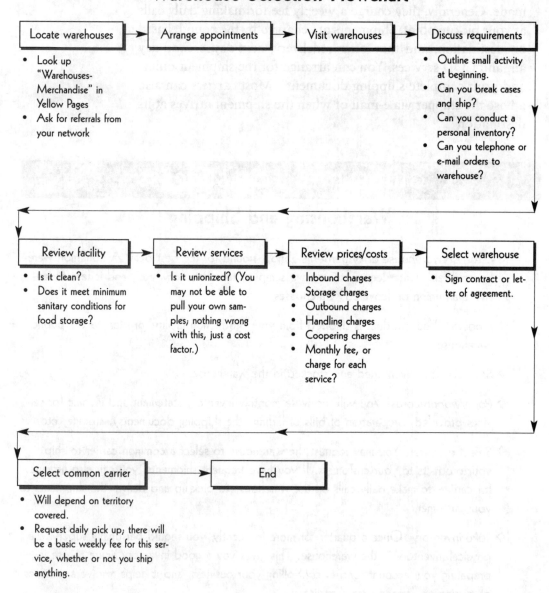

Warehouse Selection Flowchart

Locate warehouses → **Arrange appointments** → **Visit warehouses** → **Discuss requirements**

- Look up "Warehouses-Merchandise" in Yellow Pages
- Ask for referrals from your network

- Outline small activity at beginning.
- Can you break cases and ship?
- Can you conduct a personal inventory?
- Can you telephone or e-mail orders to warehouse?

Review facility → **Review services** → **Review prices/costs** → **Select warehouse**

- Is it clean?
- Does it meet minimum sanitary conditions for food storage?

- Is it unionized? (You may not be able to pull your own samples; nothing wrong with this, just a cost factor.)

- Inbound charges
- Storage charges
- Outbound charges
- Handling charges
- Coopering charges
- Monthly fee, or charge for each service?

- Sign contract or letter of agreement.

Select common carrier → **End**

- Will depend on territory covered.
- Request daily pick up; there will be a basic weekly fee for this service, whether or not you ship anything.

CHAPTER THREE

Taking Your Product to Market

This chapter offers a comprehensive review of the most fundamental aspect of specialty food marketing—taking your product to market. The chapter addresses the following elements:

✧ Six principles of marketing

✧ The role of the Internet

✧ Preparing sales literature

✧ Designing point-of-purchase materials

✧ Promoting the product

✧ Publicizing your product

✧ Advertising the product

✧ Finding buyers

✧ Establishing distribution channels

✧ Arranging the deals

✧ Appointing brokers

✧ Locating distributors

✧ Making the sale

✧ Exporting

You've come a long way in developing your product, because you have:

✧ Continued to listen to your customers,

✦ Developed partnerships with your suppliers,

✦ Your product is tried and tested, packaged and priced, and

✦ You have identified your niche and are ready to affirm why you stayed with the enterprise: to promote, market, sell, and reap your rewards by exceeding your customers' expectations.

Now you want to do a first-class job of placing your product before the consumer.

Six Principles for Marketing Success

Before you begin this undertaking, you may want to review the following six principles of marketing that will underlie all your efforts.

1. *Focus*. Ground your business on the consumer, not the distributor or retailer. Know your market and be able to identify your customer precisely. You will still have to meet the quality requirements of your distributors/retailers.

2. *Positioning*. Ensure that your product is not at a disadvantage to the competition. Differentiate sufficiently to clinch customer acceptance. How does it stand out? What is its unique selling point?

3. *Demonstrations*. Demos sell. Provide tasting opportunities as often as possible.

4. *Advertising*. Center your advertising on the one specific advantage or edge your product has over the competition. Employ proven advertising methods.

5. *Distribution*. Establish distribution sufficient to the needs of the market. Make sure there is sufficient product in distribution to meet consumer demand, especially if you do any consumer advertising.

6. *Promotion*. Manage your promotions to increase in-store display and produce greater consumer sales.

The Role of the Internet

The global linkage offered by the Internet is driving everything in our economy. Some reports suggest that annual Internet grocery sales total more than $1 billion. The rules of economic intercourse are changing. What effect will this have on specialty food distribution? Will there be a continuing role for the broker, or will these "middlemen" become redundant? How will you respond to issues of business-to-business services, marketer-retailer partnerships, fulfillment operations, cyber-shopping, direct-marketing techniques, electronic customer challenges, new online food trends, Web page design, customer-retention challenges, and developing key alliances? It may be time to review your long-term vision. What if your dream included the ability to market your products direct to consumers?

> ## A Note on Consumers and Customers
>
> *Important concept: Who is the primary determiner of quality? Is it the consumer? Or is it the retailer/distributor? If your product does not appeal to the consumer (as in end user), no amount of retail orders will ensure your success. If your product does appeal to the consumer, then you must also know the quality demands of your customer—the retailer/distributor.*

These are just some of the opportunities confronting specialty food marketers who wish to take advantage of the Internet. The following pages address some of the more important issues associated with doing that.

An Internet Home Page

You can create your own home page by using page-creating software provided by online services. You do not have to be technically adept, but it helps. A basic working knowledge of computers will suffice.

The real concern has to do with the effect your home page has on attracting customers. Because the cost of preparing a simple page is minimal—consisting of your time and talent and the access time charged by the online service—you might want to give it a try. Given the increasing level of Internet home page competition, a more sophisticated and complex Web page may be required. In this case, you would do well to retain the services of a professional Web page designer (see Appendix I).

Issues of privacy are mostly resolved—how to protect your customers' use of a credit card, for example—and more consumers are using the Net.

Putting the Web to Work for You

Rita Wilhelm, president of the Web site development firm SnapMonkey.com, weighs in with the following:

The Internet has become an important part of our lives and has become widely used, both in business and at home. Yet many people still seem unsure of how to use the Internet to market and grow their businesses. There are so many options available that at times the whole process can seem a little intimidating.

The number of Web sites doubles every four to five months. By 2003, over 80 million users were logging on to the Web regularly. The Internet is here to stay, and a Web site is now a tool that is as important to a business's success as the telephone. If you don't have a Web site, get one. If you have one, use it. It's as simple as that.

How Much Should It Cost?

Web sites can be anything you want them to be. Depending on your budget and your goals, there are many options. According to a study done by *Inc.* magazine, 96 percent of all responding small businesses paid less than $3,000 for design, and averaged $71 a month in hosting fees. Design it yourself. If you can create a Word document, you can create your own Web site. With today's easy-to-use design systems, anyone can create a professional site in just a few hours. By designing it yourself, you have the control to make changes when you want, and you have ongoing control over the content of your site.

> **CASE IN POINT**
>
> *Nearly 400 (25 percent) of the 1,600 exhibitors at the 1999 Summer Fancy Food Show had home pages on the Web. By comparison, almost all the exhibitors at the 2004 Summer Fancy Food Show reported having Web sites.*

Hire a Web Designer/Developer

A custom-designed site is the way to go if you have a complex site that needs many special features. Web designers will typically provide you with a variety of choices—but you will pay for those choices as well. Check out their references, and see what other sites they have designed before you make a commitment.

Goals for Your Site

Your Web site is an integral part of your marketing campaign. And the best thing about it is you can change it as often as you wish!

Your site should be a working product that changes and grows as you do. A Web site should be your salesperson and your order taker 24/7. That's what makes the Internet such a dynamic asset to your business!

Site Design

Make your site a part of your image. Use your logo, your colors, your theme, and your images that make your business yours. A good design is set up in a professional manner, and helps the customer along to the ultimate goal—a purchase from you!

Navigation

Good navigation is essential to a good Web site. Make it easy for your customers to move through your site, and give them easy direction to move to the next step. A good site will always provide customers with essential pages that motivate them to a purchase, and always provide them with a way to get back to your home page.

Clarity

Your home page must be clear and to the point. Don't put everything on your front page. Instead, stick with a couple of solid key facts, and then lead your viewer through your site gathering information. Evaluate your site from your customer's point of view. Better yet, have your clients tell you what they think of your site. Listen to what they say—they are the users.

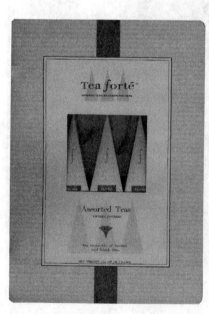

Content

Find ways to put rich and informative information on your site. Put product information, specifications, and instructions online. Information is king on the Internet.

Traffic

Traffic is the amount of people who are actually clicking into your site. And the best way to get traffic to your site is to share your Web address with everyone. Search engines are the obvious starting point. They will pull people in the first time; your content will keep them coming back. Search engines rank the placement of your site by keywords and meta tags. These are lines of coding and words or phrases that are used to help identify your site, and place you in the proper category. You will benefit much more by listing just a few phrases and keywords than by trying to think of every word combination possible for your industry. Find your true focus, and target those keywords. Every page should have keywords to ensure placement. And submit often to major search engines.

CASE IN POINT

Mark T. Wendell's (tea importer) president Elliot Johnson reports: "I have found it fascinating that our new six-week-old "wholesale" Web site has created more new customers and orders than the last two shows combined. Perhaps the times, they are a-changing. Food for thought."

E-Mail

The fastest-growing form of marketing today is e-mail marketing. Unfortunately, it's also one of the most abused because of its ease and low cost. According to Jupiter Communications, the average U.S. Internet user received 40 commercial e-mails in 1999. That number will be up to 1,600 by 2005. Your clients will gladly accept your e-mails if they are of true benefit to them. When you get their e-mail addresses, let them know you will be sending them periodic announcements of sales and happenings in your business. Don't abuse that trust.

Newsletters

The obvious transition from e-mail is to begin creating an online newsletter. Determine your purpose first: Why are you sending a newsletter? Let your clients know, and stick with your original purpose. Always have opt in/opt out options on each newsletter, allowing your clients to easily choose to remove themselves from your newsletter database. And then stay in contact with them! Give them what they want—information and sales promotions from your business!

Promote Your Site

Five tips to get your site in front of your target customer:

1. Promote your site everywhere. Include it in all your brochures, ads, letterhead, business cards, voice-mail messages and order forms and invoices.

2. Give them a reason to visit your site. Provide them with information. Information is what sells on the Internet. When people move from site to site, they are in search of someone who can help answer their questions, in ways that may never have occurred to them. Give them the information, and the sale will follow.

3. There are only three ways to increase business: Increase the number of customers, increase the initial order of each client, or increase the number of times each client purchases from you. Make sure your site includes ways to accomplish each of these. Offer "refer a friend" links from your popular pages. Create packages that include several of your top sellers, and offer your clients a discount if they buy the packages instead of items one at a time. Include reoccurring orders, similar to fruit-of-the-month programs. The key is to get the sale, and make it easy through your site.

4. Launch an e-mail campaign. Collect e-mail addresses from every one of your clients and gather addresses from people who inquire about your products. Then send e-mail promotions regularly. Make sure you have direct links to the products you promote, and verify the links before you send. Put short deadlines on your offers; e-mail is an instant function—make your client take action quickly.

5. Keep your Web site current. This is the number-one turnoff of surfers. Changing your site shows its importance in your business structure. It tells your potential clients that you value their business, and you want to provide them with the most up-to-date information. And by changing your Web site often, you can promote current events. Your site will become a relied-upon resource, and

will be looked at and referred to by many people. Include the date each time you change your Web site.

What Should I Do with My Web Site?

Begin by creating a site that contains information. Think about what content would benefit your clients the most. Add your company background and history. Include directions, maps, office hours, contact names, and best ways of getting in touch with you. Also provide instructions and guidelines on using your product or service. Add articles, resource pages, and frequently-asked-questions (FAQ) pages.

When your site is complete and offers your clients the information they're looking for, begin thinking of your site as a sales representative. What could be better than a sales rep that works for you 24/7? Put together an online product catalog, and include each of your products with photographs, key descriptions, and customer testimonials. Then move your client from the description to a shopping cart, where they can confirm their purchases with just a few simple clicks.

How can you bring your clients together online, and share ideas about your product and the way they can benefit from your company? Create an online community. Use a message board to supply advice about happenings in the specialty food market, and then lead discussions on current topics. This is a great reason for people to return to your site again and again. Ask yourself: How can I make full use of my site in my current business?

A Web site is just like any other marketing tool you use in your business. For it to be effective, you must use it. A clever site entices people to visit often. Just like your brochures and advertisements, your site should be attractive to your target audience. Find

CASE IN POINT

Internet Directory—DexMonkey.com offers a robust searchable multimedia directory program. Any organization can add a DexMonkey directory to their existing Web site. DexMonkey will categorize, and allow members of the directory to showcase their product or service. See Appendix I for more detail.

out why people are visiting your site, and give them as much of what they want as you can. One of the best things about a Web site is its ease and flexibility. It's easy to add daily tips, weekly specials, and monthly promotions right on to your front page. Keep building and keep trying. Give people what they're looking for!

Think about getting together with your state's business development or specialty foods group. Use the Internet to set up a combined sourcing site for supplies. You and your fellow marketers could take advantage of the economies of scale such larger trading offers.

The Internet and Cybershopping

Home shopping via the Internet will dramatically increase in this century. Specialty food marketers increasingly selling their products straight to consumers via the Internet will effect new product introductions. The large companies, of course, can't do the same. Their size makes it difficult for them to adopt an adaptive and flexible approach to quickly changing market conditions. What they do instead, is find ways to convince those cybershoppers to go to the supermarket via samples, coupons, and refunds for debuting products.

Cybershopping has a long way to go before bricks-and-mortar stores become obsolete. Tech-savvy consumers are becoming increasingly aware of shopping sites, but are wary that what might have been a private transaction at a local specialty food store is now part of a statistical abstract being developed by these companies. This is called user "profiling," by which the site owner attempts to collect information about the buyers' interests, habits, frequency of use, etc. The resulting profile aids the supplier in matching its products and services with the perceived consumer wants and needs.

Of all the factors influencing the specialty foods market, cyber-shopping has the most to gain and lose. As consumers become more comfortable using the Internet to make purchases, there will be a greater likelihood that distribution patterns will change. Figure 3.1 gives you an idea of the number of food-related shopping Web sites.

FIGURE 3.1: Number of Food-Related Web Sites in Summer 2004 Compared with Spring 2000

Search Engine	Number of Specialty Food Sites		Number of Gourmet Food Sites	
	2000	2004	2000	2004
Google	N/A	4,100,000	N/A	4,600,000
Yahoo	20	6,820,000	2,400	5,360,000
MSN	N/A	1,448,827	N/A	1,119,538
AOL	N/A	1,411,593	N/A	1,116,964
Alta Vista	71,134	3,245,904	263,925	2,565,854
About	N/A	8,917	N/A	233
Netscape	N/A	833	N/A	782
Ask	N/A	210	N/A	212
Web Crawler	38,577	1,540	110,957	2,680
Northern Light	498,826	N/A	251,016	N/A

Thousands of other sites are listed in the Excite and HotBot search engines. How does one get seen among so many? Select the Google search engine, for example. How realistic is to expect that anyone would wade through 4,100,000 sites? Research reports that most viewers only look at the top 20 or so listings before either selecting one or leaving. There are a number of consulting organizations which develop Web pages and which have learned how to select words that give their clients top billing on these pages (see Appendix I).

Web Site Uses

Recently, Rita Wilhelm and her partner, Lori Osterberg, created SnapMonkey.com to provide affordable and easy-to-create Web sites that small businesses can build online. (By Rita Wilhelm.)

Use Your Web Site as Great Marketing Tool

How do most of your clients find you? Is it by word of mouth, or maybe some advertising media? Whatever means they use to find you, adding a Web site can have a huge impact on your sales. For example, a gift basket business is unique in the sense that your customer never really sees the end product. What they receive is the goodwill of the recipient and an appreciative telephone call. So think about that. Naturally, your potential customers want to make the best buying decisions, and a Web site will help educate them as to their choices.

Visual information is a key component. Most of you probably distribute brochures for this purpose. And although a brochure can be an effective educational tool, potential customers will not always have one at their disposal when they are ready to make a purchase. A Web site, however, is easily accessible and affords your customer an opportunity to leisurely get an idea of your business's offerings, and learn about the quality and type of service you provide. This in turn will help you become more efficient and save time on telephone orders.

Using Your Web Site Effectively

In order for your Web site to realize its potential, you must promote it. The goal is to broadcast your Web site address in every possible venue so that your existing and future clients will begin to recognize it, use it, and pass it on. The following suggestions will help you promote your Web site.

✧ Attach a label or tag with your business's name and Web address to every product you make. This is a free marketing opportunity for you.

✧ A Web site address is simple to remember and makes it easier for your clients to share your wonderful service with the people around them. Word of mouth is always great in any business.

✧ Include your Web address on all printed material, including brochures, business cards, seasonal mailers, and advertisements.

✧ Invite customers to visit your Web site: "Visit our Web site to see our full selection." With the overwhelming number of choices your potential customers face, they will appreciate an opportunity to obtain more information to help them make their purchases.

Guidelines for Success, continued

✧ When you are selling, taking other calls, making more products, or otherwise unavailable, and calls are being received by your voice mail, invite your caller to visit your Web site. For example, you might record: "Thank you for calling ABC Company. We will be back at 3:00. In the meantime, feel free to visit our online studio at www.ABCCompany.com."

✧ Remind your clients to add your site to their "Bookmarks" or "Favorites" so they can continue to visit your updated Web site.

✧ Encourage visitors to your site to sign up for monthly e-mails on topics such as important gift-giving dates and special promotions.

✧ Having your products for sale online can also increase your productivity. During busy times such as before the holidays, you will be able to take orders online as well as by phone.

Remember, using and promoting your Web site effectively can expand your business. Keep it updated with useful information and products. Broadcast your Web address constantly.

Issues to Address in Marketing Specialty Foods Over the Internet

You may wish to consider the following issues associated with responding to the challenge and opportunity of online specialty food sales:

Strategic planning

✧ Clarifying how Internet use can add value to achieving your corporate long-range dream.

✧ Understanding and developing useful tools for measuring your Internet performance and comparing it to your strategic goals and objectives.

✧ Understanding the implications of Internet security (both credit card and your computer).

Product development

✧ Use the Internet to conduct consumer research, competitive research, and find packaging, labeling, and production services.

Web Site Hosting

There is a huge variety of Web site hosting services. For example, the "100 Best Web Hosting" Web site— http://www.100best-web-hosting.com/top100/1.html—lists 243 World Wide Web hosting services by rank, host name, and reviewer comments.

Marketing

❖ Understanding the impact Internet sales will have on the role of distributors, brokers, and retailers.

❖ Establishing simple, yet effective, Internet relationships with retailers, brokers, and distributors.

❖ Branding your product name on the Internet.

❖ Using the Internet for market research, determining specific customer needs, trends, etc.

Merchandising

❖ Effectively matching the right product with the right customer at the right time.

❖ Developing a community market where your products can be marketed along with complementary, noncompetitive products (called multistore architecture).

Customer relations

❖ Developing effective means of cultivating prospects and turning them into repeat customers.

❖ Understanding the methods required for creating an outstanding customer experience.

❖ Providing frequently-asked-questions (FAQ) sections on your Web site.

Administration

❖ Developing easy and customer-friendly order entry and fulfillment processes.

There is the issue of consumer wariness to buy sight unseen. Some of us would be happy to refill our larders with a half-dozen of that specialty mustard we like, but there are two problems with this. One is that the product is being offered to the consumer at the same (or even higher) price offered by the nearby food store. An example: The eight-ounce crock of Kieller's Dundee Marmalade is sold at Trader Joe's for $3.29. The same product is available on the

> *Have you developed an Internet strategy to turn your Web site visitors into customers?*

Internet for anywhere from $4.50 to $7.80! This is puzzling. The seller can take a greater profit than if it were sold to a distributor or retailer, and still offer a really good deal to the consumer. The other problem is that not many specialty food marketers are using the Internet to actually sell their products to consumers. They fear the negative reaction that might arise from distributors and retailers who would view direct sales to consumers as competitive.

> ### A Consumer Vision
>
> *You are the consumer. Using a hand-held scanner, you scan key ingredients in your cupboard, then download that information to your home computer. The computer conducts a search of all the appropriate Internet sites. Missing ingredients are added to your shopping list, and the food is delivered to your home.*

A report by the University of Maine shows that nearly eight million consumers purchased *something* online during the 1998 holiday season. The National Conference of State Legislatures reports that 32 million people bought something online in 1999. And that number is expected to reach $200 billion in 2005. If this behavior continues, it will naturally include more and more opportunities for Internet purchases of specialty foods.

Most of the industry is viewing the Internet with some reservation. While some agree to sell to an Internet retailer, such as GreatFood.com, many seem to be limiting use of the Internet to e-mail and reorders from their existing trade clients. In addition, food entrepreneurs can use Web site directories such as www.specialtyfoodresource.com to locate suppliers, vendors, retailers, and distributors, and to avail themselves of extensive Internet networking opportunities.

Preparing Sales Literature

Product sales literature is essential to your sales effort. A sales kit may consist of a price list, catalog (product presentation) sheet, product information sheet, and point-of-purchase material.

Typically, a catalog sheet and a price sheet will suffice. The catalog sheet is generally an 8½" by 11" four-color, product photograph accompanied by approximately 50 words of copy that describe the product. Include company name, postal and Web site addresses, email, telephone, and fax numbers.

In addition to price lists and catalog sheets, you may use a fact sheet to highlight promotable elements of your company and its products. Such elements as testimonials from famous people, historical anecdotes about your company, claims to fame, etc., can be included in the fact sheet.

Also, this is where you can amplify statements regarding recipes, applications, and health claims that relate to your product. These provide even more reinforcement of your sales message. Information that you include on your fact sheets may also be included on your price sheets. Lose no opportunity to impart your sales message!

Much of your sales material can be prepared with the aid of your PC. There are several good software packages that are both easy to master and cost-effective. Ask your local software dealer for advice. With digital imagery, one can capture product, then download it, add copy, and print. Using your computer and a good color laser printer, you have the advantage of working with and testing a number of different promotional devices.

> ### Effective Sales Literature Can Help
> ✧ improve distributor and broker knowledge of your product.
> ✧ convey preferred use.
> ✧ promote the product.
> ✧ make sales.

You can also prepare a color leaflet or mailer on your computer. Complete the design using your desktop software and burn it to a CD. Take this to your local photocopy or stationery supplies store. You can have them print your color product using their computer and color printer. (Alternatively, you can buy your own ink jet color printer for under $300, or a laser printer for under $1,000).

✧ GUIDELINES FOR SUCCESS ✧

Sales Literature

What to Include

Product description	Make it sizzle! Include the facts and figures (sizes, net contents, case lots, etc.) on the reverse side of the catalog sheet. Use the front for general presentation, and the back for the details.
Photography/graphics	Topnotch, upscale.
Copy	Sell the product benefits.
Contact information	Company name, mailing, e-mail, and Web site address, telephone number (don't forget area code), and fax.

What Not to Include

✧ Prices

✧ Dates

✧ Any time-sensitive material (e.g., "just in time for Valentine's Day 2005")

Selecting Point-of-Purchase Materials

Many retailers find point-of-purchase materials (also referred to as POP) useful in attracting attention to products they stock. POPs not only attract consumer attention, they also inform and educate the prospective buyer about the product's benefits. POPs may include tent cards (used primarily in restaurants), posters, shelf talkers, product information neck tags attached to bottles and other packages, and recipe handouts.

✧ *Tent cards* are small, tent-shaped cards that can be placed on counters, tables, and shelves. You may have seen these used in restaurants to promote specials of the day. Retailers use them to promote new products and to alert customers to items on sale.

✧ *Posters* are used in store windows, on store walls, and, when properly mounted, on shelves and counters. Because of the size of most posters, many retailers are hesitant to use them, but they are especially useful during in-store promotions and in trade show exhibits.

✧ *Shelf talkers* are used extensively in the grocery trade. They are small signs that are designed to protrude from underneath the product they describe. They can be effective for new-product introductions and are more likely to be utilized than posters. Also, they are placed under the product, rather than nearby, making a clear connection between the message they impart and the product they promote.

✧ *Product information tags* are most often used in the form of neck tags, which provide all kinds of promotional data. They may include recipes, company history, product uses, recommendations, ingredient descriptions, coupons, and free offers. The benefit is that you can ensure their use because they require no extra effort on the part of the retailer—they are already affixed to the product.

✦ GUIDELINES FOR SUCCESS ✦

Point-of-Purchase Materials

	Tent Cards	Posters	Shelf Talkers	Neck Tags
Size (approx)	5" x 7"	18" x 36"	6" x 10"	2¾" x 2½"
Color	2-color	4-color	2-color	2- or 4-color
Number to prepare	1,000	500	1,000	One run's worth
Distribution	Food service/ retailers	Retailers	Distributors	With the product
When to use	Demos/special events	New products/ new retailers	New products/ new retailers	During intro stage/new products

Notes

Size: Tent cards are used on tables, so the size is small and the message brief. I have used posters with cardboard backing that can stand alone or be placed on a wall. In both cases, the posters were 9" x 14". The number of shelf "facings" available for your product may limit shelf talker size. You don't want your shelf talker to use space occupied by another product. Neck tags are small and can be unfolded to reveal several pages of product information.

Color: Two-color products are recommended, where possible, to save money. (You can produce some four-color media on your own color printer or one available at your local copy shop.)

Number to prepare: Go slowly; prepare as few as economically feasible.

Distribution: Tent cards, posters, and shelf talkers can be shipped either with the product or via your broker and/or distributor. Neck tags may be used all the time.

Promoting the Product

One of the most important elements of niche marketing is product promotion. Product promotion often means the difference between success or failure. Getting your product before the consumer and having it recognized is the first step to making a sale. The most often-used means of promotion are trade show exhibitions, in-store demonstrations, giveaways, mailings, tie-ins, testimonials, show awards, and the Internet.

Trade Shows

Trade shows rate high on the list of important promotional vehicles. Other promotional possibilities are described later in this section.

Benefits of food show participation

- ✧ Meet customers.
- ✧ Learn about competition.
- ✧ Experiment with product ingredients.
- ✧ Evaluate product packaging.
- ✧ Test product pricing.
- ✧ Rate various promotion techniques.
- ✧ Identify important trends.
- ✧ Solicit customer reaction.
- ✧ Make sales.

Food show participation offers a cost-effective means of introducing a new product, gathering market research, learning about competition, and making sales. There are numerous food shows, but few offer real value to most specialty food producers. See Appendix C for a listing of some of the more prominent food shows.

The major shows held in the United States attract buyers from most specialty food markets. The level of exposure at these shows

✧ GUIDELINES FOR SUCCESS ✧

Trade Show Milestones

One year before show

✧ Commit to attending the trade show.

✧ Begin work on total promotion campaign.

✧ Review booth design. Look for imaginative, inexpensive display schemes/materials.

Six months before show

✧ Make plane reservations and hotel accommodations.

✧ Develop sales literature for show.

Three months before show

✧ Check on sales literature produced by both your firm and the show sponsor.

✧ Review results in search of prospective brokers and distributors.

✧ Initiate contact and establish appointments with key prospects.

Two months before show

✧ Arrange shipment of any display equipment and samples (all display materials must be fireproofed).

✧ Prepare press kits.

✧ Verify with freight forwarder that equipment has arrived. (Note: You can hand-carry samples/display materials from your car to the show booth. Generally, you cannot use any luggage carts or trolleys.)

✧ Confirm with show management that all arrangements have been made regarding shipping, electricity, extra tables/chairs, table drapes, signs, etc.

✧ Determine method for lead qualification following the show.

✧ Hand-carry a just-in-case package of samples, price sheets, and literature.

Upon arrival

✧ Set up booth display (table covers, samples, signs, etc.).

✧ Become familiar with show layout, transportation, special events, etc.

Guidelines for Success, continued

✧ Deliver your press kits to the show press room.

✧ Survey competitors' products, booths, and product literature.

Upon returning home

✧ Write thank-you notes to the appropriate people.

✧ Record recommendations for successive shows.

✧ Begin business follow-up with potential customers.

can be met or surpassed only by taking the time and expense of traveling to many of the leading specialty food markets.

Certain trade shows require exhibitors to be members of the sponsoring association. Some associations require you to be in business for at least two years in order to be accepted as a member. If a member distributor or broker takes on your product, and thereby develops a client-business relationship with you, then your products can be exhibited in that distributor's or broker's booth.

Before attending a trade show, you will have to consider the appropriateness of your sales literature for the target market, including the illustration and timeliness of information. You will have to consider booth design, layout, signs, demo equipment requirements (you will have to order display risers, electricity, and floodlighting). A standard booth order generally includes tables, chairs, and booth carpeting.

The estimated cost for a 100-square-foot booth, with minimum spot lighting, drayage, table covers, freight in and out, travel, accommodations, and meals for one person is *at least* $5,000.

As promotional tools, trade shows should be part of a fully integrated and well-managed campaign. For full effect, they should be incorporated into other promotional efforts. Aside from the all-important trade shows, specialty food promotion can take many forms. Some of the most common are described in the next sections.

In-Store Demonstrations/Tastings

Consumers tend to buy products they have sampled, usually at sample tastings conducted at the point-of-purchase. These can involve a demonstrator, your product, and the means of sampling (crackers with cheese, for example). The demonstration is conducted during high-traffic periods, over the course of three to six hours. Consumers have the opportunity to taste your product, to comment on it, to hear a pitch from the demonstrator, and to purchase. Often, demonstrations are accompanied by a special product price used to entice the consumer into making an immediate purchase.

A typical demonstration might be conducted from 10:00 AM to 3:00 PM on a Saturday. The idea is to get as much public attention as you can, so peak shopping hours are best for demonstrations.

Demonstrator costs will be in the neighborhood of $15 to $25 per hour, with a $100 to $125 minimum fee per day.

◆ GUIDELINES FOR SUCCESS ◆

How to Reduce Trade Show Expenses

◆ Share booth with another food producer.

◆ Share booth with broker/distributor.

◆ Take your own (flameproof) table drapes, backdrop, and riser covers. (Use a colorful oilcloth-type table cover for easy cleaning.)

◆ Use your own posters and signs.

◆ Order one double-neck floodlight per 100 square feet of exhibit space.

◆ Hand-carry your samples (no luggage carts with freight permitted through show doors, but you can carry boxes).

◆ Bring a hand-held vacuum to clean your carpet (touch up).

◆ Survival gear:

_____ Packaging tape/dispenser	_____ Fishing line (to hang posters)	
_____ Cellophane tape	_____ Paper napkins	_____ Marking pens
_____ Pliers	_____ Stapler/staples	_____ Ballpoint pens
_____ Clipboard	_____ Screwdriver	_____ Business cards
_____ Cell phone	_____ Laptop computer	

◆ Take a cooler (for samples, cold drinks, snacks, etc.).

◆ Use ice from outside exhibit hall for your cooler.

◆ Take a hot plate (if required for sample tasting).

◆ Bring serving materials (plastic plates, bowls, spoons, forks, etc.).

◆ Consider a less expensive hotel, and commute to the show.

Giveaways

One of the least expensive forms of advertising and promotion is a product giveaway. A carefully managed program of free merchandise can place your product in front of the consumer, while attracting the attention of the retailer.

Usually, free merchandise is offered with in-store demonstrations, introductory deals, and sampling allowances. Free merchandise may also include specially packed sample containers for distribution at the point-of-purchase and during trade shows.

Mailings

A mailing can consist of a price list, a sample, and a catalog sheet sent to several retailers and/or distributors. Or it can consist of a mass mailing with multiple inserts, full-color slick catalog sheets, and samples to thousands of prospective consumers. In entry-level niche marketing, mailings will be more than likely limited to selected retailers and distributors.

It is very difficult for a new supplier to sell a new and unseen food product via the mail. Mailings should be made to prospective distributors in accordance with a complete marketing promotion. In other words, generate more than just a mailing! Devise a follow-up program that will include telephone screening and sales calls. A mailing should sell as well as inform.

Mailings to retailers are slightly different than mailings to distributors. Usually, they do not include the follow-up telephone call or the sales call. You will be mailing to many retailers, instead of a couple of dozen distributors, so you design a different mail campaign. The inserts you use should include a postage-paid return order form for easy use by the retailer. Mailings to retailers are best used as: information providers, invitations to visit your trade show booth, invitations to request free samples or more information, and inducements to reorder.

GUIDELINES FOR SUCCESS ✦

Postal Mailings to Distributors

✦ Develop a mailing list. May be purchased through a mailing list broker.

✦ Prepare the mailer. Include a cover letter, catalog/price sheet, and a sample (if possible). The cover letter should be brief, informative, and to the point. Be sure to state that you will telephone the buyer next week.

✦ Prepare the envelope.

✦ Mail the materials.

✦ Follow up by telephone in about seven days.

✦ Qualify the buyer (discern level of interest).

✦ Arrange an appointment.

✦ Send a brief note confirming appointment details, and stressing a benefit of your product.

✦ Call on the prospect, stress the benefits, and make the sale!

✦ Follow up with a brief note about sale details.

E-Mail Mailings to Distributors

E-mails to distributors involve the same process as regular mail, except that you can mail to a larger audience less expensively and with fewer moves. Large e-mail address-listings can be obtained from the same mailing list brokers as regular mail address listings.

Tie-Ins

You can get more out of your promotion dollar by sharing the costs with another food producer. This is accomplished by "tying" your product with another, complementary product. For example, tea with pastries/cakes/cookies; cheese with crackers; preserves with special muffins/breads.

Arrange to have a series of in-store demonstrations where both products are being served. Share the costs of the demonstration with the other producer. Presenting the two products in a special promotional package can support the tie-in concept.

Testimonials and Show Awards

One of the most effective, and least expensive, promotional tools is to get someone who is in the public eye to say something nice about your product.

Send your samples and product information to all the important food editors in your major markets, as well as food-preparing personalities who appear on radio and television. Include a press kit with press release, sample (if possible), company history/data, and a listing of where the product can be purchased. To assist you, if your budget permits, you may wish to have this accomplished by a professional public relations firm.

Submit your product to trade show managers who have product award committees. Your product will be evaluated against many others, but if you win "best new product for such-and-such year," you can use this in your product literature, trade show exhibits, and advertisements. Both the testimonials and show awards offer third-party endorsements that attest to the quality of your product.

CASE IN POINT

The following is an example of possible overkill in a mailing to retailers.

The following materials were received in an 8¾" by 6" envelope sent via bulk mail to retailers by a two-year-old specialty food company that specializes in distinctive baked goods and confectionery:

✦ *Two empty cookie boxes, each with one-cookie capacity (75 ounces).*

✦ *One deal sheet describing two deals.*

✦ *One empty cheesecake box (to hold one miniature 4-ounce cheesecake).*

✦ *One empty 1.5-ounce cookie box, to hold two cookies.*

✦ *One mailing list inquiry return card with special offer.*

✦ *One valuable coupon to save $10 off the regular price of a national retailer directory.*

✦ *One corporate logo "private label offer" and sample cookie box (for your logo, their cookie, and a cookie carton company's carton).*

✦ *One six-page, four-color, 8½" x 11" brochure that includes a price list and order form.*

Note: This is a very expensive, major mailing. Such direct mailings—in which "more is more"—are atypical in the specialty food trade, simply because they cost so much to conduct.

Publicizing Your Product

A prominent public relations firm offers the following information about public relations.

Cost Effective

Public relations is a cost-effective way to draw attention to your product from a group of people who influence consumers. The targets of a public relations campaign are the editors and writers for newspaper and magazine food sections, and producers and hosts of radio and television shows that feature cooking and food products. A positive feature or mention in the press can be even better than advertising because it carries the implied "seal of approval" from a respected source—the food journalist.

While consumer media reach the ultimate purchasers of food products, public relations can also be effective in expanding distribution by reaching retailers, brokers, and distributors through food industry publications.

Public relations should be a part of any total marketing plan, and, because of its relatively low cost, it can be especially important when marketing funds are scarce. In some cases, public relations can even replace advertising (see Case in Point).

Components of a Public Relations Campaign

There is no formula for a public relations campaign. It should be tailored to your needs, whether you are introducing a product in just one area or nationwide. The critical elements are an informative, well-written press release and an up-to-date, targeted mailing list. Depending on budget, include

> **CASE IN POINT**
>
> *Nantucket Off-Shore Seasonings, a start-up operation manufacturing a unique line of blended herbs and spices, relied solely on public relations via trade show sales and telephone/mail order to support its entry into the specialty food market. The news of the product's benefits (as told by a public relations firm) was one of the first of its kind and fit into current consumer desires for quality, taste, convenience, and low-fat cooking. The effort resulted in features in The New York Times, Family Circle, Food & Wine, Parade, and other publications. The favorable publicity convinced top retailers and catalog distributors that the product was worth carrying. The increased availability generated further publicity.*

a photograph, tips on how to use the product, recipes, and a feature that ties your product to an emerging food trend. All of these elements, especially the photograph, can increase chances of pickup.

Many top editors want personally to try any product before writing about it; however, sending hundreds of samples can become prohibitive in terms of the postage alone. Consider sending samples to the top 100 prospects on your media list; return-addressed postcards requesting samples to the next 250 names; and a line on the release itself, offering a sample to the remaining names who call for one.

Increase Your Visibility

While product announcements and endorsements can lead directly to sales, raising general visibility can be accomplished in other ways. A small ice cream company made the front page of a large metropolitan newspaper by handing out ice cream samples the night of April 15 to thousands of people waiting to mail their income taxes; and a small company importing sparkling waters gained the same sort of name recognition by giving T-shirts to runners in a race. Other public relations vehicles include recipe contests and production of recipe newsletters.

If you are introducing a product nationally, consider retaining a small public relations agency that specializes in food products. Such an agency already will have researched and organized the mailing lists you will need and can advise on the most effective materials to use in your press package.

> **CASE IN POINT**
>
> *Colt Chocolates—won three NASFT product awards. The owner got famous media cowboy Roy Rogers to endorse one of their products (Happy Trail Chocolates). He met Rogers when the company founder was a regular on "Hee Haw," a country comedy television show.*

How to Know If a Press Release Is Successful

Knowing where and when a story has appeared is important for two major reasons—first, to know in which areas your potential customers are likely to have read about your product, and second, to see how the product is being received. This information can be used to fine-tune your sales messages.

Clipping services, such as Burrelle's and Luce, monitor newspapers, magazines, and radio and television programs nationally. They provide their clients with an original copy of each story that mentions the product name—or messages specified by the client—complete with the name of the publication, date the story appeared, and the circulation.

How to Write a Press Release

When writing your product announcement release, keep in mind the needs of the recipient. Food editors and writers want to know the "Five W's"—who, what, where, when, and why—of your product so they can decide whether to pass the information along to their readers. You should also tell them about its advantages over competitive products and tips for using it, as well as any interesting facts about the development of the product.

The release can be printed on your letterhead. The general format should look something like the sample press release in Figures 3.2 and 3.3.

FIGURE 3.2: **Sample Press Release**

For Immediate Release:

Contact: (Your name, telephone number, and e-mail address)   Date:

WILD RICE EXCHANGE APPOINTS ENCORE SPECIALTY FOODS

Gourmet Valley, a California-based producer of wild rice and specialty blended rice and dried heirloom beans, has named Encore Specialty Foods, LLC, as its U.S. master distributor. The joint announcement was made by Wild Rice Exchange General Manager Carlos Zambello and Encore Specialty Foods President Ron Johnson. The appointment extends a 14-year collaboration between the two executives.

The Gourmet Valley line includes organic Giant Canadian, and California extra-fancy wild rice, plus blended rice for both retail and food-service market sectors. Gourmet Valley recently introduced their heirloom beans to the line, and new three-pound stand-up jumbo packs of both beans and rice.

Johnson says the Gourmet Valley line is a good strategic fit with his company's lines of European imported specialty foods. "The healthful nature of this line and its attractive retail packaging and reasonable price, position it perfectly with our other products. Whether you're a professional chef or a creative at-home cook, the line appeals to all who are looking for healthful and cost-effective ingredients to use in the kitchen."

Encore will trim costs for the line by shipping to Midwestern and Western distributors from the packer's Sacramento-area warehouse. "We're lowering previous pricing by as much as 18 percent," said Johnson.

#

FIGURE 3.3: Another Sample Press Release

For Immediate Release:

Contact: (Your name, telephone number, and e-mail address)   Date:

UNIQUE RUBS TURN EVERY BACKYARD CHEF INTO A GRILLING GURU

Now almost any food destined for the grill—not to mention the kitchen broiler or oven—can get "rubbed the right way." Rubs—uniquely blended dried seasonings that impart heavenly flavors to meat, poultry, fish, and vegetables—are destined to become the ticket to healthy, flavorful foods in the new century.

While grilling imparts its own heady flavor, the reason why grilled food seems to taste better when it comes from a restaurant kitchen is that the chef has usually treated it with herbs and spices to enliven the inherent taste of the food.

Now, these flavor blends—from green garden herbs and colorful peppers for fish to authentic Scotch bonnet chilies and allspice berries for heady Caribbean flavors—are available to the home cook.

Nantucket Off-Shore Seasonings, Inc., has created a line of salt-free, all-natural, pre-blended herb and spice rubs to make everyone a grilling guru. The spectacular formulas are the work of Nigel Dyche, an island transplant who used Nantucket's quiet winter months to recreate the savory sensations of his summer memories.

Like fine caviar, the equally precious rubs are packed in handsome tins, because light is one of the primary reasons dried herbs and spices lose their color and potency. The terrific rubs come in six varieties:

- Nantucket Rub. A blend of delicate herbs such as dill, tarragon, and fennel, flecked with whole pink peppercorns and given depth with garlic and onion. Whether rubbed on fishermen's favorites such as swordfish or tuna, on crustaceans like shrimp, or on the famed bay scallops from Nantucket's waters, the rub brings out all the best qualities of fish and shellfish. It makes a dynamite herbed chicken, and works equally well on whole pieces and boneless, skinless breasts. For a new

FIGURE **3.3: continued**

twist, use Nantucket Rub to add zing to herbed garlic bread, as well as dips and salad dressings.

(Continue with description of other products in the line.)

They are available at a suggested retail price of $_____ at select specialty food stores nationally, by calling (insert contact telephone number) or at (insert Web site).

# # #

✦ GUIDELINES FOR SUCCESS ✦

Public Relations

What Gets an Editor's Attention

✦ Write a headline that tells the story in two lines or fewer.

✦ Include all information: company and product name, product benefits, size and/or weight, kind of package, where and when available, and price.

✦ Include a photo if possible—5"x 7" color glossy. Be sure to identify the photos—they can get separated from the release.

✦ Provide a separate fact sheet so the editor can get the basic information at a glance.

✦ Be aware of publication deadlines. Newspaper food sections work weeks in advance, and magazines need three to four months lead time prior to their publication date. When in doubt, call and ask.

✦ Send the information to the right person. If necessary, call the general office number and ask who covers food and/or new products at the media outlet.

✦ Follow your release with a phone call to ask if you can answer any questions. But don't make a pest of yourself; leaving one message is sufficient.

Advertising Your Product

We tend to think that consumer advertising is the easy way to draw attention to our product. In the first place, your product has to be on the market before an advertisement directed at the consumer will work.

Occasionally, consumers will see inserts in the likes of *Gourmet*, *The New Yorker*, *Smithsonian*, and other magazines that advertise fancy foods; however, in the specialty food industry, the only advertisements that seem to be directed to consumers with any regularity in those magazines are ones that offer product via mail order instead of through retail stores. Successful consumer advertising requires ingenuity and deep pockets. According to the American Association of Advertising Agencies (http://www.aaaa.org), the average American is exposed to approximately 7,000 advertising stimuli a day.

You are well advised to tread lightly when it comes to consumer advertising, especially if you are considering television or radio. Stick with advertising inserts in specialty-food trade journals. See Appendix A for a listing of trade journals devoted to this industry.

Media Selection

Several of the trade journals will work with you to save money in preparing your advertisement. Consider retaining a small and hungry advertising agency. It will cost a little more, but the result will be better than cutting and pasting on your own. Make sure that advertising costs are figured into your overall budget in an amount equal to 10 to 15 percent of sales, or projected sales.

Some advertising can be accomplished using local radio and newspapers, but this is best done in

---

CASE IN POINT

DeMedici Imports, Ltd.— NASFT Outstanding Product Line Award winner (French Provencal Olives). Founded in 1979 as the importer of Badia a Coltibuono, the first Tuscan extra-virgin olive oil to be marketed in America, De Medici Imports provides the specialty food trade with premium products from Italy, France, Spain, Argentina, and America. De Medici products have won 15 product award trophies at the International Fancy Food Show.

connection with larger retailer promotions, such as those conducted by department stores.

What you undertake in the form of advertising will be determined by available funds. You will depend more on your own resources if you have a $1,000 budget and more on outside help if you have a $10,000 budget.

Advertising Costs

✧ *Insert preparation ($2,000 to $4,000)*. An insert is the actual advertisement you will have "inserted" into the magazine/newspaper. Many specialty-food trade journals will take your camera-ready artwork and produce it as an advertisement. You can expect to pay upwards of $4,000 for a black-and-white ad with about 50 words of copy. Illustrations and photography will cost extra. Cost factors in a one-half-page black-and-white insert include: artwork, copywriting, design, and layout.

✧ *Photography ($600 to $1,000)*. If you have a photograph made of your product, or product line, then arrange to use the same photograph in your catalog sheets and other promotional materials.

✧ *Typical costs of insert space ($2,000 to $3,300 and up)*. Media costs (the magazine or newspaper space) to insert a half-page (vertical or horizontal) black-and-white ad, for example, will range from $3,000 to $3,100, depending on the magazine/newspaper. Color ads will cost more. These costs can be discounted by running the ad more than once.

CASE IN POINT

Fenton & Lee Confections— 1992 Outstanding Confection (Espresso Crunch Wafers). Founded in 1982 by Janele Smith who, by running a petite business, offers customers the benefits of a true artisanal product. Located in the historic Tiffany Building in Eugene, Oregon, where customers have a clear view of the chocolate-making process, Fenton & Lee sells and ships chocolates all over the world. Their confections have been featured in national magazines and have won a number of awards, from "Best Confection of the Year" to their most recent award, "Outstanding Confection of the Year 1999–2000" for Pistachio Buttercrunch. The "Outstanding Confection Award" is presented by the NASFT.

✧ GUIDELINES FOR SUCCESS ✧

Advertising Hints

✧ Use the advertisement over the course of 12 months, or longer, and in a number of issues of different trade journals.

✧ Make certain the artwork and materials designed for the advertisement can be used in point-of-purchase posters and other promotional materials.

✧ Use the advertisement in combination with a well-planned and effectively managed advertising and promotion program.

✧ Coordinate advertising inserts with press releases, in-store promotions, show displays, mailings, and point-of-purchase posters.

✧ Don't waste money by running one fancy advertisement only once or twice in a single journal.

✧ Coordinate promotions with current and prospective retailer and distributor promotions.

Finding Buyers

Now that you have had your product produced, packaged, and labeled, how do you find the specific buyers identified as a category during your initial market research? The type of customer you identify will depend on the type of product you sell.

Whether the product is canned, fresh, frozen, or refrigerated will affect its distribution possibilities.

Identifying the Potential Customer

We have identified approximately 23,000 retailer prospects as potential buyers of your product. This figure presumes a product not requiring special handling and display, thus eliminating frozen and refrigerated foods. It presumes also an ability to get the product to all these prospects. About 15,000 of them will be able to stock refrigerated items such as cheese and fresh pâté. The competition for that space will be keen.

The number of retailer prospects swells substantially if your product can be sold in a gift store, of which there are approximately 74,000! Our 23,000 retailer figure includes only 10 percent of these as devoting any shelf space to specialty foods. More often than not, a gift store will carry a food product, notably candy, and will merchandise it as a gift, rather than food.

There are approximately five dozen distributors that specialize in selling specialty food to retailers.

In addition, full-line grocery distributors, of which there are hundreds, are carrying more specialty foods every year.

✧ GUIDELINES FOR SUCCESS ✧

Hints for Finding Buyers

✧ Exhibit in major (national and regional) specialty-food trade shows.

✧ Arrange for one of the specialty-food trade journals to conduct a mailing on your behalf.

✧ Contact the NASFT for information about their retailer and distributor members.

✧ Purchase a mailing list of gourmet food retailers from available business list consolidation services (Appendix P).

✧ Contact Specialty Food Distributors and Manufacturers Association for member list (Appendix B).

✧ Contact National Food Brokers Association for member list; brokers can help you find buyers (see Appendix E).

Qualifying Potential Buyers

Qualifying a buyer involves assessing the potential interest and likelihood of that buyer making a purchase. In the case of distributors, you do this by reviewing the product lines currently carried, mailing information, sending samples, and following up by telephone. Once you have qualified your buyer, you can then make arrangements to set an appointment for a sales call.

You can rely on your broker to qualify retailers, or you can make the call yourself to determine the interest level and to make the sale.

Establishing Distribution Channels

You will employ various channels of distribution to get your product to the consumer. Understanding these distribution options will enable you to refine your marketing plans. In the specialty food trade, you will use either distributors (also called store-door distributors, full-service distributors, jobbers, and wholesalers), retailers (including gourmet food stores, warehouse clubs, department stores, and mass merchandisers), direct mail, and/or catalog houses.

The exact type of distribution used will depend on a number of factors, some of which include:

✧ the market segment (by product type, geographic region, etc.).

✧ the expected sales volume (large volume may require different distribution capabilities).

✧ the nature of the product promotion.

The profusion of specialty foods has made the process of obtaining distributor interest in carrying new products increasingly difficult. As a result, distribution often will require that you do all the pioneering yourself (selling direct to retailers) in order to attract the attention of a distributor. If you are lucky, your product may have sufficient appeal to attract a distributor as soon as you introduce it.

Before you approach a distributor, you should review certain aspects of the specialty foods business.

This list includes the topics you should be familiar with and which are contained in this book. Consult the table of contents or index for page numbers.

In order to successfully negotiate with potential distributors, you need to be well-versed in the following areas:

✦ Pricing/deals

✦ Length of contract

✦ Post-sales support/training

✦ Performance measurements

✦ Territory

✦ Promotional activities—who pays

✦ How specialty foods get to the consumer

✦ The role of the distributor in this process

✦ Required profit margin/promotion support

✦ The relevance of introductory deals

✦ Details of your competition

✦ Specialty food pricing strategies

✦ Specialty food promotion strategies

✦ Marketing elements specific to the territory

Distributor Options Vary by Annual Sales Volume

Your distribution options will be more sophisticated at higher levels of gross revenues. Also, higher revenues will mean a greater commitment to funding advertising and promotion programs. The following describes the approximate distinctions between varying levels of sales and distribution schemes.

❖ *High-volume sales (+$1 million)*. The buyer has a warehouse and is involved with mass merchandising for which significant advertising dollars are required. Generally speaking, this is not a major factor in specialty food distribution.

❖ *Medium-volume sales ($500,000 to $1 million)*. The product goes to supermarkets via rack jobbers (they do all the shelf work). Costs can include demos and free merchandise. Some specialty food distributors have established relationships with both independent and major supermarket chains.

❖ *Low volume sales (generally under $500,000)*. Products are delivered to a store's back door via wholesaler/distributor who uses brokers and own sales force, or direct to store via your broker. This is the primary distribution option used in the specialty food trade.

How Distribution Works

Distribution depends on the product, season, market segment, region, product stage of development, and consumer

awareness/perception/attitudes. As mentioned in the introduction to this guide, as soon as you find a profitable way to distribute your product, someone else will be doing just as well with a similar product, but with an entirely different distribution strategy. There are a number of distribution avenues open to you.

You can sell direct to the consumer by running your own retail operation, either in a permanent setting, or at special holiday fairs, for example. You can also do this via mail order. Send a mailing to prospective customers or take out a mail-order advertisement.

You can reach the consumer via a retailer, which will probably be your initial means of entering the specialty food industry. You put the samples in the trunk of your car and call on as many retailers as possible to make sales. Or make the sale and then ship to the customer.

HIGHLAND SUGARWORKS
INCORPORATED

Selling to a retailer through a broker is similar to the above, but instead of doing it yourself, a commissioned broker takes your samples to the retailers in his or her territory and makes the sales calls.

You may also reach your retail market through a distributor. The distributor buys your product and sells it to the retailer. Some products, especially heavy products in jars, generally require distribution in this manner. It tends to be too expensive to design the containers required to ship a dozen jars via UPS so they arrive undamaged at the retailer's door. (Nevertheless, direct-to-retailer sales are often necessary for the beginner, in order to inspire interest in the distributor.)

Sales are also made via a broker to a distributor to a retailer. Again you employ a commissioned broker to take your samples and make sales calls on distributors.

Your product may be sold via a catalog house, although very few catalogs have been successful in selling retail packaged specialty foods. Those that are successful usually sell products that can be used as gifts. Some catalog companies will ask you to "drop-ship." This means that they send you the order and a mailing label, and you ship the individual product directly to the consumer. The catalog company pays you. You may also use a broker to make sales to a catalog house.

Significance of Exclusivity

All brokers and many distributors will ask for an exclusive territory. With brokers, the exclusive arrangement is to your advantage. It makes little sense to have two brokers competing for the same buyer with the same products.

Distributors often request exclusivity, especially when introducing a new product. It will make some sense to work closely with a distributor in a given market on an exclusive basis. This helps rationalize your marketing and distribution strategy. You might want to limit the arrangement, depending on the distributor and on the market, to six months.

Some strategies work for some producers and not for others. Many successful specialty food producers have never offered any exclusive arrangements. Once again, it depends on the timing, territory, product, price, etc. One way to ascertain distributor interest in an exclusive arrangement is to ask what sort of volume is guaranteed.

Food Service

A growing segment of the specialty food trade consists of selling to hotels, restaurants, and institutions offering better food service. Distribution in this market segment requires the use of brokers and distributors who sell to food service accounts. Food service opportunities exist for specialty food producers who supply fancy jams, preserves, and syrups and the like in single servings for use on hotel restaurant tables, in room service and other situations, such as takeout orders and picnic baskets.

Offering single-serving food products to food service outlets adds an opportunity to attain sampling and brand awareness because single-serving packages will be labeled with your brand name.

Providing your product for use as a prepared food ingredient will meet increasing demand by restaurants that are preparing more foods with specialty food ingredients. It is also a way to generate revenue during your start-up stage, and to reduce product costs by arranging for larger production runs. On the

✧ GUIDELINES FOR SUCCESS ✧

Specialty Food Distribution Channels with Incremental Profit Margins/Commissions

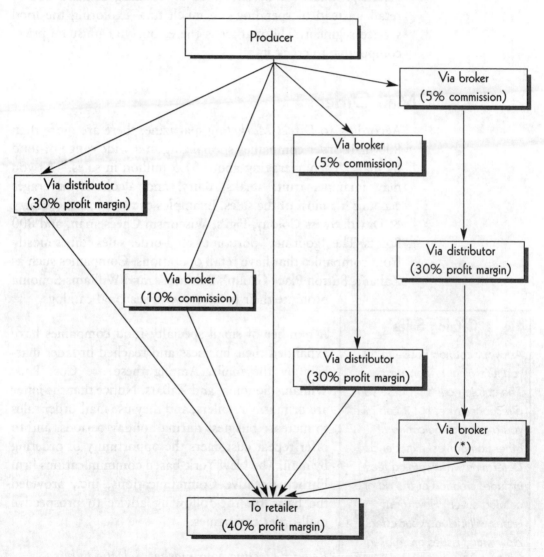

*Commission paid from distributor's share of profit margin.

other hand, there is little branding opportunity for your products sold in institutional containers, and you will be subject to the vagaries of food service trends.

The food service sector is extremely price-conscious. High-priced products are better served by creating demand first at retail, instead of spending too much time exploring the food service segment. The market is there, but you must be price-competitive to crack it.

Mail Order

According to *Direct Marketing* magazine, there are more than 800 mail-order companies specializing in a wide range of food by mail, "each averaging about $1.5 million in sales." As you may imagine, fruit, steaks, dairy, and alcoholic beverages account for most of the sales. Examples of these include: Harry & David, Swiss Colony, Figi's, Wisconsin Cheeseman, and 800 Spirits. The "gourmet" portion of mail-order sales comes mostly from companies that have retail operations. Companies such as Zabar's, Sutton Place Group's Balducci's, and Williams-Sonoma promote their products with seasonal catalogs.

Catalog Sales

Ask your catalog house to tell you its typical response rates. The catalog can't promise you a response rate, but it can give you a general indication of other companies' experiences. Determine what catalog fees include: creation of the ad or catalog cover? How many issues will include your offer? How many issues are mailed each year?

A number of small specialty food companies have expanded their business and reached broader markets by the mails. Among these are Cost Plus, Williams-Sonoma, and Zabars. Notice that the latter are primarily retailers, and they use mail-order sales to increase business during holiday periods, and to offer repeat customers the opportunity of ordering by mail. The New York-based communications firm Ehrlich Creative Communications, Inc., provided the basis for the following advice to prospective mail-order companies:

Begin by testing your market. Select a publication you think your customers read. If they are well-off and live in small towns, for example, try something like Country Living; if you plan to sell to a professional market (chefs, librarians, etc.), buy an ad in one of the trade publications, and so on.

If you profit from the returns on the ad, then you may want to try it again. Advertising won't tell you much about the size of your market. If you get 100 responses to your ad, and 12 people eventually buy, is that good? The only way to know is through experience over time. You will be able to compare ad results from different publications, at different times of the year, etc.

You could try a co-op mailing. This involves using a catalog that advertises other catalogs, or using co-op mailings that include card packs and coupon mailings. The advantage of these types of mailings is that you get to compare your results with others in the program. They can help you determine some aspects of the market for your product; however, it is not particularly scientific (you have very little control over who gets the mailing, or whether they read it).

Another option is to get your products into someone else's catalog. This is one of the more cost-effective ways of getting into a new mail order market. Your advantages include no upfront costs, no requirement for a full product line (you can run with just one product), a reasonably accurate idea of the demand for your product, and you may be able to get demographic and other information about the people who order your product.

Finally, you can conduct your own mailing. This is the most expensive option, but it is the most reliable. You will control all the variables—who receives your offer,

> **CASE IN POINT**
>
> General Foods Corporation, with all its resources, was unable to make a success out of its much ballyhooed Thomas Garroway, Ltd., mail-order specialty foods division. The company spent millions of dollars on full-page, four-color advertising in major consumer magazines in an effort to sell gourmet foods by mail. I know of no successful gourmet-foods-by-mail enterprise in which a company ships a variety of different foods direct to consumers.

when they receive, how it is presented, etc.—and you will get all the results. If you elect to go it on your own (produce your own catalog), then you will want to purchase a mailing list of at least 50,000 names.

The list is the most crucial part of your mailing. Test the list first, then your prices, offer, and copy. The rule of thumb for your test should be to generate 50 responses, or a return of 1 percent. This means a list of at least 5,000 names. You can get these lists from other catalog companies that serve markets similar to the one you want to enter.

You can count on spending about $15,000 for a 50,000-piece mailing, plus costs for producing the catalog or mailing piece.

Arranging the Deals

Because of the risks involved, both in terms of wasted time and expended resources, few of your potential customers will be willing to carry a new product automatically.

Consequently, most retailers, and particularly distributors, require special deals in order to earn extra profit during start up and to introduce your product successfully.

The most common is the introductory deal. This can involve some combination of those described below.

With all deals, you can offer a "60-day buy-in" that allows the buyer to purchase up to a predetermined credit limit for 60 days and get the introductory deal.

Competition is so stiff in this industry that getting retailers and distributors to even try your

✧ GUIDELINES FOR SUCCESS ✧

Selling to Mail-Order Catalogs

(Adapted from an outline developed for the Roundtable for Women in Foodservice by Nina Dorsett, Director of Sales and Marketing, Plaza Sweets Bakery.)

✧ The good news—mail-order buyers are accessible! Review catalogs and pursue those who seem a likely fit.

✧ Know your products well. Know their limitations. Understand what they will be put through. Do they require specialized shipping?

✧ Do you drop-ship? What does this involve?

✧ Can you do business via e-mail?

✧ Private label—yes or no?

✧ Properly price your product to cover all your costs and make a profit, yet allow enough room for the catalog to make its margin.

✧ Sales projections—how accurate are they? How do you plan?

✧ Be prepared to come through at all times.

✧ After the selling season, review catalog sales with the buyer. Try to get a commitment to continue with the product and take the opportunity to introduce new items.

✧ When exhibiting in shows, set aside a separate area to feature your mail-order products. Make sure your mail-order items are clearly identified.

✧ Remember, catalog sales can mean volume orders and seem resistant to economic downturns. With more people having less time to shop, there is an increasing reliance on catalogs for gift-giving and entertaining. The catalog market business is on the upswing, and you should do your best to become a part of it.

product can be a major undertaking. The reasoning behind the deals is to help the buyer justify some of the costs and risks associated with introducing, or pioneering, the product. Most distributors, for example, would like to be assured of their normal profit at the outset of a product introduction, in the event the product does not succeed. In this way, they do not suffer a loss. They do not have to wait until the product takes off before they make a profit. The cost of deals is a cost to you, just as are ingredients, and must be budgeted and controlled accordingly.

Deals offer extra profits to the buyer, lower selling prices to attract customers, sources of funding for advertising/promotion, and assistance in gaining attention over competing brands.

Note: Many of the following deals/allowances should be offered only if asked for by the buyer, and considered only if you feel the overall benefit is worth the expense. Weigh your decision carefully.

You will want to develop a long-term relationship with the buyer that may not evolve if at first you give the product away, and then later withdraw the deal.

The Overall Best Deal: Guaranteed Sales

As a rule, most food marketers only guarantee that their product is packed properly, and will replace any broken or damaged merchandise. Here's a thought: Think of how much you appreciate your local appliance/electronics store policy that allows you to return almost any product within 30 days of purchase for an exchange, credit, or full refund—no questions asked. Such a policy develops tremendous store loyalty (Safeway does it). Wouldn't it be terrific if the food industry did that? What if you allowed your consumer to return the unused portion of your product for a full refund, no questions asked? If you did this, you could quickly carve out a niche that would appeal to almost any distributor or retailer. The offer would be for the consumer only.

Of course, the matter is tricky in that we are dealing with a consumable. The CD player you bought can be returned, no questions asked, and then sold at clearance, thereby offering the seller an option to recoup at least the cost of the product. On the other hand, you are stuck with the half-used jar of mustard that was returned by an unhappy consumer.

Another twist would be to guarantee the sale, within a specific period, to both the distributor and the retailer. In other words, if your product failed to move, for whatever reason, the distributor or retailer could return it for a full refund or credit. In this case, it would be fair if the retailer or distributor who returns the product pays the return freight.

> **CASE IN POINT**
>
> *The Fancy Foods Gourmet Club formerly sold gourmet food via the Internet. It offers a 100 percent satisfaction guarantee. The company would replace the product or issue a credit if the consumer notified them within seven days of receipt. The guarantee, however, only covered spoilage, spillage, damage, or error. The company did not offer credits or exchanges if the product "did not appeal to one's palate." Is this a 100 percent satisfaction guarantee?*

Free Merchandise

"One free case with 10, the 11th case is free." Distributors or retailers may use the free product in any way they wish. Retailers may choose to pass the savings along to the consumer, or distributors may pass it along to the retailers, or either may take the difference to defer the cost of introducing the product and to increase profits.

Note that this differs from the offer "one free case in ten." Offering the 11th case free is preferred because you ship more product, which is, after all, the point. One free case with ten amounts to a 9.1 percent discount. Figure 3.4 shows the discount percentages with free merchandise.

If you specify that the free goods are for the retailer, then obtain proof of delivery for free merchandise shipped from the distributor to the retailer. In this way, you have greater assurance that your product gets to the customer, and you get the names and addresses of the customers.

FIGURE 3.4: Discount Percentages on Free Merchandise

Here are some other free merchandise discount percentages:

1 free with 2	=	33.3%
1 free with 3	=	25.0%
1 free with 5	=	16.7%
1 free with 12	=	7.7%
1 free with 20	=	4.7%
1 free with 25	=	3.8%

Sampling Allowance

Another free merchandise offer involves providing free product to the distributor (or retailer) so that free samples can be offered to consumers. This can also help the distributor get a retailer to purchase for the first time.

Demonstration Allowance

The demo allowance can combine free product along with a cash discount to cover the cost of a demonstrator. The demonstrator is retained either by you, the retailer, or the distributor, to serve and promote your product in the retail store. Ascertain beforehand the demonstrator's abilities, and the day and time for the intended demonstration. If possible, control and monitor the demonstration carefully, for experience shows that the absence of active producer involvement in control of demonstrations can waste time and money.

Prepare a standard demonstration kit that contains procedures you want to be followed in order for the demonstrator to be paid. It should include detailed instructions and an evaluation form that must be sent to you after the completed demonstration.

Demonstration costs vary, depending on the store and on the nature and length of the demonstration. Please refer to the section on promotion earlier in this chapter for a discussion of demonstration costs.

Special Terms

Many companies offer a discount for payment within ten days. This can be expressed as 2 percent, 10 days, net 30 days, FOB warehouse. This means that the distributor and retailer will pay the freight (either freight collect, or added to the invoice), and that you must receive their payment on the 10th day, with a 2 percent discount, or in the full amount by the 30th day after delivery.

> **CASE IN POINT**
>
> *A new hitch in the food industry is the so-called success fee. When a producer introduces a new product, both the producer and the distributor agree to establish sales goals over a defined period. When the goal is achieved, the producer pays the distributor a success fee. Some industry participants have predicted that the success fee will replace the slotting fee over the next five years.*

As an introductory deal, you can offer special terms to the distributor, such as: 2 percent, 30 days, delivered, which means that you pay the freight, and the buyer takes a deduction of 2 percent from the FOB invoice amount, which is due within 30 days.

You can offer any combination of these to the distributor or to the retailer. My recommendation is that you stick to your original terms, unless it is a major purchase that would not work without special terms.

Freight Allowance

You can peg these to volume orders. For example, you might offer a 5 percent freight allowance for any order over 50 cases of assorted product. This means that the buyer may deduct 5 percent of the FOB invoice amount from the payment. The idea is to encourage larger purchases by offering the benefit of economy to the buyer.

You can also calculate freight into your prices. Link these with three geographic zones—East, Central, and West—so that you will have three different, delivered prices depending on customer location.

Your terms of FOB warehouse mean that the buyer is responsible for the freight costs from your loading dock to his or her warehouse or store. When selling to distributors, you may have occasion to ship freight collect. This means that the trucking company will pick up and deliver your merchandise and will collect for the freight costs on delivery.

When shipping to a retailer, you may add the freight costs (usually a United Parcel Service-type shipper) to your invoice. Further discussion of shipping procedures and theory appears under Warehousing and Shipping, in Chapter Two.

Slotting Allowance

Many supermarket chains and specialty food distributors will require that you pay them a slotting allowance (also called push money and placement fees). This is a dollar amount that may be paid in the form of cash, cash discounts, or free merchandise, to cover the cost of slotting the product in the distributor's warehouse.

Ostensibly, the slotting allowance is exacted from the distributor by the supermarket chain in order to justify the costs, and risks, of taking on a new product. The result is that many new specialty food producers have had to seek other means of distribution, such as direct sales to small retailers, and thereby experience considerable difficulty in establishing full distribution.

Here's one way this works: Your distributor will not even take your product to the selection committee unless you offer an appropriate slotting allowance.

> ### CASE IN POINT
>
> *"Slotting allowances allow chains and distributors to make money on the buy versus the sell; therefore, success is being measured not by product performance, but by product profit. This has led to virtually flat growth for supermarkets as opposed to nearly double-digit growth within the specialty/ gourmet food sector."*
>
> *—Industry leader Richard Worth*

You can expect that the distributor will deduct up to 10 percent of the gross value of your invoice. Often, distributors will deduct an amount equal to THEIR gross profit (your price plus their profit margin).

If you agree to a slotting fee, you should demand proof from the distributor that the product has actually reached the store shelves. The requirement for slotting allowances is a hotly debated, and not a universally popular phenomenon.

Advertising and Catalog Allowances

Advertising allowances should be agreed to in advance, with specific elements of proof requested. Such proof of performance can include copies of the advertising inserts or circulars.

Another form of advertising allowance is cooperative advertising, wherein you and the buyer agree to share the cost of an advertisement in a local newspaper, or on a local radio station. You may be requested to provide copy, and black-and-white slicks (camera-ready artwork on glossy stock), or high-resolution scans that depict your product and/or logo.

The use of advertising allowances (the buyer deducts the allowance from the invoice) and bill backs (you request the buyer to remit a bill to you at the end of the period) should be restricted to those opportunities that offer the best potential for sales.

Using catalog houses is a good way of promoting your product. In order to defray some of the cost of producing a catalog, an allowance, usually 10 percent, is required by the catalog companies that will carry your product. This is a promotional cost to you because the catalogs generally carry your product only

✧ GUIDELINES FOR SUCCESS ✧

Deals in Review

✧ *Free merchandise*. A broadly employed, and cost-effective, means of getting new business.

✧ *Sampling allowance*. Similar to free merchandise.

✧ *Demonstration allowance*. A useful promotional tool. Requires effective management.

✧ *Special terms*. Not encouraged. Use only if in special circumstances (e.g., the buyer is planning a major promotion and requests an extended payment period).

✧ *Freight allowance*. Used to encourage a larger order.

✧ *Free freight*. Use as a special arrangement (trade shows, seasonal specials, etc.).

✧ *Slotting allowance*. Mostly required by supermarket chains and larger distributors. Try to avoid.

✧ *Advertising allowance*. Use for special promotions (e.g., ethnic foods). Monitor carefully.

✧ *Catalog allowance*. For catalog sales.

---

once, but you do get the residual benefit of putting your product before a large audience.

Appointing Brokers

Brokers are manufacturers' representatives. They do not buy your products. They take your product literature, samples, and pricing information and make sales for you in a given territory. Brokers receive a commission for sales made, based on your FOB invoice value. They generally receive 10 percent commission for sales to retailers, and 5 percent commission for sales to distributors. These arrangements, and commissions, can differ depending on the product and the market.

Brokers obtain supermarket authorizations and monitor distributor activity on behalf of the principal. Often referred to as food reps, food brokers also sell to individual retail accounts, small boutiques, specialty food shops, and gift shops. As food reps, they often maintain a showroom.

Note that most experienced brokers already have extensive lines to represent. On the one hand, a broker with several lines may not be able to devote much attention to your line; on the other hand, a new broker may not be able to make a living just selling your product alone. Nevertheless, the system works, and most brokers are interested in exploring new opportunities.

Brokers can exercise an important influence on developing sales for your products. They have access to buyers, knowledge of territories, and experience that you probably could not afford to replace in the form of a full-time sales staff. Brokers carry a number of lines, and they often provide the only cost-effective way for you to get your product to stores in regions away from home base.

> **CASE IN POINT**
>
> *Bittersweet Pastries, Inc.—1991 Outstanding New Product (Raspberry Almond Tart). Bittersweet Pastries was created in 1984 as a retail pastry shop/tearoom by Phyllis Trier, who, with her husband, Bob, runs the company today. In 1985, with the development of their chocolate truffle cake, a mail-order business was begun. Over the years Bittersweet Pastries created many new products, specializing in tarts, and began selling their desserts to restaurants, hotels, country clubs, and gourmet stores. Many of these desserts have won awards considered to be among the best in the country.*

Because of this, there is a trade-off. Depending on the situation, you may have to take second place in a product line-up carried by a broker who is interested in your product. Unless the broker can see potential for high volume (read: "high commission income"), it will be unlikely for the broker to devote much attention to pioneering your product.

Brokers can help implement your promotion plans, including in-store demonstrations and new product introductions. You will not require a broker if you can manage the territory yourself.

Locating Brokers

Broker listings are available from the National Association for the Specialty Food Trade (see Appendix E), and from advertisements in various specialty food industry journals (Appendix A). In addition, brokers regularly present themselves for consideration at the fancy food shows.

I do not recommend advertising for a broker in trade journals. It is more effective to ask other producers, retailers, and distributors for recommendations and leads, than to take a "shotgun" approach through an industry trade journal. Make certain the prospective broker understands your product, and knows how to sell it. You should meet with the broker to achieve a sense of how effectively you can do business together.

Broker Management Hints

◆ Visit the broker and make joint calls on key customers at least twice a year.

◆ Send monthly, or bimonthly, product information notes.

◆ Inform your broker of new products, testimonials, and all success stories.

◆ Work with the broker on planning your product promotions.

◆ Ask the brokers to visit and work your booths in the major trade shows.

Managing Brokers

Once you have selected a broker, you will prepare a contractual agreement or appointment letter, (Appendix E) that stipulates the territory to be covered, conditions of sales, terms, commissions, payment procedures, etc. Remember, brokers work for you in specific, designated territories.

Send the broker a supply of samples, catalog sheets, price sheets, press kits, and other descriptive literature in the quantity requested by the broker.

To some extent, you may rely on your broker to provide information regarding the credit history of new accounts. You should also be able to rely on the broker to make a personal attempt to collect any overdue invoices. (Make sure the broker is amenable to this before you retain her/his services.)

Essentially, brokers are your representatives in the field. Treat them well, pay their commissions on time, and keep them informed. You will attain a span of attention to your product directly proportional to the amount of time and effort you expend on maintaining the broker's interest. Make it easy for them to make money, and you too will be rewarded.

Generally, brokers are paid monthly, or after the customer invoice has been paid. This is something you will negotiate when the broker is appointed.

Specialty Food Broker Enigma

Offered by Kirk Camoriano, Camoriano and Associates, Inc.

With little or no fanfare within the trade and absolutely no identity recognition from the public, the Specialty Food Broker plays an important role in bringing high-quality products to the American home. Misunderstood by customers and principals alike, the Specialty Food Broker actually lowers the cost of food distribution. If there were no food broker in the chain, the manufacturer would have to field his or her own sales staff at a much higher cost. The broker provides the efficient way to bring a product to the marketplace. Because brokers are independent businesspersons, they pay their own way—covering their

GUIDELINES FOR SUCCESS

Broker Evaluation

✧ *Years in business.* A well-established broker may not have room for your line.

✧ *Territories covered.* Are they adequate to your needs?

✧ *Major accounts called upon.* Do they include your prime targets?

✧ *Account requirements for deals, etc.* Can you accommodate them?

✧ *Lines currently represented.* Do any compete with yours?

✧ *Number of sales staff.* Sufficient to meet your needs?

✧ *References.* Contact three of them for comments.

✧ *Success stories.* Especially with lines similar to yours.

---

office, payroll, insurance, telephone, and car expenses as well as pension and taxes. They do not receive a penny unless a sale is made. Today's modern broker has become, in addition to a sales force, a full-service organization. Brokers provide cost-effective professional representation that most manufacturers could not afford on their own. Brokers must negotiate the best deal and promotion for the customer while protecting the integrity of the product they represent. The successful brokers' inventory includes their code of ethics, their credibility, integrity, and the services they provide, as well as their product knowledge and salesmanship.

Locating Distributors

Specialty food distributors (direct store distributors) buy your product for their own accounts and sell it to retailers and to other distributors, using their own sales force and independent brokers.

As a rule, they offer the specialty food producer a higher volume and profit-generating alternative to direct retailer sales. The grocery food distribution system is very efficient. Because of this, it leaves little room for the lower volume specialty food product. Specialty food distributors fill this niche by carrying products that have not yet reached the level of consumption experienced by products in the grocery trade.

Many newer specialty food processors begin by selling direct to the retailer. A number of them retain this method of distributing their products, even after they have gained a foothold in the market. With the increasing incidence of slotting allowances (see "Arranging the Deals," earlier in this chapter), most small companies will be unable to afford the cost of introducing a new product through distributors.

Distributors will let you know what they require. To attract their attention, you will most likely have to develop some of their territory first. This means selling direct to retailers. You will have to assess your circumstances carefully, and be prepared for the long haul, if you wish to continue selling direct to the retailer.

Distributor Services

Specialty food distributors offer a variety of services to the producer and to the retailer. Many, but not all, specialty food distributors perform the following services:

✧ Make sales calls on retailers and chain buyers.

✧ Purchase, inventory, and deliver your product to the retailer.

✧ Stock retailer shelves (usually only at chains).

✧ Oversee instore demos.

✧ Prepare shelf diagrams for optimal display of the product (usually done only at chains).

✧ Provide product sales and profit data to the retailer.

✧ Distribute point-of-purchase (POP) materials (obtained from you).

✧ Instruct store personnel in the benefits of your product.

✧ Rotate shelf stock and remove unsalable merchandise (usually done only at chains).

✧ GUIDELINES FOR SUCCESS ✧

Appointing Distributors

Consider the following elements before you appoint a distributor:

✧ *Length of appointment*. Your letter of appointment should stipulate the period covered. Example: One year from signing, renewable annually thereafter.

✧ *Territory covered*. Stipulate which state, region, or large metropolitan area you are assigning to the distributor.

✧ *Promotional support*. Determine which combination of advertising allowances, special deals, free merchandise, etc., will be required by the distributor. Negotiate the details that are best suited to your mutual requirements and circumstances.

✧ *Frequency of contact*. You should attempt to be in regular contact with all your distributors. Use mail, telephone, e-mail, and fax, plus personal visits and combined sales calls.

✧ *Termination provisions*. Your appointment letter should provide the means for terminating the contract. Either party with 30 or 60 days' advance notice can effect this in writing.

Note: In many instances, you may have to take what is available and proceed without any formal appointment. If a distributor wants to buy your product, you cannot refuse on the basis of other distributor arrangements. This can be considered restraint of trade, and is against the law; however, you can always appoint your distributor in a given territory as master distributor. That distributor would then sell to other distributors. In fact, once the distributor buys your product, you have no legal control over what he/she decides to do with it!

Making the Sale

Now that you have an appointment, remember to take product samples, price lists, catalog sheets, pens, and a hand-held calculator. You will need the latter to verify your mental gymnastics. These will come about as you respond to fast questions about various discounts and quantity orders as well as other details from the buyer.

Use your price list as an order form. This will make it easier to process the order when you return to the office. Generally, you will not be required to give a copy of the order to the buyer. Many distributors will provide you with their own computer-generated order form.

Closing the Sale

The single greatest obstacle to closing a sale, aside from ignorance, is the fear of rejection! We all want friendly environments. We all want everybody to love our product, but we tend to avoid asking the most important question: "How many cases may I ship you?"

A great salesperson goes for the jugular! He or she never cries "uncle," no matter how many rejections, insults, or refusals are received. The process is constantly being improved. No salesperson rests on laurels. All salespeople love selling. Learn about the importance of stressing benefits to the buyers instead of simply pointing out product features.

Listen to the buyer and learn how to handle objections (most of which can be turned to your advantage, once you know what to say).

> **CASE IN POINT**
>
> *Cherith Valley Gardens—1995 Outstanding Food Gift Pack (The Grand Sampler: garden-fresh products, hot and spicy dill pickles, hot and spicy baby carrots, hot pepper sauce). In 1986, Alan Werner was a principal in an independent oil company, which funded, drilled, and operated gas and oil wells in West Texas. The stock market plunge of October 1987 precipitated the eventual collapse of the company. Out of this trauma, the firm's founders discovered a desire to "return to the land." They began gardening in order to produce vegetables to feed their families. Family members prepared the soil, planted, watered, weeded, harvested, and canned the garden's bounty for the year's consumption. After using their canned items as gifts, they were strongly encouraged to market them as specialty products. On May 8, 1993, they officially produced the first Cherith Valley Gardens product.*

Do not impugn your competition, especially if the competing product is carried by the company you are trying to sell to. This puts the buyer in an awkward position, for he/she probably made the decision to carry the other product, and putting the buyer's judgment in question may impede your ability to sell your product.

Your first goal has been achieved. You are in the company of a qualified buyer who has expressed an interest in hearing your pitch. Don't lose sight of your objective, which is not to make friends or have an informal chat. Your sole objective is to make that sale!

Keep in focus! So many of us go off on tangents. When you are stressing the benefits of purchasing your product, it is easy to react defensively when the buyer asks something like: "What am I going to do with just another _____?" The buyer is not tearing down your "baby." Instead, the buyer is looking for ammunition to help him/her make a favorable decision. Who else but you should know why it is important to purchase your product? Remember that you are providing a solution (benefit) to the buyer.

It does not take a lifetime to master the successful sales pitch. Sales ability is acquired. We do it in all walks of life. Only make the call once you are solidly prepared, and practice beforehand. Don't let your pitch sound canned.

Specialty food buyers appear to want the deal. They are not interested, ostensibly, in product quality, variety, choice, or newness, per se. They want the product line that offers them the best deal—one with the most upfront profit.

The buyer/seller dialogues on the following page provide a small sampling of how you could respond to some of the more common objections.

✧ GUIDELINES FOR SUCCESS ✧

Handling Buyer Objections

Buyer: "I already have a dozen brands of mustard."

You: "Offering variety and choice is a specialty food trade strength. This is especially true in the mustard and condiment category."

Buyer: "Your competition offers a better deal."

You: "Let's compare the two deals, and I will consider meeting or bettering it."

Buyer: "Your product is just too expensive."

You: "Ours offers the highest quality of any product in its category. It is more than worth the money. Why not let your customers decide?"

Buyer: "I have no more room in my product assortment."

You: "You can purchase a smaller beginning order of the unique item(s) in my line." (For example, if your line consists of five different condiments, offer the one that is really different, not readily available from other suppliers, as the lead.)

Buyer: "Not now." (This is very common.)

You: "If not now, then when?" Or, "What would it take to make the offer of interest now?" (There may not be much you can do about this, except to offer to come back, call, or make contact by mail later.)

Buyer: (a retailer) "I don't want to deal with another supplier."

You: "I can ship COD, and save you the time and cost of setting up a new file/account."

Buyer: (a retailer) "I don't want to deal with another supplier."

You: "Can you give me the name of a distributor with whom you like dealing, and from whom you would consider buying my product?"

Buyer: (a distributor) "I don't want to do the pioneering your product requires in my territory."

You: (having made several successful sales calls in the distributor's territory) "Here are a half dozen orders from retailers in your territory. All you have to do is deliver my product in your next shipment to them."

Buyer: (distributor who doubts worth of product) "We don't have any call for this product."

You: "People (retail customers) won't ask for products they know you don't have. Why not poll your retailer customers by phone or mail to determine the product's potential?"

Buyer: (who already buys similar products): "Why should I change suppliers and give you the business?"

You: "We're not asking you to abandon your current supplier—just let us supply you with a few items and let us prove our service and value to you."

Buyer: "Will you guarantee the product?"

You: "We will guarantee the product against defects and will replace or refund. We do not guarantee the sale of the product." (See earlier comments about guaranteed sales.)

Exporting—Sales in Nontraditional Markets

Food exporting can be both profitable and challenging. You will encounter requirements for pull dates in the European Economic Community, for example, and you will have to provide labels in a number of languages.

Nevertheless, always be on the lookout for opportunities to sell your product overseas. For most specialty food products, this will mean sales opportunities generated by overseas visitors to your booth in U.S. trade shows.

This is especially the case with the shows sponsored by the NASFT and the National Association of State Departments of Agriculture (NASDA). The latter organization focuses exclusively on promoting U.S.-made food products in overseas markets. The NASDA show is called "U.S. Food Export Showcase," and is held in concert with the Food Market Institute's Supermarket Industry Convention. (See Appendix M.)

Your first point of contact should be the staff of your home state's Department of Agriculture. They will direct you to the

local resource for export assistance. In Massachusetts, for example, the Executive Office of Environmental Affairs—Department of Food and Agriculture, coordinates export assistance.

At the national level, the U.S. Department of Agriculture's Foreign Agricultural Service (FAS) is the best source of information and assistance for entering overseas markets. Be advised, though, that the FAS has focused most of its energies on agricultural commodities. Only recently has the service begun to offer aid to what they call high-value food products.

The FAS offers marketing assistance that includes trade leads, low-cost advertising in its weekly newsletter, buyer and supplier listings, and U.S. pavilions at major international trade shows.

A good point of contact is the Trade Assistance and Program Office, USDA/FAS, 3101 Park Center Drive, Suite 1103, Alexandria, Virginia 22302, phone: 703-305-2772, http://www.fas.usda.gov/agexport/exporter.html.

CASE IN POINT

The author's company, Food Marketing International, was involved actively in exporting. The company formed The American Gourmet Food Export Association, and took several specialty food lines to display at Salon International de Alimentation (SIAL) in Paris, the NASDA-sponsored show (see Appendix C), and at special shows in London and Zurich. Even though one of our lines was Newman's Own, we were unable to make large sales of any of the products. Most were limited to occasional (seasonal) sales to high-powered retailers in the major trade areas— Fortnum & Mason and Harrods in London, Hediard's, and Au Fauchon, in Paris. We focused on exports mostly when the U.S. dollar exchange rate was favorable. The rest of the time we imported and devoted our attention to the domestic specialty food market.

CHAPTER FOUR

Running Your Business

Many new food producers spend too much of their time on food production and marketing, and not enough time focusing on the business and how to set it up. There are any number of ways to organize the structure of your business; you just need to take the time to define what works best for you.

Organizing Your Business

Your choices include a sole proprietorship, partnership, subchapter S corporation, limited-liability corporation (LLC), and other, somewhat complicated arrangements. Most of the companies in the specialty food trade are proprietorships. If you want to form a corporation, you can do so by calling a corporation-forming service in Delaware. Costs run around $75; however, I would recommend that you seek counsel from a qualified attorney before you proceed.

Partnerships: What Are They all About?

If you are producing and marketing a product with a colleague, then you may want to form a partnership.

Benefits

Along with sharing profits, you also share the workload, expenses, liability, and taxpaying. Doing this takes a great deal of thought. If you are considering forming a partnership, you should find answers to several important questions:

Why do I need a partner?—It may be as simple as needing additional money to invest in your business, or you might just want another person's expertise, experience, and industry contacts to help your business grow.

Each partner brings individual talents to the business. For example, one partner may bring sales and marketing skills, while the other brings design skills, development of new products, and warehouse management.

Is the chemistry right?—Partners have to be sure of compatibility. Each partner brings a different perspective. Similar guiding principles and moral philosophy will ensure respect for each other. Having the same philosophy is very important to a successful partnership.

One way to find out if the organizational fit is right before forming the partnership is to set up a trial period. Avoid committing yourself financially until you are sure you and your partner(s) are compatible.

Can you trust your potential partner?—A lot of your business activities will be based on trust. Business in the specialty food trade is done at arm's length. Partners who don't trust each other will suffer the

---

Focus

Creating a business partnership takes work, especially since entrepreneurs tend to be very independent. People with such zeal find it difficult to fuse their efforts in one direction, which can be very costly.

consequences. Similar abilities and skill levels help, but understanding among the partners has to take place in an environment of trust.

Can partners be friends?—Many a friendship has ended when friends live together or go into business together. Two or more people who get along as friends will not necessarily make good business partners. And, when you are friends before you are partners, it may be more difficult to offer opposing opinions for fear of hurting each other's feelings. Dissolving a partnership can be messier than the messiest divorce.

Successful partnerships are based on professionalism and attitude, as well as a burning desire to succeed. This doesn't mean you have to sacrifice your friendship to profit; it just means you have to base your decisions on business needs, not the friendship.

You must make a conscious decision, with each partner agreeing not to make business decisions unilaterally. This is where respect for each other's talents comes in.

Can you and your partners reach consensus?—Partners must be able to compromise and reach consensus in decision making. Once you are in agreement on your company vision, the direction you take will be clear to all concerned. Regular communication is essential to avoid the usual misunderstandings. Make time to talk about your business ideas only. Learn how to become an effective listener.

Financing the venture—who invests what?—The amount of money you allot to the business can be determined by a clear understanding of who will be doing what. If the partnership work is not evenly distributed, will this mean a greater investment for one than the other? And, how will profits be distributed?

> ## Consensus
>
> Consensus, according to the Saturn Automobile Company
>
> "70% comfortable, 100% committed."

Will you need a formal agreement?—Ultimately, no amount of paper will replace the basic trust and understanding between you and your partners, the kind of understanding that is sealed with a handshake. However, drawing up a formal agreement with the advice of a lawyer will clarify the issues and settle any future disputes should one of the partners decide to quit. All parties should write down all the issues each thinks are important. See where the issues converge and where they diverge. Negotiate the details. Reach consensus.

Figure 4.1 lists some of the elements your partnership agreement should contain. It is advisable to consult with a lawyer once you have worked out the various articles of your agreement.

FIGURE 4.1: Some Elements of a Partnership Agreement

✦ Date of agreement

✦ Names of all partners

✦ Business name

✦ Place of business

✦ Term of partnership

✦ Nature of the business

✦ Partner roles

✦ Finance and investment details

✦ Compensation details

✦ Who has authority to do what

✦ Termination provisions

✦ Special provisions

Processing Orders and Office Management

Many new food producers devote too much of their time and energy to producing the product. They think about marketing the product only after it is produced. But, once the orders are in hand, what then? Order processing and office management are employed in preparing the paperwork associated with shipping and paying for orders.

Accounts Receivable Bookkeeping

It will be important for you to understand some basic accounting. It is called double-entry accounting, and it is easy to learn. Perhaps it will be easier for you to retain the services of an accountant or bookkeeper; however, many of you will not be able to afford this luxury in the early stages of your business development. Also, it will be necessary for you to understand the principles so you can communicate effectively with the bookkeeper.

Mr. Carl A. Lindblad, founder of the Needham, Massachusetts, financial systems company, Rubicon, Inc. (specializing in small business service), offers the following guidance:

From the very start, it is essential that you set up an accurate and informative bookkeeping system. An exhaustive study has revealed that of the eight primary causes of business failure, six are financial. They are: insufficient capital, inventory mismanagement, overspending on fixed assets, too liberal a credit policy, taking too much out of the business, and too rapid growth. The other two are lack of experience and wrong location.

Furthermore, it should go without saying that your business should have a bank account separate from your personal account. Personal funds should not be comingled with business funds, and all transactions should go through the bank account and not through distant cash or other accounts.

If you do not have a good working knowledge of bookkeeping, you should hire the services of a competent professional to set up your books and teach you how best to use them. This applies even if you are unable to afford a bookkeeper or ongoing services in the early stages of your business.

In seeking professional help, check with friends and acquaintances to find a well-recommended accountant or bookkeeping professional. They may have designations all the way from CPA (Certified Public Accountant) to public accountant to bookkeeping service.

In your discussions with these firms, you will want to ascertain what sort of financial programs each offers. The more important systems include income statements, balance sheets, the general ledger, and budget statements. A brief description of each follows.

Statement of activities *(the* income statement*)* is an historical report showing how your business did during a certain period. It is a primary source for business planning, and should contain such vital information as sales by product, cost by product, gross profit, expenses by type, and ratios used to monitor the financial health of the business.

Statement of financial position *(the* balance sheet*)* is a snapshot of the financial condition of the business at the time stated. It not only shows the net worth or "book value" (assets minus liabilities) of your business, but also provides the remaining figures needed to calculate the important ratios of business analysis. Such ratios include liquidity, safety, profitability, and asset management. The ratios are important for financial control, and are used by bankers and other lenders when considering loans to the business. Your bookkeeping firm should be able to analyze the ratios of your business.

The general ledger, commonly called the "books" of the company, records all of the day-to-day financial transactions. The more detail, for later understanding, the better. Supporting the general ledger are subsidiary ledgers and records that may include: the employee ledger, sales journal, purchase journal, and inventory report.

Budget statements are estimates of future results. A carefully prepared budget will enable you to plan marketing strategy, production criteria, personnel needs, and financing requirements. A good budget not only supplies a reasoned road map for future operations but also yields essential information for potential lenders or investors. This is where you "plan your work, then work your plan."

The vital consideration in selecting a financial services professional is not the university degree or designation but the quality of training and the amount of experience such a person can bring to get your particular business headed in the right direction. Interview and compare the prices and experience of several such firms, and don't necessarily pick the cheapest one.

Your system should include a complete set of books, monthly financial statements, required tax returns (which do *require a professional), and an accurate and aged tracking of accounts receivable and accounts payable transactions. Anything less puts your business at risk.*

Essentially, accounts receivable bookkeeping is simply keeping track of who owes you money during a period in time. Usually, you will work on a monthly basis. I recommend that you employ a one-write system that reduces the chance of error, and saves time. With a one-write system, you use an Accounts Receivable Control Sheet and individual account ledger cards, along with a one-write binder. The control sheet allows you to keep track of sales and receivables during the month, and to allocate the funds involved using the columns provided.

You make entries when transactions occur: sales (or debits) and receipts (or credits). Each account ledger card is filed alphabetically by customer name, which offers you an easy way of keeping track of each customer account. Much of the accounts receivable bookkeeping can be accomplished with the use of computer software programs.

Dunning

Dunning is what you do when the account you thought was going to pay on time doesn't. If your terms are net 30 days, then around the 35th day, mail the first of three dunning letters/notes. See Appendix O for sample dunning letters.

About ten days after the final letter/telephone call, place the account into collection. There are a number of firms that provide this service. At the level of your activity, these firms will charge as much as 40 percent of the invoice amount to make the collection. If they fail, they will recommend that you seek legal recourse (as a rule, this is only practical when used for amounts over $5,000). This can be very costly, usually more than either the invoice amount or the amount that may be awarded in court. Consider writing the outstanding amount off as a bad debt (a factor that should be considered in your pricing under a "reserve for bad debts" category).

Tax Considerations

Depending on the type of company you establish (proprietorship, partnership, corporation, limited liability or subchapter S corporation), you may be required to file certain types of tax returns, both with the IRS and with your state revenue service. The important thing to remember is to keep accurate and complete records of all your business income and expenditures. You will be well-advised to seek the advice of an accountant when you first set up your books. The process of meeting your tax obligations will be less cumbersome if you get the paperwork in order from the start.

Forms Usage and Filing

Many of your basic supplies including invoices, envelopes, price sheets, letterhead stationery, address labels, credit check forms, and dunning letters/forms can be designed with the help of a personal computer. Use a rubber stamp if you do not want to have 1,000 copies of something printed.

Invoices can be generated by your computer. Forget about running your business without a personal computer, because the 21st century is upon us and no business can be in the least way professional—or profitable—without the application of computers. Figure 4.2 suggests some tips to get maximum mileage out of your invoice.

> ### CASE IN POINT
>
> *Pasta Fresca took the 1994 Outstanding Pasta Award for its Jalapeño and Cheddar Ravioli with a Sweet Bell Pepper Shell. It was also honored in 1999 for Outstanding Pasta: Black Bean and Salsa Ravioli with Corn in a Jalapeño Shell. Well, these people didn't suffer from winning in 1994. In fact, they have grown to where their products are being carried in a number of Kroger stores, plus Giant, Heinens, and Food Emporium. The company has a complete line of easy-to-prepare, upscale flavored, easy-to-eat pasta with fresh, natural ingredients.*

FIGURE 4.2: Tips to Get Maximum Mileage Out of Invoices

The invoice copies may be used for some or all of the following purposes:

Part 1. Customer via mail

Part 2. Broker via e-mail

Part 3. Accounts receivable (There's no need to produce a hard copy; use your electronic file.)

Part 4. Shipping confirmation via e-mail

Part 5. Warehouse copy via e-mail

Part 6. Packing slip via e-mail

See Appendix O for sample forms.

Naturally, you will want to maintain files of all your business correspondence, accounts receivable, accounts payable, completed sales transactions, etc. Generally, files are kept current for one year, then placed in a different drawer. Keep one current-year file drawer, plus two others for the past two years. Files from earlier years may be retired to boxes and should be stored for at least seven years (for tax purposes).

Filing should be set up in accordance with what makes life easier for you. Files should have some rationale that is easy to remember and easy to employ. A file set up for completed sales transactions alphabetically by geographic location is one of the easiest to use. (The actual filing of paper will not be necessary for most of the aforementioned because the same thing can be achieved with your computer and accounting software.)

Notwithstanding my statement about computer importance, we still need some paper backup for our records. Make certain to back up your computer files—in fact, you may want to "zip" them up instead. (There are a number of software titles that can do this. I recommend winzip.exe, for example, or use a special zip drive and disk, or write your files to a CD-ROM.) This saves the whole file, and you do not have to confront the troubles sometimes experienced with backed up files.

Order-Processing Flow

For the computer user (you), there are a number of good software packages that you can employ to keep track of your transactions. (Quicken, CashGraf, and One-Write Plus Accounting offer full business accounting systems.) Until you get the requisite software, you will need the following order-processing supplies: A "one-write" accounting system, consisting of binder, journal forms, and ledger cards. The accompanying flow-chart shown on the following pages can be applied to understanding and clarifying both manual and computer applications.

Notes to Order-Processing Flow

The flow shows both hard copy and computer software processing. You will not have to place invoice copies in a hold file if you are using a software-generated invoice. Simply file the information in the customer's computer account. No need for hard copies beyond those mailed to the customer.

> ### CASE IN POINT
>
> *The Elegant Apricot—1993 Outstanding Jam, Preserve, Spread or Topping (Apricot Pepper Jelly). This company is part of Martin Family Farms in California. Founder Jo Martin reports that they experienced a big surge after winning the award, then a big falloff in sales. They were unprepared for success. She wants new-comers to know that the initial investment is JUST the beginning. Today her focus is mostly on supplying sun-dried toma-toes to other processors. She stopped exhibiting at fancy food shows to fully focus on market-ing her farm's tomatoes. She advises that newcomers must also be prepared to take the next big step. Think about alter-native ways of getting into the grocery chains. Think outside of the box; i.e, don't overdo your own version of the "elegant apricot" concept.*

GUIDELINES FOR SUCCESS

Order-Processing Flowchart

(Many of the processes described below will not be required if you use order-processing software;
e.g., entering an order number, deducting from inventory, and invoice distribution.)

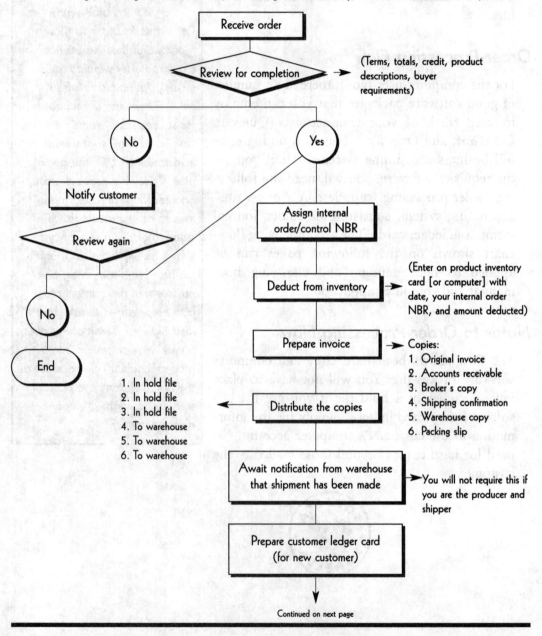

Receive order

Review for completion → (Terms, totals, credit, product descriptions, buyer requirements)

No

Yes

Notify customer

Review again

Assign internal order/control NBR

No

End

Deduct from inventory → (Enter on product inventory card [or computer] with date, your internal order NBR, and amount deducted)

Prepare invoice → Copies:
1. Original invoice
2. Accounts receivable
3. Broker's copy
4. Shipping confirmation
5. Warehouse copy
6. Packing slip

1. In hold file
2. In hold file
3. In hold file
4. To warehouse
5. To warehouse
6. To warehouse

Distribute the copies

Await notification from warehouse that shipment has been made → You will not require this if you are the producer and shipper

Prepare customer ledger card (for new customer)

Continued on next page

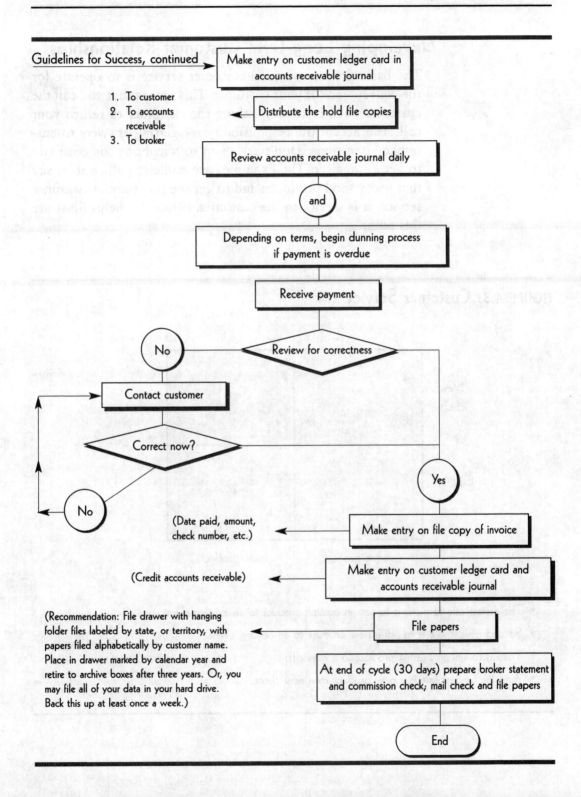

Guidelines for Success, continued

1. To customer
2. To accounts receivable
3. To broker

Make entry on customer ledger card in accounts receivable journal

Distribute the hold file copies

Review accounts receivable journal daily

and

Depending on terms, begin dunning process if payment is overdue

Receive payment

Review for correctness

No

Contact customer

Correct now?

No

Yes

(Date paid, amount, check number, etc.)

Make entry on file copy of invoice

(Credit accounts receivable)

Make entry on customer ledger card and accounts receivable journal

(Recommendation: File drawer with hanging folder files labeled by state, or territory, with papers filed alphabetically by customer name. Place in drawer marked by calendar year and retire to archive boxes after three years. Or, you may file all of your data in your hard drive. Back this up at least once a week.)

File papers

At end of cycle (30 days) prepare broker statement and commission check; mail check and file papers

End

Developing Long-Term Customer Relationships

The basic premise of good customer service is to operate for the convenience of your customer. This means that you call the customer back instead of asking the customer to return your call. You accept the responsibility for getting answers to customers' questions. Don't ask them to telephone someone else to get an answer. The examples are endless. Suffice it to say that many food producers fail to get the point about customer service: it is service to the customer. Figure 4.3 helps illustrate this point.

FIGURE 4.3: Customer Service

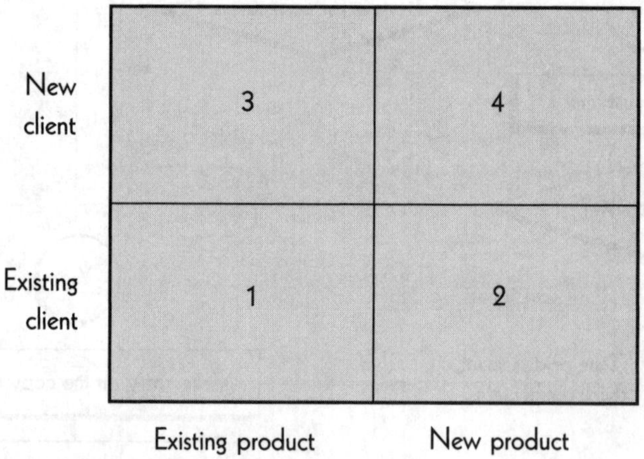

- The easiest sale to make is to sell an existing product to an existing client.
- Second easiest sale is to sell a new product to an existing client.
- Third is to sell an existing product to a new client.
- And the hardest sale is a new product to a new client.

One often overlooked aspect of marketing is the follow-up process after the order is shipped. Sometimes this is simply a telephone call or visit to see that all arrived in good order. This helps cement your professional relationship and it creates goodwill. You impress the customer as someone who will stay around, and not run off with the check.

Consider telephone marketing to ensure that customer contact is maintained. In those areas where you are not using a broker, you can generate continued sales over the telephone. You can use the telephone and the mails to contact all your customers, regardless of broker use, regarding special promotions. Alert your broker to any subsequent interest so that a sales call can be made.

> ### Customer Feedback Hint
>
> Include a customer satisfaction card in your shipment or with your invoice to retailers. This can be a form that allows the customer to comment on the condition of the product or the nature of any of your services. It can also be designed as a convenient and easy-to-use reorder form. Consider having it postage-paid, or invite the recipient to reply via e-mail.

Earlier we talked about the distinction between customer and consumer. The consumer consumes your product; the customer buys it for resale. The latter determines the quality of your service/product. Your success can be measured only by how you meet your customers' quality needs.

CHAPTER FIVE

Creating Your Own Success Niche

This book began by testing your motivation. You learned that obtaining nationwide distribution—in every grocery on every corner in every city and town—costs the market leaders a fortune. There are more than 15,000 new food products introduced every year, and there is a 96 percent failure rate over the first three years. Yet here you are, now versed in the methods and procedures for marketing your specialty food product. Or, armed as you are with the knowledge, you have decided, or are about to decide, that it is just not for you. Perhaps you are going to give it a good think before proceeding.

In either case, you are ahead of the game. You now know the importance of developing a clear vision, how to become a focused niche player, and what is needed to get your product on the food store shelf.

How to Know If You Are Successful

Add up your revenues, deduct your costs, and if something is left over, you might be successful. This is the traditional means of determining success in business. A better and more long-term way is to measure the effect you and your company are having on your customers. Have you, in fact, delighted them?

There are tools you can use to measure your efforts at quality planning, and exceeding your customers' quality needs.

The Malcolm Baldrige National Quality Award, administered by the U.S. Department of Commerce, incorporates criteria that you can use to evaluate your forward movement. The award was established in 1987 to promote awareness of the importance of quality improvement, to recognize organizations that made substantial improvements in competitive performance, and to foster sharing of best practices information among U.S. organizations. Only one food industry firm has won the award: Stay Fresh Foods, a manufacturer and distributor of more than 160 egg-based food products.

Whether or not you apply, a review of the award criteria may help in your search for excellence. The following is a brief summary of key elements of the award criteria.

Leadership.—This category examines how you and your key managers create and sustain clear quality values, and whether you have developed an appropriate supporting management system that promotes management excellence. An example of a quality value is your willingness to treat all customers equally. Another is to involve all members of your team in your product development and promotion planning. If you do it all alone, you risk the possibility of someone on whom you rely not having a stake in the outcome and, therefore, not giving his or her share of the effort.

Questions to ask yourself. Describe your personal involvement in setting directions and in developing and maintaining a leadership system that fosters excellence. Do you create and reinforce high expectations throughout your company? Do you set performance goals and measures through strategic planning? Do you maintain a climate conducive to continuous learning?

Information and analysis.–This category examines the use of data and information to support overall performance excellence.

Questions to ask yourself. Are you in regular contact with your customers to obtain data on their needs? Do you use data as a basis for making decisions, or are you a seat-of-the-pants decision maker? The food industry tends to be product-driven: "We grow it in Kansas, we can sell it anywhere." This is a short-sighted approach that ignores the importance of the voice of the customer. A market-driven company will succeed because it uses information gained from listening to the customer.

Strategic quality planning.–This looks at how you set strategic direction, and how you determine key planning requirements.

Questions to ask yourself. Describe your strategic planning process and how this process determines and addresses key customer performance requirements (one might be a rapid turnaround of orders). Do you translate these requirements into critical success factors (24-hour order processing, for example)?

Human resource utilization.–Examines how your sales, operations, and administrative staff are aligned with your company's overall performance objectives. Also examined are your efforts to build and maintain a climate conducive to performance excellence, full participation, and personal growth.

Questions to ask yourself. Describe the training in quality concepts you provide for your sales,

---

CASE IN POINT

The King's Cupboard is a company started by a husband-and-wife team who are molecular biologists in Red Lodge, Montana. They loved Montana and wanted to start a business so they could stay there. The company produces very high-end chocolate sauces that retail for around $8. In business for eight years, and winner of six NASFT Outstanding Product Awards, The King's Cupboard became successful at the four-year mark.

operations, and administrative staff. Are your resource planning and evaluation aligned with your company's overall performance improvement plan? Do you evaluate your sales staff, for example, on how effectively it meets customer needs, as opposed to just the number of sales made? Do you reward high-performing individuals or high-performing teams? Do you treat your employees as costs to be reduced, or as assets to be developed?

Business process management.—Key aspects of process management are examined, including design and delivery of services and business operations.

Questions to ask yourself. Describe how you develop new products, or line extensions, in response to customer needs. Is current information on customer requirements disseminated to the employees responsible for product development and improvement? Do you involve everyone in discussing possible alternatives?

Performance results.—Examines your company's results (outcomes) in terms of how you met your customer needs.

Questions to ask yourself. How do you measure your success? (Return on investment, stockholder equity, gross profit margin, gross revenues, trends, number of repeat orders, new customers, complimentary letters, low employee turnover, etc.)

Customer satisfaction.—Examines how you determine customer (both internal and external) satisfaction. Your primary customers (those without whom your company would not exist) are the food buyers. Other customers include companies that buy your products for resale (distributors and retailers), your employees, and any other entity for whom your company provides a product or service.

CASE IN POINT

Marrakesh Express developed a bean cuisine concept consisting of low-fat and healthy products. Co-packed in beautiful packages, Marrakesh made sales to retailers and distributors. They hit the market at a time when Mediterranean foods were in demand. After extending the line, they reached the $2 million sales mark in about two years. The company and brand were purchased by Hormel Foods.

Questions to ask yourself. How do you develop and maintain awareness of the needs and expectations of your current and future customers? Understanding the voice of the customer is essential to achieving customer satisfaction.

The Deming Chain Reaction

Dr. W. Edwards Deming—considered one of the first leaders in the global quality movement—noted that when we focus on quality, our operating costs are reduced and our productivity improves. The process he described is a very simple chain reaction that can be best shown in the following chart, Figure 5.1.

FIGURE 5.1: The Deming Chain Reaction

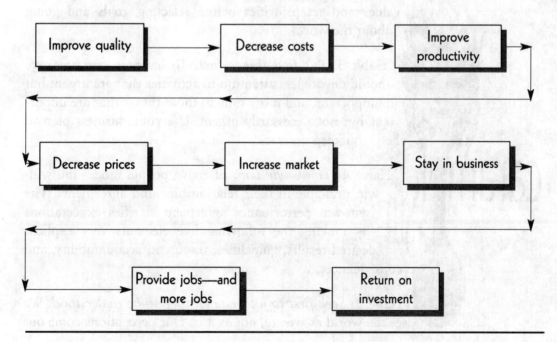

When you focus on quality, you improve the quality of your product, reduce its price, expand your market, and reap the profits.

Cultivating Effective Habits

If you have decided to go ahead, then take a lead from Stephen Covey's book, *The Seven Habits of Highly Effective People* (Free Press, 2004), and incorporate these habits into your repertoire.

Habit 1: *Be proactive*. Proactive people develop the ability to choose their response, making them more a product of their values and decisions than their moods and conditions.

Habit 2: *Begin with the end in mind*. Effective people realize that things are created mentally before they are created physically. They write a vision or purpose statement and use it as a frame of reference for making future decisions. They clarify values and set priorities before selecting goals and going about the work.

Habit 3: *Put first things first*. To leverage our time, we should devote less attention to activities that are urgent but unimportant, and more time to those things that are important but not necessarily urgent. Use your business plan to help you keep on track.

Habit 4: *Think win-win*. Effective people model the win-win principle in their relationships and agreements. The win-win performance agreement clarifies expectations by making the following five elements very explicit: desired results, guidelines, resources, accountability, and consequences.

Habit 5: *Seek first to understand, then to be understood*. We see the world as we are, not as it is. Our perceptions come out of our experiences. Most credibility problems begin with perception differences. To resolve these differences and to restore credibility, one must exercise empathy, seeking first to understand the point of view of the other person. Remember to operate for the convenience of your customer.

> Gourmet food marketing, like the frog, can be dissected, but in the process, the beast dies.

Habit 6: *Synergize*. This is the habit of creative cooperation or teamwork. For those who have a win-win abundance mentality and exercise empathy, differences in any relationship can produce synergy, where the whole is greater than the sum of its parts.

Habit 7: *Sharpen the saw*. The habit of sharpening the saw regularly means having a balanced, systematic program for self-renewal in the four areas of our lives: physical, mental, emotional-social, and spiritual.

Take these seven habits to heart. They will be useful in everything you do.

❖ ❖ ❖

Throughout this book, I have tried to make sense of some of the more complex issues of specialty food cost accounting, market research, pricing, and distribution. The rest of it—production, packaging, and labeling, for example—are all pretty matter of fact, save the visceral issues of what is or is not aesthetically appealing (taste, packaging, labeling, etc.).

Ultimately, you will have to just put your foot in the water. To paraphrase a famous saying, "Gourmet food marketing, like the frog, can be dissected, but in the process, the beast dies." Death by analysis. If you have that fire in your belly, and if you have the willpower, perseverance, motivation, focus, and self-discipline . . . and if you have the money, and the health, and the idea, the concept, the fever, the VISION . . . then Do it, and Good Profits to You!

I invite you to comment on this book, and/or to make any recommendations for future editions. Please see www.specialty-foodresource.com. If you are a service provider, please submit your company name and description of your service to be considered for listing in the next edition of *From Kitchen to Market*. Send comments to:

Stephen Hall
c/o Dearborn Trade Publishing
A Kaplan Professional Company
30 South Wacker Drive, Suite 2500
Chicago, IL 60606
800-621-9621 http://www.dearborntrade.com

Trade Journals

The following list is not all-inclusive, nor does it mean to serve as an endorsement. Ask for sample copies and rate sheets. Please see http://www.specialtyfoodresource.com for updates.

Fancy Food & Culinary Products Magazine

20 North Wacker Drive, #1865
Chicago, IL 60606
312-849-2220; Fax: 312-849-2174
e-mail: fancyfood@aol.com

Primary focus: Specialty food and gourmet food products.

Food Product Design

Executive/Editorial Offices
3400 Dundee Road, Suite #100
Northbrook, IL 60062
847-559-0385; Fax: 847-559-0389
e-mail: contactus@foodproductdesign.com
Web site: http://www.foodproductdesign.com

Primary focus: Business-to-business magazine edited for those individuals who design new and reformulated food products for the retail and foodservice markets.

Gift Basket Review Magazine

815 Haines Street
Jacksonville, FL 32206
904-634-1903; Fax: 904-633-8764
e-mail: http://www.festivities-pub.com

Primary focus: Gift basket marketing and promotion. Design features, tips, industry news, and new products.

Gourmet News

P.O. Box 1056
106 Lafayette Street
Yarmouth, ME 04096
207-846-0600; Fax: 207-846-0657
e-mail: rrector@gourmetnews.com
Web site: http://www.gourmetnews.com

Primary focus: "The business newspaper for the gourmet industry." Reports timely and newsworthy stories and events, issues, trends, and other happenings among the specialty food and natural-food retailers, supermarkets and department stores, specialty distributors, and suppliers to the trade.

The Gourmet Retailer Magazine

Specialty Media, Inc.
3301 Ponce de Leon Boulevard, #300
Coral Gables, FL 33134
305-446-3388, 800-397-1137
Fax: 305-446-2868
Web site: http://www.gourmetretailer.com

Primary focus: A monthly trade publication that blends coverage of specialty food, kitchenware, coffee, and tea in a comprehensive source of news and information about the industry.

> *The Gourmet Retailer Online* features all the latest industry news, access to online market research, editorial archives, comprehensive trade show information, and much more. Visit them at: http://www. gourmetretailer.com

Specialty Food Magazine

120 Wall Street
New York, NY 10015
212-482-6440, 800-627-3869
Fax: 212-482-6459
e-mail: lstefanofs@nasft.org
Web site: http://www.fancyfoodshows.com

Primary focus: Specialty food. Strong retailer emphasis.

Prepared Foods

1050 IL. Route 83 Suite 200
Bensenville, IL 60106
630-694-4344; Fax: 630-227-0527
e-mail: pfeditors@bnpmedia.com

Primary focus: Grocery trade, with a new products news section.

Trade Associations

This list is not all-inclusive, nor does it mean to serve as an endorsement. Some references will be of minimal value to the food entrepreneur, but I have included them on the outside chance that you find one of interest. Please see http://www.specialtyfoodresource.com for updates.

General

American Association of Candy Technologists
175 Rock Road
Glen Rock, NJ 07452
201-652-2655
Web site: http://www.aactcandy.org

American Cocoa Research Institute
7900 Westpark Drive, Suite A-320
McLean, VA 22102
703-790-5011

American Culinary Federation
P.O. Box 3466
St. Augustine, FL 32085
800-624-9458; Fax: 904-825-4758
e-mail: acp@acfchefs.net
Web site: http://www.acfchefs.org

American Frozen Food Institute
2000 Corporate Ridge
Suite 1000
McLean, VA 22102
703-821-1350; Fax: 703-821-1350
Web site: http://www.affi.com

American Institute of Wine & Food
1550 Bryant Street, #700
San Francisco, CA 94103
415-255-3000; Fax: 415-255-2874
800-274-AIWF
Web site: http://www.aiwf.org

American Wholesale Marketers Association
1128 16th Street, NW
Washington, DC 20036-4808
202-463-2124; Fax: 202-467-0559
e-mail: info@awmanet.org
Web site: http://www.awmanet.org

Association of Food Industries
3301 Route 66, Suite 205
Neptune, NJ 07753
732-922-3008
e-mail: info@ifus.org
Web site: http://afi.mytradeassociation.org

The Food Institute
American Institute of Food Distribution, Inc.
28-12 Broadway
Fair Lawn, NJ 07410
201-791-5570; Fax: 201-791-5222
Web site: http://www.foodinstitute.com

The Food Institute is a trade association and information reporting organization that follows trends, changing legislation, and market statistics in the food industry. It publishes the weekly *Food Institute Report* and numerous food-related reports, including *Food Retailing Review, Food Mergers & Acquisitions, Complying with the Nutritional Labeling & Education Act, Food Markets in Review, Supermarket Analysis Series,* and many more.

Food Marketing Institute
800 Connecticut Avenue, NW, #400
Washington, DC 20006
202-452-8444; Fax: 202-429-4519
Web site: http://www.fmi.org

The Food Marketing Institute is a nonprofit association conducting programs in research, education, and public affairs on behalf of its 1,600 members, composed largely of multistore chains, small regional firms, and independent supermarkets.

General Merchandise Distributors Council
1275 Lake Plaza Drive

Colorado Springs, CO 80906
719-576-4260

The Grocery Manufacturers of America Inc. (GMA)
1010 Wisconsin Avenue, NW, Suite 800
Washington, DC 20007
202-337-9400; Fax: 202-337-4508
e-mail: info@gmabrands.com
Web site: http://www.gmabrands.com

GMA is a trade association of the manufacturers and processors of food and non-food products sold primarily in retail grocery stores in the United States. Readers may wish to request a copy of their 2002 report "E-Commerce Opportunities in Direct Store Delivery." There is no charge for this, and the report can be obtained on line at: http://www.gmabrands.com at their publications page.

Institute of Food Technologists
525 West Van Buren, Suite 1000
Chicago, IL 60607
312-782-8424, Fax: 312-782-8348
e-mail: info@ift.org
Web site: http://www.ift.org

International Association of Culinary Professionals
304 West Liberty, #201
Louisville, KY 40202
502-581-9786, Fax: 502-589-3602
e-mail: iacp@hqtrs.com
Web site: http://www.iacp-online.org

International Foodservice Manufacturers Association
180 North Stetson Avenue, Suite 4400

Chicago, IL 606016710
312-540-4400, Fax: 312-540-4401
e-mail: ifma@ifmaworld.com
Web site: http://www.ifmaworld.com

International Mass Retail Association
1700 N. Moore Street, Suite 2250
Arlington, VA 22209
703-841-2300
Web site: http://www.imra.org

Kosherfest
241 West 30th Street
New York, NY 10001
212-643-1623; Fax: 212-643-164
e-mail: info@kosherchannelone.com
Web site: http://www.kosherfest.com

National Association for the Specialty Food Trade (NASFT)
120 Wall Street, 27th Floor
New York, NY 10005-4001
212-482-6440 or 800-627-3869 (outside NY)
Fax: 212-482-6459
e-mail: custserv@fancyfoodshows.com
Web site: http://www.fancyfoodshows.com

The NASFT is a nonprofit business trade organization that has been fostering trade, commerce and interest in the specialty food industry since 1952. It has more than 1,800 U.S. and overseas members composed of food manufacturers, importers, distributors, and brokers involved in marketing specialty foods and beverages, fine confections, wine, cooking accessories, and publications. The association sponsors two major annual trade shows and an educational conference, and publishes *Showcase* magazine, which tracks industry trends, presents processor and retailer profiles, and pertinent government rules and regulations. Be warned: NASFT has one of those frustrating unattended voice messaging systems. For example, if you get it wrong, the system will say "good-bye" and hang up on you.

National Association of Concessionaires
35 East Wacker Drive
Chicago, IL 60601 USA
312-236-3858
Web site: http://www.naconline.org

National Food Processors Association
1401 New York Avenue, NW
Washington, DC 20005
202-639-5900, Fax: 202-639-5932
Web site: http://www.nfpa.food.org

A primary scientific and technical association of the food industry, the National Food Processors Association (NFPA) has more than 90 years of experience and expertise in food issues. NFPA members manufacture the nation's processed/packaged fruits and vegetables, juices and drinks, meat and poultry, seafood, and specialty products.

The Food Processors Institute is the nonprofit education arm of the NFPA. Its primary educational goal is to provide a curricula of workshops, seminars, materials, texts, and leadership training in support of the food processing industry.

Member dues in NFPA start at $3,000 per year and go up, depending on member company annual revenues.

National Frozen Food Association
4755 Linglestown Road, Suite 300

Harrisburg, PA 171120069
717-657-8601; Fax: 717-657-9862
e-mail: info@nffa.org
Web site: http://www.nffa.org

National Grocers Association
1005 North Glebe Road, Suite 250
Arlington, VA 22201
703-516-0700; Fax: 703-516-0115
e-mail: info@nationalgrocers.org
Web site: http://www.nationalgrocers.org

National Restaurant Association (NRA)
Headquarters
1200 17th Street, NW
Washington, DC 20036-3006
202-331-5900; Fax: 202-347-2989
Web site: http://www.restaurant.org

National Restaurant Association (NRA)
Convention Office
150 North Michigan Avenue
Suite 2000
Chicago, IL 60601
312-853-2525; Fax: 312-853-2548

Pennsylvania Manufacturing Confectioners'
Association
2980 Linden Street, Suite E3
Bethlehem, PA 18017
610-625-4655; Fax: 610-625-4657
e-mail: Yvette.Thomas@pmca.com
Web site: http://www.pmca.com

Philadelphia National Candy Gift &
Gourmet Show
P.O. Box 496
Abington, PA 19001
888-226-3989
Web site: http://www.rcaphila.org

Private Label Manufacturers Association
(PLMA)
369 Lexington Avenue
New York, NY 10017
212-972-3131; Fax: 212-983-1382
Web site: http://www.plma.com

Retail Confectioners International, Inc.
1807 Glenview Road, Suite 204
Glenview, IL 60025
708-724-6120
Web site: http://www.retailconfectioners.org

Snack Food Association
Western Association of Food Chains
825 Colorado Boulevard, Suite 203
Los Angeles, CA 90041
213-254-7270
Web site: http://www.snax.com

Snack Food Association
1711 King Street, Suite 1
Alexandria, VA 22314
703-836-4500
Web site: http://www.sfa.org

Baking

American Bakers Association
1350 I Street, NW, #1209
Washington, DC 20005-3305
202-789-0300, Fax: 202-898-1164
e-mail: info@americanbakers.org
Web site: http://www.americanbakers.org

American Institute of Baking
1213 Baker's Way
Manhattan, KS 66502
785-537-4750; Fax: 785-537-1493
Web site: http://www.aibonline.com

Retailer's Bakery Association
14239 Park Center Drive
Laurel, MD 20707
301-725-2149; Fax: 301-725-2187
e-mail: rba@rbanet.com
Web site: http://www.rbanet.com

Beans/Legumes

Idaho Bean Commission
P.O. Box 2556
Boise, ID 83701-2556
208-334-3520; Fax: 208-334-2442
e-mail: rtway@bean.state.id.us
Web site: http://www.state.id.us/bean/

USA Dry Pea & Lentil Council
2780 West Pullman Road
Moscow, ID 83843
208-882-3023; Fax: 208-882-6406
e-mail: pulse@pea-lentil.com
Web site: http://www.pea-lentil.com

Beverages

INTERBEV
1101 16th Street, NW
Washington, DC 20036
202-463-6795; Fax: 202-833-2484

International Bottled Water Association
1700 Diagonal Road, Suite 650
Alexandria, VA 22314
703-683-5213; Fax: 703-683-4074
Web site: http://www.bottledwater.org

National Beverage Association
1101 16th Street, NW
Washington, DC 20036
202-463-6732; Fax: 202-463-8277

e-mail: mcavanagh@nsda.com
Web site: http://www.nsda.com

New York Wine & Grape Foundation
350 Elm Street
Penn Yan, NY 14527
315-536-7442; Fax: 315-536-0719
Web site: http://www.nywine.com

Wine Institute
1127 Eleventh Street, Suite 900
San Francisco, CA 95814
916-441-6974; Fax: 916-441-7890
Web site: http://www.wineinstitute.org

Cheese/Dairy

American Cheese Society
304 West Liberty Street, Suite 201
Louisville, KY 40202
502-583-3783; Fax: 502-589-3602
Web site: http://www.cheesesociety.org

American Dairy Association
10255 West Higgins Road, #900
Rosemont, IL 60018-5616
708-803-2000; Fax: 708-803-2077
Web site: http://www.realseal.com/home.html

American Dairy Products Institute
300 W. Washington Street, Suite 400
Chicago, IL 60606-1823
312-782-4888; Fax: 312-782-5299
Web site: http://www.americandairy
products.com

California Milk Advisory Board
400 Oyster Point Boulevard
Suite 214
South San Francisco, CA 94080

650-871-6455; Fax: 650-583-7328
Web site: http://www.calif-dairy.com

Cheese Importers Association
488 Madison Park Avenue
New York, NY 10022
212-753-7500; Fax: 212-688-2870

Dairy Management, Inc.
O'Hare International Center
10255 West Higgins Road, Suite 900
Rosemont, IL 60018-5616
847-803-2000
Web site: http://www.dairyinfo.com

The Eastern Perishable Products Association, Inc.
(Formerly: Eastern Dairy Deli Association)
411 Route 17 South, #320
Hasbrook Heights, NJ 07604
201-288-5454; Fax: 201-288-5422
e-mail: eppa@eppainc.org
Web site: http://www.eppainc.org

International Dairy-Deli-Bakery Association
313 Price Place, #202
P.O. Box 5528
Madison, WI 53705
608-238-7908; Fax: 608-238-6330
e-mail: iddba@iddba.org
Web site: http://www.iddanet.org

International Dairy Foods Association, Milk Industry Foundation, National Cheese Institute, International Ice Cream Association, American Butter Institute
1250 H Street, NW, Suite 900
Washington, DC 20005
202-737-4332; Fax: 202-331-7820
Web site: http://www.idfa.org

National Dairy Council
10255 West Higgins Road, #900
Rosemont, IL 60018-5616
708-803-2000; Fax: 708-803-2077
Web site: http://www.nationaldairycouncil.org

National Dairy Council of Canada
221 Laurier Avenue East
Ottawa, Ontario, Canada K1N 6P1
613-238-4116; Fax: 613-238-6247
Web site: http://www.ndcc.ca/english/main.htm

New England Dairy-Deli-Bakery Association
20 Scanlon Drive
Randolph, MA 02368
781-963-9726
Web site: http://www.neddaweb.org

Western Dairy Council
12450 North Washington
Thornton, CO 80241
303-451-7711, 800-274-6455
Fax: 303-452-5484
Web site: http://www.wdairycouncil.com

Wisconsin Cheesemakers Association
3 South Pinckney, #620
Madison, WI 53703
608-255-2027; Fax: 608-255-4434
e-mail: office@wischeesemakersassn.org
Web site: http://www.wischeese makersassn.org

Wisconsin Milk Marketing Board
8418 Excelsior Drive
Madison, WI 53717
608-836-8820; Fax: 608-836-5822
Web site: http://producer.wisdairy.com

Coffee

National Coffee Association (NCA)
15 Maiden Lane, Suite 1405
New York, NY 10038
212 766-4007
Web site: http://www.ncausa.org

Specialty Coffee Association of America (SCAA)
One World Trade Center, Suite 1200
Long Beach, CA 90831-1200
562-624-4100; Fax: 562-624-4101
Web site: http://www.scaa.org

Confections

Chocolate Manufacturers Association
7900 Westpark Drive, Suite A-320
McLean, VA 22102
703-790-5011; Fax: 703-790-5752
Web site: http://www.candyusa.org

National Candy Brokers Association
710 East Ogden Avenue, Suite 600
Naperville, IL 60563-8603
630-369-2406
Web site: http://www.candynet.com

National Confectioners Association
7900 Westpark Drive, #A320
McLean, VA 22102
703-790-5750; Fax: 703-790-5752
Web site: http://www.ecandy.com

Philadelphia National Candy, Gift & Gourmet Show
P.O. Box 496
Abington, PA 19001
888-226-3989
Web site: http://www.rcaphila.org

Fish/Seafood

Alaska Seafood Marketing Institute
1111 West Eighth Street, #100
Juneau, AK 99801-1895
907-465-5560; Fax: 907-465-5572
Web site: http://www.alaskaseafood.org

National Fisheries Institute
1525 Wilson Boulevard, #500
Arlington, VA 22209
703-524-8880; Fax: 703-524-4619
Web site: http://www.nfi.org

Flavors

Flavor & Extract Manufacturers Association
1620 I Street, NW, #925
Washington, DC 20006
202-293-5800; Fax: 202-463-8998

Fruit

Calavo Growers of California
15661 Red Hill Avenue
Tustin, CA 92680
714-259-1166; Fax: 714-259-4810

California Apricot Advisory Board
1280 Boulevard Way, #107
Walnut Creek, CA 94595
510-937-3660; Fax: 510-937-0118

California Dried Fig Advisory Board
P.O. Box 709
Fresno, CA 93712
209-445-5626; Fax: 209-224-3449

California Kiwifruit Commission
1540 River Park Drive

Sacramento, CA 95815
916-924-0530; Fax: 916-929-3740

California Strawberry Commission
P.O. Box 269
Watsonville, CA 95077
408-724-1301; Fax: 408-724-5973
e-mail: info@calstrawberry.com
Web site: http://www.calstrawberry.com

California Table Grape Commission
392 W. Fallbrook, #101
Fresno, CA 93711
559-447-8350; Fax: 559-224-9184
e-mail: info@tablegrape.com
Web site: http://www.tablegrape.com

California Tree Fruit Agreement
975 I Street, P.O. Box 968
Reedley, CA 93654
559-638-8260; Fax: 559-638-8842
e-mail: info@caltreefruit.com
Web site: http://www.caltreefruit.com

Cherry Marketing Institute
2220 University Park Drive
Okemos, MI 48864
517-347-0010; Fax: 517-347-0605
Web site: http://www.cherrymkt.org

Cape Cod Cranberry Growers, Cranberry Institute, Cranberry Marketing Committee
3203-B Cranberry Highway
East Wareham, MA 02538
508-295-4132; Fax: 508-291-1511
Web site: http://www.cranberryinstitute.org

Dried Fruit Association of California
P.O. Box 270A
Santa Clara, CA 95052
408-727-9302; Fax: 408-790-3833

New Zealand Kiwifruit
2001 W. Garfield, Pier 90
Seattle, WA 98119
604-284-1705; Fax: 604-282-0533
e-mail: zespri@oppy.com
Web site: http://www.zespri-usa.com

North American Blueberry Council
4995 Golden Foothill Parkway, Suite 2
El Dorado Hills, CA 95762
916-933-9399; Fax: 916-933-9777
e-mail: bberry@blueberry.org
Web site: http://www.blueberry.org/
nabcmainpage.html

Oregon Cherry Growers
1520 Woodrow Street, NE
P.O. Box 7357
Salem, OR 97303
503-296-5487; Fax: 503-296-2509
e-mail: mrm@orcherry.com
Web site: http://www.orcherry.com

Oregon Blueberry Commission, Oregon Raspberry and Blackberry Commission, Oregon Strawberry Commission
712 NW Fourth Street
Corvallis, OR 97330
503-758-4043; Fax: 503-758-4553

National Watermelon Promotion Board
P.O. Box 140065
Orlando, FL 32814-0065
407-895-5100; Fax: 407-895-5022

Processed Apples Institute
5775 Peachtree-Dunwoody Road, #500-G
Atlanta, GA 30342
404-252-3663; Fax: 404-252-0774
e-mail: info@appleproducts.org
Web site: http://www.appleproducts.org

Raisin Administrative Committee
3445 North 1st Street
Fresno, CA 93726
559-225-0520; Fax: 559-225-0652
e-mail: info@raisins.org
Web site: http://www.raisins.org

Washington Red Raspberry Commission
1626 North Atlantic
Spokane, WA 99205
509-328-7307

Washington State Apple Commission
P.O. Box 18
Wenatchee, WA 98807
509-663-9600; Fax: 509-662-5824

**Wild Blueberry Association of North
America (WBANA)**
50 Cottage Street
Bar Harbor, ME 04609
800-233-9453; Fax: 207-288-2656
e-mail: info@wildblueberries.com
Web site: http://www.wildblueberries.com

Grain

California Wild Rice Advisory Board
c/o The Thacker Group
1008 Second Street
Courtyard Level
Old Sacramento, CA 95814
916-444-8363; Fax: 916-444-3536

Flax Council of Canada
465-167 Lombard Avenue
Winnipeg, Manitoba
Canada R3B 0T6
204-982-2115; Fax: 204-942-1841
e-mail: flax@flaxcouncil.ca
Web site: http://www.flaxcouncil.ca

Kansas Wheat Commission
2630 Claflin Road
Manhattan, KS 66502-2743
785-539-0255; Fax: 785-539-8946
e-mail: dfrey@kswheat.com
Web site: http://www.kswheat.com

USA Rice Federation
Houston, TX 77074
713-270-6699; Fax: 713-270-9021
e-mail: riceinfo@tx.usarice.com
Web site: http://www.usarice.com

Wheat Foods Council
10841 South Crossroads Drive, 105
Parker, CO 80138
303-840-8737; Fax: 303-840-6877
e-mail: wfc@wheatfoods.org
Web site: http://www.wheatfoods.org

Hot and Spicy

The Chili Pepper Institute
Box 30003, Department 3Q
Las Cruces, NM 88003
505-646-3028; Fax: 505-646-6041
e-mail: hotchile@nmsu.edu
Web site: http://www.chilipepperinstitute.org

Jams/Jellies/Preserves

International Jelly & Preserve Association
5775 Peachtree-Dunwoody Road
Atlanta, GA 30342
404-252-3663; Fax: 404-252-0774
Web site: http://www.jelly.org

Nutrition/Organic/Health

American Council on Science and Health
1995 Broadway, 2nd floor

New York, NY 10023
212-362-7044; Fax: 212-362-4919
e-mail: acsh@acsh.org
Web site: http://www.acsh.org

American Dietetic Association
216 W. Jackson Boulevard
Chicago, IL 60606
800-366-1655 (Weekday Consumer
Nutrition Hotline)
Fax: 312-899-4899
e-mail: exhibit@eatright.org
Web site: http://www.eatright.org

Human Nutrition Program
The Rockefeller University
1230 Park Avenue, Box 246
New York, NY 10021
212-746-1617; Fax: 212-746-8310
e-mail: miller@rockefeller.edu
Web site: http://www.nalusda.gov/fnic/

Hotlines

Calcium Information Center 800-321-2681

Garlic Information Center 800-330-5922

Olive Oil Information Center 800-232-6548

Organic Trade Association
P.O. Box 547
Greenfield, MA 01302
413-774-7511; Fax: 413-774-6432
e-mail: info@ota.com
Web site: http://www.ota.com

Pasta

National Pasta Association
1156 15th Street, NW, Suite 900

Washington, DC 20005
202-637-5888; Fax: 202-223-9741
e-mail: info@ilovepasta.org
Web site: http://www.ilovepasta.org

Produce

Produce Marketing Association
P.O. Box 6036
Newark, DE 19714-6036
302-738-7100; Fax: 302-731-2409
Web site: http://www.pma.com

Salad Dressings

Association for Dressings and Sauces
5775 Peachtree-Dunwoody Road
Atlanta, GA 30342
404-252-3663; Fax: 404-252-0774
e-mail: ads@assahq.com
Web site: http://www.dressings-sauces.org

Snacks

Snack Food Association
1711 King Street, #1
Alexandria, VA 22314
800-628-1334 or 703-836-4500
Fax: 703-836-8262
e-mail: sfa@sfa.org
Web site: http://www.sfa.org

Tea

Tea Association of the USA, Inc.
420 Lexington Avenue, #825
New York, NY 10170
212-986-9415; Fax: 212-697-8658
Web site: http://www.teausa.com

Trade Shows and Services

The following appendixes list services and sources of assistance and are meant to be neither all-inclusive nor to serve as an endorsement. Please go to http://www.specialty foodresource.com for updates.

ANUGA (American Foods Pavilion)
World Food Market
Cologne, Germany
Contact: USDA, Room 4939
Washington, DC 20250-1000
202-720-7420
Web site: http://www.fas.usda.gov

Show held in October, odd-numbered years.

Boston Gift Show
Boston, MA
Boston Convention and Exhibition Center
Contact: George Little Management, Inc.
10 Bank Street
White Plains, NY 10606-1954
800-272-7469; Fax 914-948-6180
Web site: http://www.glmshows.com
April and September

The Boston Gift Show features New England specialty food products that can be successfully merchandised via the gift trade.

Attendees include retailers with strong purchasing power from a variety of gift, stationery, and department stores, as well as representatives from mail-order catalogs, specialty stores, craft shops, college stores, museum shops, garden centers, and gourmet stores.

International Gift Basket, Floral and Balloon Jubilee!
Contact: Festivities Publications, Inc.
815 Haines Street
Jacksonville, FL 32206
904-634-1903
Web site: http://www.Festivities-pub.com

International Fancy Food and Confection Show
Contact: NASFT
120 Wall Street
New York, NY 10018
212-482-6440, 800-627-3869

Fax: 212-482-6459
Web site: http://www.specialtyfood.com

These are owned and sponsored by the National Association for the Specialty Food Trade (NASFT), the largest association in the United States specializing in the representation and promotion of specialty food and confectionery products. It sponsors three very important annual food shows for its members, which attract buyers and decision makers from all segments of the specialty food industry. The association also sponsors food processor seminars devoted to food marketing and distribution issues.

International Restaurant and Foodservice Show of New York
383 Main Avenue
Norwalk, CT 06851
800-840-5612
Web site: http://www.internationalrestaurant ny.com

Heavy emphasis on foodservice with over 900 exhibitors of food, freezers, utensils, uniforms, beverages, baked goods, etc. Sponsored by the California Restaurant Association. Produced and managed by Reed Exhibitions.

NASDA—U.S. Food Export Showcase
National Association of State Departments of Agriculture
1156 15th Street, NW
Washington, DC 20005
202-296-9680
Contact: Convention Management Group at 703-876-0900
e-mail: ammccormick@cmgexpo.com

The Showcase is held each year at Chicago's McCormick Place in conjunction with the Food Marketing Institute's Supermarket Industry Exposition, the NASFT International Fancy Food and Confection Show, and All Things Organic. It attracts supermarket industry executives from around the world. The next show will be in May 2005.

NGA Annual Convention
National Grocers Association (NGA)
1825 Samuel Morse Drive
Reston, VA 22090-5317
703-437-5300; Fax: 703-437-7768
Web site: http://www.nationalgrocers.org

The NGA is the national trade association exclusively representing the retail and wholesale grocers who comprise the independent sector of the food distribution industry.

Philadelphia National Candy, Gift, and Gourmet Show
651 Allendale Road
King of Prussia, PA 19406
610-265-4688 or 610-369-1044
e-mail: rcap@rcaphila.org
Web site: http://www.rcaphila.org

Sponsored by the Retail Confectioners Association of Philadelphia

SIAL (American Foods Pavilion)
39, Rue de la Bienfaisance
75008, Paris, France
Web site: http://www.fas.usda.gov

Show held in October, even-numbered years. SIAL and ANUGA are biannual food shows that are particularly beneficial to European producers desiring to introduce products to the United States, and for U.S. producers wishing to export products to European markets. Average cost for a booth in the American Pavilion at SIAL, for example, is $14,000. Use the Web sites, above, for initial contact. USDA employs one of those wonderfully convoluted telephone answering systems that generally requires making a long-distance call, listening to a listing of options, and then getting a voice messaging system.

In addition to SIAL and ANUGA, noted above, there are numerous other international trade promotion events that may be of some value to food producers ready to explore international markets. Contact the Foreign Agricultural Service, USDA, Room 4647, South Building, Washington, DC 20250-1000, 202-690-1182; Fax: 202-690-4374.

Western Foodservice & Hospitality Expo Los Angeles
Web site: http://www.westernfood expola.com

APPENDIX D

Co-Packers

The National Association for the Specialty Food Trade (NASFT) has a listing of nearly 700 contract packaging companies (co-packers). Far too many people feel that a co-packer is a co-packer, and that any co-packer can do everything. In fact, co-packers have a variety of specific functional areas in which they excel. Please see http://www.specialty foodresource.com for updates.

Readers may wish to request the NASFT to send them a co-packer listing.
Contact: Ms. Heather Paul
NASFT
120 Wall Street
New York, NY 10005
800-627-3869, ext. 102, 212-482-6440
Fax: 212-482-6459
e-mail: hpaul@nasft.org

The listing consists only of NASFT members who have indicated to the NASFT that they are co-packers. It includes the co-packer contact information, products that they co-pack, plant locations, types of packaging they use, and specialized packing equipment (such as enrobers, form-fill and seal, smokers, vacuum packaging, etc.).

Few co-packers can provide all of the following range of services:

✧ Liquid products

✧ Dry products

✧ Ingredient preblends

✧ Labeling

✧ Packaging service only

✧ Product development/recipe conversion

Using a qualified contract packer will enable you to devote your time to management and marketing, while eliminating the enormous expense and responsibility of operating a production facility. Some will provide only the packaging, while others will help you with the entire formulation, production, packaging, and labeling process. Most offer no-cost initial consultation. Some even have marketing capability. See Chapter Two for a detailed discussion of co-packer services. Many of the companies are just food processors that have extra production capacity.

Northeast Area Small Co-Packers and Commercial Kitchens
See http://www.nysaes.cornell.edu/necfe/CoPackerKitchen/index.html
for a listing of co-packers in New York and New England.

Broker Information

The following list is not all-inclusive nor is it meant to serve as an endorsement. Please see http://www.specialtyfoodresource.com for updates.

Broker Associations

National Association of Specialty Food & Confection Brokers (NASFCB)
The National Association of Specialty Food and Confection Brokers (NASFCB) merged with the National Association for the Specialty Food Trade (NASFT). Readers may wish to request that the NASFT send them a broker listing.

Contact: Ms. Heather Paul
NASFT
120 Wall Street
New York, NY 10005
800-627-3869, ext. 102
212-482-6440
Fax: 212-482-6459
e-mail: hpaul@nasft.org

This listing consists only of NASFT broker members who have indicated to the NASFT that they are brokers. As of April 2004, the following 74 firms were listed:

A. P. Marketing
Mr. Brian W. Gilbertson
4904 Lincoln Drive
Edina, MN 55436-1071
952-931-9761; Fax: 952-936-9690
e-mail: briang@pclink.com

A.R. & Associates
Mr. Richard E. Redohl
4548 S. Square Drive
High Ridge, MO 63049
636-677-4104; Fax: 636-376-9909
e-mail: arassoc1@nuvox.net

ACB/Richard Watson
Mr. Richard Watson
501 Via Casitas, #321
Greenbrae, CA 94904-1958

415-461 9255
e-mail: rgwatson@pacbell.net

Advantage Sales & Marketing
Mr. Randy Allen
535 East Crescent Avenue
Ramsey, NJ 07446-1208
201-825-9400; Fax: 201-825-8556
e-mail: rdallen456@aol.com

Alfred H. Gledhill & Sons
Mr. Alfred H. Gledhill, Jr.
17 Selwyn Road
Belmont, MA 02478-3557
617-489-4929; Fax: 617-489-4231
e-mail: algledhill@att.net

Annie Hall Inc.
Ms. Annie Hall
5116 Coronado Ridge
Boca Raton, FL 33486
561-391-7636; Fax: 561-391-3368
e-mail: annhallinc@aol.com

Arnold H. Gitter Associates Inc.
Mr. Arnold H. Gitter
123 R Pleasant Street
P.O. Box 30
Marblehead, MA 01945
781-631-7527; Fax: 781-631-3852
e-mail: gitter.assoc@verizon.net

B & B Specialty Foods, Inc.
Ms. Mary Ann Greenawalt
4050 Stoneleigh Road
Bloomfield Hills, MI 48302-2018
248-645-2096; Fax: 248-645-6725
e-mail: magatbb@msen.com

Baron Associates, Inc.
Mr. William Baron
15 Locksley Road
Lynnfield, MA 01940
781-334-2978; Fax: 781-334-3622
e-mail: ewbaron@comcast.net

The Brauner Group LLC
Ms. Bonnie M. Brauner
32 Heron Road
Livingston, NJ 07039
973-535-3143; Fax: 973-535-3142
e-mail: bmbrauner@aol.com

Burgess, Bradstreet, Leland & Associates
Mr. Ken Leland
P.O. Box 550
Millbrae, CA 94030
650-692-1585; Fax: 650-692-1654
e-mail: bbleland@aol.com

Camoriano & Associates
Mr. Kirk Camoriano
14725 NW Tiffany Park Road
Parkville, MO 64153-1069
816-891-7755; Fax: 816-891-6474
e-mail: kirkc@camoriano.com

Cappetta Associates Sales & Marketing
Mr. Frank Cappetta
1763 East Route 70
Cherry Hill, NJ 08003-3016
856-795-4541; Fax: 856-795-9262
e-mail: cappettasales@aol.com

The Carroll Group
Mimi Carroll
2844 Dallas Trade Mart

Dallas TX 75207
214-698-1172; Fax: 214-748-3225
e-mail: carrollgroup@aol.com

Chesapeake Sales
Mr. Jack M. Epstein
11044 Wood Elves Way
Columbia, MD 21044
301-596-4859; Fax: 410-740-2958
e-mail: jechesapeakesales@comcast.net

Coastal Gourmet Sales, Inc.
Mr. Kenneth Pease
5048 Golf Club Lane
Brooksville, FL 34609
352-796-0539; Fax: 352-796-4189
e-mail: coastalgs@msn.com

The Cristol Group Inc.
Mr. Sam Cristol
4600 W. Commercial Blvd.
Fort Lauderdale, FL 33319
954-486-4129; Fax: 954-486-4133
e-mail: sam@cristolgroup.com

CS Brokers
Mr. Cyrus Settineri
53 River Street
Milford, CT 06460-2057
203-878-7788; Fax: 203-877-6649
e-mail: cyrus@csbrokers.com

Custom Gift & Gourmet
Ms. Teri E. Horn
453 Marin Avenue
Mill Valley, CA 94941-1928
415-381-5721; Fax: 415-381-5877

De Michele Associates/Fontana E De Michele
Mr. James De Michele

P.O. Box 2820
Worcester, MA 01613
508-755-9854; Fax: 508-755-9298
e-mail: demicheleassociates@charter.net

DKB Sales & Marketing, Inc.
Dianne Keeler Bruce
109 W. 70th Street
New York, NY 10023-4453
212-877-9676; Fax: 212-787-9522
e-mail: dkeelerbruce@earthlink.net

Dunn Specialties
Mr. Michael B. Dunn
4188 Weathered Oaks Lane
Fairfield Township, OH 45011
513-844-2892; Fax: 513-844-6575
e-mail: dspec@aol.com

ESM/Metro New York
Ms. Liz Connolly
2 Van Riper Road
P.O. Box 409
Montvale, NJ 07645-0400
201-307-9100; Fax: 201-782-5145

Exclusively Gourmet, Ltd.
Ms. Beth Bitzegaio
175 E. Delaware Place, Suite 4619
Chicago, IL 60611-7712
312-397-9494; Fax: 312-264-2550
e-mail: beth@egsales.biz

FOS Sales & Marketing Inc.
Doreen Faulhaber
2005 Park Street
Atlantic Beach, NY 11509
516-239-0963; Fax: 516-239-6130
e-mail: fosfoods@optonline.net

Family Foods
Mr. Joseph P. Egan
100 Elizabeth Street
Farmingdale, NY 11735
631-293-5300; Fax: 631-293-5381
e-mail: sales@familyfoodsales.com

Fine & Fancy Foods
Mr. Tom P. Smith
349 Knots Center
Woodstock, GA 30188
770-924-1760; Fax: 770-924-9634
e-mail: fandff@aol.com

Fine Food Marketing, Inc.
Ms. Meg Price Whitlock
1878 Virginia Avenue
Atlanta, GA 30337
404-766-6464; Fax: 404-766-0027
e-mail: meg@finefoodmarketing.com

Gail Kramer Associates
Ms. Gail Kramer
19 Bala Avenue
Bala Cynwyd, PA 19004
610-667-0584; Fax: 610-667-9476

Golick Martins, Inc.
Mr. Manny Martins
140 Sylvan Avenue
Englewood Cliffs, NJ 07632-2502
201-592-8800; Fax: 201-592-9196
e-mail: mmartins@golickmartins.com

Gourmet Food Inc.
Mr. Garry M. Derrick
420 Bywood Drive
Durham, NC 27712
919-477-1917; Fax: 919-479-5966
e-mail: derrickgm@aol.com

Gourmetexas, Inc.
Mr. Craig M. Beveridge
4114 Tracey Trl
Rowlett, TX 75088-6422
972-235-0303; Fax: 972-235-0311
e-mail: jason@gourmettexas.com

Green Mountain Specialty Foods, Inc.
Mr. Bill Fitzgerald
441 Wadsworth Boulevard, Suite #124
Lakewood, CO 80226
303-530-3861; Fax: 303-530-3909
e-mail: bill@gmsf.biz

Hanson Faso Sales & Marketing
Mr. Stewart H. Reich
246 E. Janata Boulevard, Suite 340
Lombard, IL 60148
630-953-9800; Fax: 630-953-9889
e-mail: hftc@aol.com

J'Ai Besoin Ltd.
Ms. Conni Kalman
20 Ridge Drive
Melville, NY 11747
631-424-5353; Fax: 631-424-0130
e-mail: c.kalman@juno.com

James V. Sidari and Associates Inc.
Mr. James V. Sidari
19291 Lorain Road
Fairview Park, OH 44116
440-356-4858; Fax: 440-356-4857
e-mail: jvsidari@aol.com

JBM Sales & Marketing
Mr. Jerry Mintz
P.O. Box 188
Foxboro, MA 02035
508-543-3611; Fax: 508-543-8178
e-mail: jerry@jbmsales.com

Joel Van Emelen Company
Mr. Joel R. Van Emelen
5750 E. Greenlake Way North
Seattle, WA 98103-5954
206-632-1935; Fax: 206-632-4162
e-mail: vanem@wolfenet.com

Karam Foods
Ms. Lorrie B. Karam
17 Magnolia Drive
Dobbs Ferry, NY 10522-3508
914-693-6338; Fax: 914-479-0067
e-mail: karam.food@verizon.net

Ken Rabin & Associates
Mr. Ken Rabin
114 San Rafael Avenue
San Rafael, CA 94901-3645
415-485-0162; Fax: 415-485-0371
e-mail: kenrabin@attbi.com

Kenyon & Kenyon, Inc.
Mr. Michael C. Kenyon
50 Pearl Road, Suite 111
Brunswick, OH 44212
330-220-9814; Fax: 330-220-8505

M & Y Sales Associates Inc.
Mr. John W. Yates
1 Central Avenue
Tarrytown, NY 10591
914-332-1414; Fax: 914-332-4882
e-mail: mysalesassoc@aol.com

Maximum Marketing, Inc.
Mr. Brad Magaro
7710 NW 56th Way
Pompano Beach, FL 33073-3509
954-725-3700; Fax: 954-725-3400
e-mail: brad@maximummarketing.com

Michael Azurak Brokerage
Mr. Mike Azurak
17 Domino Road
Somerset, NJ 08873
732-356-3826; Fax: 732-356-6057

Mid America Sales Co.
Mr. William Antognoli
1750 Dewes Street
Glenview, IL 60025
847-729-4500; Fax: 847-729-4503
e-mail: info@midamericasales.com

Milmark Sales
Mr. Allen Rosenberg
1223 Ligurian Road
Palm Beach Gardens, FL 33410-2130
561-624-1422; Fax: 561-624-7155
e-mail: milmarksales@adelphia.net

Morton Schweitzer Sales
Mr. Morton F. Schweitzer
5582 Pocusset Street
Pittsburgh, PA 15217-1913
412-521-3674; Fax: 412-421-2595
e-mail: schweitzersales@aol.com

Mullen Marketing, Inc.
Mr. Dwight O. Mullen
6232 Old York Drive
Plano, TX 75093-6168
972-608-0717
e-mail: domullen@aol.com

Murdock & White
Charlene Murdock
6100 Fourth Avenue S. #437
Seattle, WA 98108-3234
206-767-9175; Fax: 206-767-3755
e-mail: murdockwht@aol.com

Nancy's Fancy Foods
Ms. Nancy K. Waterhouse
166 Crescent Avenue
Waldwick, NJ 07463
201-670-1000; Fax: 201-670-1811
e-mail: nffds@aol.com

O'Leary and Company
Ms. Carolyn S. O'Leary
31 Shepard Hill
Danielson, CT 06239
860-774-8384; Fax: 860-779-1135
e-mail: doleary@myeastern.com

Peter Blatchford Company
Peter Blatchford
28 Middle Street
South Dartmouth, MA 02748-3414
508-994-5557; Fax: 508-994-5579

Pinski-Portugal & Associates Inc.
Ms. Lynn Portugal
1933 South Broadway
Suite 311
Los Angeles, CA 90007
213-763-5722; Fax: 213-763-5747

Preferred Marketing
Mr. Gene R. Portz
600 N. Mountain Avenue
Upland, CA 91786
909-949-1116; Fax: 909-949-7179
e-mail: prfmkt@aol.com

R.J. Bickert Associates Inc.
Mr. Roger J. Bickert
10205 Main Street
Clarence, NY 14031
716-759-8876; Fax: 716-759-2823
e-mail: rbickert@msn.com

R.J. Muccillo & Associates
Mr. Robert J. Muccillo
1307 Touchstone Drive
Indianapolis, IN 46239
317-894-2352; Fax: 317-894-2422
e-mail: rjmuccillo@netzero.net

RJM Trading
Mr. Ron Maiorino
374 N. Greeley Avenue
Chappaqua, NY 10514
914-238-6902; Fax: 914-238-0498
e-mail: rjmtrade@bestweb.net

S & S Brokerage
Mr. William C. Stephens
8 Magnolia Drive
Newnan, GA 30263
770-253-6365; Fax: 770-304-1902
e-mail: billstep02@aol.com

Santucci Associates Inc.
Mr. Gerald Santucci
1010 Millcreek Drive
P.O. Box 326
Feasterville-Trevose, PA 19053-7321
215-355-1117; Fax: 215-355-0986

Schnakenberg Associates, Inc.
Mr. John H. Schnakenberg
230 Oak Tree Road
Mountainside, NJ 07092
908-654-1133; Fax: 908-654-3737

Seidman Hudon Food Brokerage, Inc.
Mr. Gary Seidman
7684 Wiles Road
Coral Springs, FL 33067-2069
954-345-6622; Fax: 954-345-8384
e-mail: gary.seidman@earthlink.net

Shaw Specialty Foods
Ms. Susan Shaw-Weaver
5227 N. Shoreland Avenue
Milwaukee, WI 53217
414-332-5950; Fax: 414-332-5958
e-mail: shawandassoc@cs.com

Signature Specialty Sales & Marketing Inc.
Mr. Andrew J. Paul
305 Quail Ridge Drive
Westmont, IL 60559
630-654-2100; Fax: 630-654-2130
e-mail: andy@signaturessm.com

Specialty Products, Inc.
Mr. Jose D. Teigeiro
P.O. Box 320123
Franklin, WI 53132
414-425-6225; Fax: 414-425-4560
e-mail: jose@candyspi.com

Strand Specialty Sales
Mr. Jon Strand
551 Monroe Court
River Edge, NJ 07661
201-261-6347; Fax: 201-261-6638
e-mail: strand1@aol.com

Susan Frierson and Staff
Ms. Susan B. Frierson
3848 Ivy Road NE
Atlanta, GA 30342
404-261-0375; Fax: 404-814-0385
e-mail: pnstsu@aol.com

Taste Bud's, Etc., Inc.
Ms. Gennie Tull
3052 Greyfield Place
Marietta, GA 30067-5530
770-951-9435; Fax: 770-951-0258
e-mail: tastegt@aol.com

Tom Manning Associates
Mr. Thomas R. Manning
220 Pascack Avenue
Emerson, NJ 07630
201-262-3578; Fax: 201-634-1298

Tomales Bay Foods
Ms. Sue Conley
80 Fourth Street
P.O. Box 594
Point Reyes Station, CA 94956-0594
415-663-9335; Fax: 415-663-5418
e-mail: cowgirls@srn.net

Valley Food Specialties LLC
Mr. Steve Auerbach
40 River Road
Chatham, NY 12037
518-392-6851; Fax: 914-992-7278
valleyfoodspecialties@ix.netcom.com

Wallish Assoc.
Mr. Charles Patton
227 W. Grand Avenue
Bensenville, IL 60106
630-860-0770; Fax: 630-860-0832
e-mail: cpatton@wallish.com

Wild Rose Marketing, Inc.
Ms. Rose Pierro
P.O. Box 21276
Boulder, CO 80308
303-448-9556; Fax: 303-448-9762
e-mail: info@wildrosemarketing.com

Woolf Associates
Ms. Maureen Woolf
41 Milk Porridge Circle
Northborough, MA 01532-2308
508-393-8173; Fax: 508-393-2496
e-mail: maureenwoolf@aol.com

Wright Choice
Mr. Chris Wright
3608 Sherwood Avenue
Fort Worth, TX 76107-1040
817-626-1462; Fax: 817-624-1411
e-mail: wrightchoice01@hotmail.com

Sample Broker Appointment Letter

This is a very formal version. You may use a simpler form to suit your needs.

AGREEMENT between [your company], a [corporation, proprietorship, partnership, as appropriate] ("Company"), whose principal office is located at [your address], and [broker name], a [corporation, etc., as appropriate] of [state] with principal office located at [address].

In consideration of the mutual covenants contained herein, the parties agree as follows:

Article I

APPOINTMENT
Company hereby appoints [broker name] its exclusive representative for sales of all the Company's [indicate product types, if necessary] throughout the Territory, as designated below, on the following terms and conditions.

Article II

TERRITORY
Territory means the [insert territory]. [Indicate any variations, accounts not included, etc.].

Article III

AUTHORITY
[Broker name] shall promote the sale of the Company's products according to its best judgment, including carrying out the following activities:

A. Establishing and supervising all field sales;

B. Contracting and servicing dealers, suppliers, retailers, whole-salers, and other users and purchasers for resale;

C. Assessing marketing strengths and weaknesses prices, competi-tion, and other contractual terms;

D. Recommending and implementing, if requested, advertising and promotional strategies and activities;

E. Receiving and transmitting orders and other requests from cus-tomers.

Article IV

RIGHT TO SOLICIT AND ACCEPT ORDERS

[Broker name]'s authority includes the exclusive right to solicit and accept orders, either directly or through its sales agents in the Territory, for all products of the Company. Company agrees to trans-mit regularly to [broker name] all information concerning orders and sales that the Company receives or obtains directly, whether from existing customers or from third parties. [Broker name] will supply the Company its best field information on credibility for any new account and will maintain field surveillance on established accounts in terms of stability/credibility. Company has the responsibility and authority to control credit line and terms to the customer.

Article V

COMMISSION ON SALES

Unless specified otherwise:

A. [Broker name] shall be entitled on all orders shipped by the Company to a commission of 10 percent for sales to retailers, and 5 percent for sales to distributors.

B. The commission will be calculated on the total dollar amount of the order FOB [your warehouse location].

Article VI

DEVOTION OF TIME AND SKILL

A. [Broker name] agrees to use its best efforts to promote the sales and use of, and to solicit and secure orders for, the products of the Company within the Territory.

B. [Broker name] shall observe Company policies, as provided in writing by the Company, as regards the sales of Company's products and shall be furnished regularly with sales literature, technical data, and sample products by the Company, in reasonable quantities and without charge.

C. [Broker name] shall not participate in the sale of any product that would conflict with the products of the Company included in this agreement without the authorization of the Company.

Article VII

EXPENSES

Except as herein provided, [broker name] agrees to assume all expenses of its own employees, and all expenses of maintaining its organization as the sales representatives of the Company's products within the Territory and all expenses of sales agents or brokers retained by [broker name]. [Broker name] will identify and recommend advertising and promotional opportunities which, if agreed to by the Company, will be paid for by the Company.

Article VIII

COMPANIES REPRESENTED

[Broker name] will provide to the Company a list of all companies that it represents.

Article IX

DURATION OF AGREEMENT: TERMINATION

This agreement shall be effective from the execution hereof, and shall be binding on the parties hereto and their assigns, representatives, heirs, and successors. This agreement shall continue in effect for one year, and be automatically renewable annually thereafter until terminated by either party on thirty (30) days' written notice to the other, provided that in the event of insolvency or adjudication in bankruptcy or on the filing of a petition therefore by either party, this agreement may be terminated immediately at the option of either party on written notice to the other. Termination shall be without prejudice to the rights and obligations of the parties hereto that have vested prior to the effective date of termination, except that, on termination, the Company shall pay [broker name] the commissions provided only on orders received by the Company prior to the effective date of such termination and delivered to customers within ninety (90) days following the effective date of such termination. The acceptance, however, of such orders and the liability of the Company for the payment of commissions thereon are to be subject to the terms and conditions herein before provided.

Article X

CHANGES; ALTERATIONS

No change, alteration, modification, or amendment to this agreement shall be effective unless in writing and properly executed by the parties hereto.

Article XI

APPLICABLE LAW

This agreement and any disputes relating thereto shall be construed under the laws of [your state], United States of America.

Article XII

CONTRACT TERMS EXCLUSIVE

This agreement constitutes the entire agreement between the parties hereto and the parties acknowledge and agree that neither of them has made any representation with respect to the subject matter of this agreement or any representations inducing the execution and delivery hereof except as specifically set forth herein and each of the parties hereto acknowledges that it has relied on its own judgment in entering into the same.

IN WITNESS WHEREOF, the parties have executed this agreement:

This _____ day of _____, 20_____

By: _____   By: _____
   (your company name)   (broker name)

_____   _____
          title   title

Catalog Sheet Preparation

These companies offer a complete package, from photography to printed sheets. You can order 2,000 to 2,500 catalog sheets with a color photograph, up to 50 words of designed copy, electronic art, and full-color printing on one side of an 80-pound coated stock for prices that range from $375 to $500, depending upon which supplier you select. Each of the following companies was invited to provide particulars as to its services. Only those that responded have descriptions beyond the name, address, and telephone number. This list is not all-inclusive nor is it meant to serve as an endorsement. Please see http://www.specialty foodresource.com for updates.

Colorlith Corporation
900 Jefferson Street
Fall River, MA 02721
508-837-6100, 800-556-7171
Fax: 508-677-4466
Web site: http://www.colorlith.com

Cosmos Communications Inc.
11-05 44th Drive
Long Island City, NY 11101
800-969-2676, ext. 225
e-mail: info@cosmosinc.net
Web site: http://www.cqprint.com

GenoaGraphix
1485 Bayshore Boulevard
San Francisco, CA 94124
415-330-3582, 800-546-8494
Web site: http://www.genoagraphix.com/
services/catalogs.html

GenoaGraphix specializes in creating professional and high-quality catalogs of all sizes. Their creative team has over 16 years of experience in catalog design and management, and offers a comprehensive catalog management service that includes:

❖ digital photography

❖ copywriting

❖ complete layout and design

❖ index creation

199

✧ one through six color printing

✧ fulfillment and mailing

Mcolor Corporation
1498 Northwest Third Street
Deerfield Beach, FL 33442
888-333-8507 or 954-782-3600
Fax: 954-247-0083
e-mail: info@mcolor.com
Web site: http://www.mcolor.com/home.htm
Contact: Stan Cohen

Studios for photography are in:

Arizona	Minnesota
California	Missouri
Colorado	Nevada
Connecticut	New Jersey
Florida	New York
Georgia	North Carolina
Illinois	Ohio
Maine	Pennsylvania
Maryland	Rhode Island
Massachusettes	Texas
Michigan	Washington

Primary focus: MegaColor specializes in photography and full-color printing of brochures, catalog sheets, posters, and post-cards. They guarantee the best prices and quality in the country.

Packaging Design

These companies supply and design packages. This list is not all-inclusive nor is it meant to serve as an endorsement. Please see http://www.specialtyfoodresource.com for updates.

Institute of Packaging Professionals
1601 North Bond Street
Suite 101
Naperville, IL 60563
630-544-5050; Fax: 630-544-5055
e-mail: info@iopp.org

Krepe-Kraft, Inc.
4199 Bay View Road
Blasdell, NY 14219
888-826-8581, 716-826-7086
Fax: 800-826-7239
e-mail: sales@krepekraft.com
Web site: http://www.krepekraft.com

Packaging Graphics
5732 Milentz Avenue
St. Louis, MO 63109
314-457-9095
e-mail: sales@packagingGraphics.net

Presentation Packaging
870 Louisiana Avenue South
Minneapolis, MN 55426-1614
800-326-2698 or 612-540-9544
Fax: 612-540-9522
e-mail: customerservice@presentation
packaging.com
Web site: http://www.presentation
packaging.com
Contact: Carol Sylvester, Connie Maloney, and/or Lori Pearson

Primary focus: Presentation Packaging designs and manufactures imaginative corrugated packaging for the food, mail order, retail, giftware, and direct mail industries. The company reports that its stock collection is the largest available in the industry, combining colorful preprints, litho-label, and direct print patterns, with a huge selection of shapes and sizes. All boxes ship and store flat.

Packaging and Labeling Materials

These companies provide specialty food containers, labeling services, and related materials. There are hundreds of others (more than five dozen exhibited at the 2004 NASFT Summer Fancy Food Show), and you should check available listings for some near you. This list is not meant to serve as an endorsement. Please see http://www.specialtyfoodresource.com for updates.

AKM Packaging, Inc.
(No glass jars)
223 Clover Hill Drive
Feeding Hills, MA 01030
800-836-6256; Fax: 413-786-8097
e-mail: akm5253@aol.com
Web site: http://www.akmpackaging.com

Berlin Packaging
435 E. Algonquin Road
Arlington Heights, IL 60005
800-4-BERLIN (800-423-7546)
Fax: 800-423-7545
Web site: http://www.berlinpackaging.com

Specific focus: Berlin Packaging is the largest U.S. distributor of glass, plastic, and metal containers plus accompanying closure systems. Call 800-4-BERLIN for a free catalog

with more than 3,100 bottles, jars, tubs, etc. All orders placed before 3:00 PM are shipped the same day. There are no minimum quantity requirements. Professional customer service representatives are available to answer packaging questions and help you locate the ideal container for your product.

Driscoll Label Co., Inc.
1275 Bloomfield Avenue
Fairfield, NJ 07004
973-575-8492; Fax: 800-342-1195
Web site: http://www.cpcpkg.com

Label Graphics Manufacturing
175 Patterson Avenue
Little Falls, NJ 07424
973-890-5665; Fax: 973-890-1164
Web site: http://www.labelgraphicsmfg.com

Labels Plus
2407 106th Street
Everett, WA 98204
206-745-4592, 800-275-7587
Fax: 206-523-1973
e-mail: trace@labelsplus.com
Web site: http://www.labelsplus.com

You can contact MOD-PAC at either address:

MOD-PAC Corporation
Custom Sales/Manufacturing
1801 Elmwood Avenue
Buffalo, NY 14207-2496
716-873-0640; 800-666-3722
Fax: 716-873-6008
e-mail: sales@modpac.com

MOD-PAC Corporation
Stock Box Sales Office
4199 Bayview Road
Blasdell, NY 14219-1907
800-666-3722

Primary focus: Quality paperboard folding cartons for every day and every season. Special stock run and custom run programs.

Olshen's Bottle Supply Co.
2331 NE Argyle Street
Portland, OR 07211
800-258-4292; Fax: 503-290-4260
e-mail: trooper731@aol.com
Web site: http://www.richardspackaginginc.com

Primary focus: A family-owned business since 1925, Olshen's distributes stock glass and plastic containers and closures. It also offers special order and custom-designed items.

Pohlig Brothers, Inc.
8001 Greenpine Road
Richmond, VA 23237
804-275-9000; Fax: 804-275-9900
Web site: http://www.pohilg.com

Specific focus: Manufacturer of custom-designed paperboard boxes.

Polyfoam Packers
3751 Sunset Avenue
Waukegan, IL 60087
800-800-0359; Fax: 847-263-0350
Web site: http://www.polyfoam.com

Specific focus: Products for the shipment, storage, and distribution of perishables.

Presentation Packaging
870 Louisiana Avenue South
Minneapolis, MN 55426
800-818-2698; Fax: 612-540-9522
Web site: http://www.presentation
packaging.com

Western Specialty Container
Independent Can Company
2040 South Lynx Place
Ontario, CA 91761
909-923-6150; Fax: 909-923-6052
e-mail: sales@westernspecialty.com
Web site: http://www.westernspecialty.com

Specific focus: Decorative tins, glass, and plastic containers, including PET wide-mouth jars and bottles, tamper-evident bands, and a wide assortment of packaging concepts.

Internet Resources

The following list is neither all-inclusive nor meant to serve as an endorsement. Please see http://www.specialtyfoodresource.com for updates.

References

American Demographics
A good source of consumer trend information for business leaders.
Web site: http//www.demographics.com.

Easy World Wide Web with Netscape
by Jim Minatel, 1995
Que Corporation, Indianapolis, IN
800-428-5331

A an easy to follow, step-by-step guide with full-color illustrations and screen shots on every page. Very useful if you are browsing the World Wide Web.

The Food Channel
Web site: http//www.foodchannel.com.

This World Wide Web forum provides trend information, reports, and other food-industry facts plus online forums, links to other food sites, and a direct link to Food Channel staff.

NASFT
Web site: http://www.specialtyfood.com

The NASFT produces an online specialty food catalog that helps consumers find the products they're looking for. It does not offer the products directly, but connects the consumer with a search capability more than 200 listings of specialty food companies' Web sites.

Poor Richard's E-Mail Publishing
Chris Pirillo and Peter Kent

Covers everything about e-mail publishing including the mechanics of publishing and an extensive resource directory. Top Floor Publishing. Available from Amazon.com

Web Site Development and Directory

Deep River Interactive
Web site: http//www.swarlick.com

Deep River Interactive is a wholly owned subsidiary of Swardlick Marketing Group, working with companies and organizations to create new business models based on the transformative power of the Internet. They help businesses reinvent themselves using new technologies and integrated marketing solutions to achieve powerful and measurable results.

DexMonkey.com
820 S. Monaco Parkway, #277
Denver, CO 3703
303-338-1552, Fax: 303-489-2248
e-mail: Info @Snapmonkey.com

The firm offers a robust searchable multimedia directory program. Any organization can add a DexMonkey Directory to their existing Web site. DexMonkey will categorize, and allow each member of the directory to showcase their product or service. See Appendix I for more details.

Members have their own control panel, allowing them to update their content 24/7. They may add a video or a flash presentation to their listing, as well as photos, a 500-character description of their product and service, a Web link, and more. In addition, the DexMonkey program is designed to be a profit center for the organization. The directory administrator may set pricing

for different types of listings. The collection of funds each month from the members is automated, and funds are deposited into the Administrator's account. Directory Administrators also have the option of putting the entire Directory presentation, complete with member profiles, onto a CD. They can then duplicate this CD and use it as a marketing tool to hand out at tradeshows, to add to the back of books or publications, etc.

Elfin Creative
374 E. Main #1
Ashland, OR 97520
541-840-5906
e-mail: brandon@elfincreative.com
Web site: http//www.elfincreative.com

Elfin Creative provides high-end Web site design, development, and consultation.

E-Zine University: Learn to Make and Promote E-Mail Publications
Web site: http//www.ezineuniversity.com

An electronic magazine that provides information on creating and maintaining an online newsletter. Comprehensive newsletter.

Kellen Interactive
(Formerly: HQ Cyberservices)
5775 G Peachtree-Dunwoody Road
Suite 500
Atlanta, GA 30342
Contact: Josh Linard, Business Development Manager
404-836-5050; Fax: 404-252-0774
Web site: http//www.hqcyberservices.com

Offices in Atlanta; Washington, DC; New York; Tucson; and Brussels. From conceptualization of strategies and budgets, to implementation and ongoing support, Kellen Interactive is committed to exceeding your expectations. They provide daily services as Webmasters and Internet consultants for over 200 companies and organizations. Kellen offers one-on-one customer service and project management every step of the way. They are committed to client budget, objectives, and deadlines for every project.

OpSys Interactive
Miami, Florida
305-503-3000
Web site: http//www.opsys.com

SnapMonkey
820 S. Monaco Parkway, #277
Denver, CO 3703
303-338-1552; Fax 303-489-2248
e-mail: Info @Snapmonkey.com
Web site: http//www.SnapMonkey.com

Build your own Web site using SnapMonkey's easy-to-use "Point and Click" technology. Sign up for SnapTo It Tips in a weekly e-mail that shares with you great ideas on promoting your Web site and your business to more people on the Web!

Yahoo! Merchant Solutions
Web site: http://smallbusiness.yahoo.com

Offers a service that helps you build, manage, and market an online store.

The Web Marketing Resource Center
Web site: http//www.zeromillion.com

This is a free resource developed to help Web site owners, advertisers, and marketing professionals get the most from their marketing activities. The site includes details of the latest Web marketing techniques being used by many of the most successful sites on the Net, and features articles, reviews, and links to hundreds of the best Web site promotion resources available.

Miscellaneous
Resources for Promoting on the Internet

Here is a list of resources that can help you create and implement a Web site marketing program.

General/Business
Inc. Magazine
Web site: http//www.inc.com

An online resource center with a wide variety of resources for small businesses.

SnapMonkey.com
Web site: http//www.SnapMonkey.com

Provides a full resource center full of ideas on how to bring your small business online, and grow it to success.

U.S. Chamber of Commerce
Web site: http//www.chamberbiz.com

Listing of all chambers in the United States.

U.S. Small Business Administration
Web site: http//www.sba.gov

Provides information and guidelines for small businesses.

U.S. Patent & Trademark Office
Web site: http//www.uspto.gov

Provides information on applying for and researching patents and trademarks.

WebTrends
Web site: http//www.webtrends.com

Provides analysis services and Web site statistics.

Marketing/Promotion

Directory of Associations
Web site: http//www.associationscentral.com

Provides a comprehensive list os associations for trade industries.

Directory Guide
Web site: http//www.directoryguide.com

A listing of over 400 search engines and directories that accept search engine submissions.

PR Newswire
Web site: http//www.prnewswire.com

An informational site on how to create press releases, and have them distributed to your target market.

SearchEngineWatch.com
Web site: http//www.searchenginewatch.com

Search engine marketing and optimization techniques.

SmallBusiness.com
Web site: http//www.smallbusiness.com

An incredible resource directory listing all kinds of advice for small businesses.

Federal Government Sources

Please see http://www.specialtyfoodresource.com for updates.

Code of Federal Regulations

The Code of Federal Regulations (CFR) contains the specific laws governing labels and ingredient statements for food products. Copies of the appropriate chapters may be purchased from your local government printing office.

Small Business Administration (SBA)

1441 L Street, NW
Washington, DC 20416
800-368-5855 or 202-653-7561
Web site: http://www.sba.gov

The SBA provides business counseling and has a government-guaranteed loan program for small businesses. You can only qualify for such loans if you have been refused by your local bank. Don't hold your breath. Very few food entrepreneurs are able to access these funds. Ask for the address of the regional office nearest you.

Small Business Development Centers (SBDC)

Web site:http://www.sbaonline.
sba.gov/sbdc/

The U.S. Small Business Administration (SBA) administers the Small Business Development Center Program to provide management assistance to current and prospective small business owners. SBDCs offer one-stop assistance to small businesses by providing a wide variety of information and guidance at centrally located branch locations.

Alabama SBDC

William Campbell Jr, State Director
2800 Milan Court Street, #124
Birmingham, AL 35211-6908
205-943-6750; Fax: 205-943-6752
e-mail: williamc@uab.edu
Web site: http://www.asbdc.org

Alaska SBDC
Jan Fredericks, State Director
430 West Seventh Avenue, Suite 110
Anchorage, AK 99501
907-274 -7232; Fax: 907-274-9524
e-mail: anjaf@uaa.sbdc.alaska.edu
Web site: http://www.aksbdc.org

American Samoa Community College
Dr. Herbert Thweatt, Director
P.O. Box 2609
Pago Pago, American Samoa 96799
011-684-699-4830; Fax: 011-684-699-6132
e-mail: htalex@att.net

Arizona SBDC
Michael York, State Director
2411 West 14th Street, Suite 132
Temp, AZ 85281
480-731-8720; Fax: 480-731-8729
e-mail: mike.york@domail.maricopa.edu
Web site: http://www.dist.maricopa.edu.sbdc

Arkansas SBDC
Janet M. Roderick, State Director
2801 S. University Avenue
Little Rock, AR 72204-1099
501-324-9043; Fax: 501-324-9049
e-mail: jmroderick@ualr.edu
Web site: http://asbdc.ualr.edu

California
  Fresno SBDC
  Ms. Helen Sullivan, State Director
  UC Merced Lead Center
  550 East Shaw, Suite 105A
  Fresno, CA 93710
  559-241-7414; Fax: 559-241-7422

e-mail: Helen.sullivan@ucop.edu
Web site: http://www.ucmerced.edu/

Los Angeles SBDC
Dr. Michael Fronmueller/Debbie Cours,
Co-Directors
California State University, Northridge
18111 Nordhoff Street
Northridge, CA 91330-8232
818-674-0417 or 818-677-2467
Fax: 818-552-3260
e-mail: michaelf@csun.edu
Web site: http://www.sba.gov/gopher/
Local-Information/Small-Business-
Development-Centers/sbdcca.txt

Sacramento SBDC
Ms. Janice Rhodd, State Director
California State University
Chico Research Foundation
Kendall Hall, Room 114
Chico, CA 95929-0870
530-898-4598; Fax: 530-898-4734
e-mail: jrhodd@csuchico.edu
Web site: http://www.sbdcsierra.org

San Diego SBDC
Ms. Mary Wylie, State Director
Southwestern Community College District
900 Otey Lakes Road
Chula Vista, CA 91910
619-482-6375; Fax: 619-482-6402
e-mail: mwylie@swc.cc.ca.us
Web site: http://www.sba.gov/ca/sandiego/
sandiegosbdc.html

San Francisco SBDC
Mr. Blake Escudier, State Director

San Jose State University Foundation
210 North 4th Street, 4th Floor
P.O. Box 720130
San Jose, CA 95129
408-655-9487
e-mail: escudier_b@cob.sjsu.edu
Web site: http://www.sba.gov/gopher/
Local-Information/Small-Business-
Development-Centers/sbdcca.txt

Santa Ana SBDC
Ms. Vi Pham, Lead Center Director
Tri-County Lead SBDC
California State University, Fullerton
800 N. State College Boulevard, LH640
Fullerton, CA 92831-3599
714-278-2719; Fax: 714-278-7858
e-mail: vpham@fullerton.edu
Web site: http://www.sba.gov/ca/
santa/sbdc.html

Colorado SBDC
Kelly Manning, State Director
1625 Broadway, Suite 1700
Denver, CO 80202
303-892-3794; Fax: 303-892-3848
e-mail: Kelly.Manning@state.co.us
Web site: http://www.state.co.us/oed/sbdc/

Connecticut SBDC
Dennis Gruell, State Director
2100 Hillside Road, Unit 1094
Storrs, CT 06269-1094
860-486-4135; Fax: 860-486-1576
e-mail: dennis.gruell@uconn.edu
Web site: http://www.sbdc.uconn.edu

Delaware SBDC
Clinton Tymes, State Director
1 Innovation Way, Suite 301
Newark, DE 19711

302-831-1555; Fax: 302-831-1423
e-mail: tymesc@be.udel.edu
Web site: http://www.delawaresbdc.org

District of Columbia SBDC
Henry Turner, State Director
2600 6th Street, NW, Room 128
Washington, DC 20059
202-806-1550; Fax: 202-806-1777
e-mail: hturner@howard.edu
Web site: http://www.dcsbdc.com/

Florida SBDC
Jerry Cartwright, State Director
401 E Chase Street, Suite 100
Pensacola, FL 32502
850-473-7800; Fax: 850-473-7813
e-mail: jcartwri@uwf.edu
Web site: http://www.floridasbdc.com

Georgia SBDC
Henry Logan, State Director
University of Georgia
1180 East Broad Street
Athens, GA 30602-5412
706-542-6762; Fax: 706-542-7935
e-mail: HLOGAN@sbdc.uga.edu
Web site: http://www.sbdc.uga.edu

Hawaii SBDC
Darryl Mleynek, State Director
200 West Kawili Street
Hilo, HI 96720
808-974-7515; Fax: 808-974-7683
e-mail: darrylm@interpac.net
Web site:http://www.hawaii-sbdc.org

Idaho SBDC
James Hogge, State Director
1910 University Drive
Boise, ID 83725

208-426-1640; Fax: 208-426-3877
e-mail: jhogge@boisestate.edu
Web site: http://www.idahosbdc.org

Illinois SBDC
Mark A. Petrilli, State Director
Department of Commerce and Economic
Opportunity
620 E. Adams, S-4
Springfield, IL 62701
217-524-5700; Fax: 217-524-0171
e-mail: mark_petrilli@illinoisbiz.biz
Web site: http://www.ilsbdc.biz

Indiana SBDC
Debbie Bishop Trocha
One North Capitol, Suite 900
Indianapolis, IN 46204
317-234-2086; Fax: 317-232-8874
e-mail: dtrocha@isbdc.org
Web site:http://www.isbdc.org

Iowa SBDC
Lars Peterson, Interim State Director
137 Lynn Avenue
Ames, IA 50014-7126
515-292-6351; Fax: 515-292-0020
e-mail: larsp@iastate.edu
Web site: http://www.iabusnet.org

Kansas SBDC
Wally Kearns, State Director
214 SW Sixth Street, Suite 301
Topeka, KS 66603
785-296-6514; Fax: 785-291-3261
e-mail: ksbdc.wkearns@fhsu.edu
Web site: http://www.fhsu.edu/ksbdc

Kentucky SBDC
Becky Naugle, State Director
225 Gatton Business & Economic Building

Lexington, KY 40506-0034
859-257-7668; Fax: 859-323-1907
e-mail: lrnaug0@pop.uky.edu
Web site: http://www.ksbdc.org

Louisiana SBDC
Ms. Mary Lynn Wilkerson, State Director
University of Louisiana at Monroe
College of Business Administration
700 University Avenue
Monroe, LA 71209-6435
318-342-5506; Fax: 318-342-5510
e-mail: wilkerson@ulm.edu
Web site: http://www.lsbdc.org/

Maine SBDC
John Massaua, State Director
96 Falmouth Street
P.O. Box 9300
Portland, ME 04104-9300
207-780-4420; Fax: 207-780-4857
e-mail: jrmassaua@maine.edu
Web site: http://www.mainesbdc.org

Maryland SBDC
Renee Sprow, State Director
7100 Baltimore Avenue, Suite 401
College Park, MD 20740
301-403-8300; Fax: 301-403-8303
e-mail: Rsprow@mdsbdc.umd.edu
Web site: http://www.mdsbdc.umd.edu

Massachusetts SBDC
Georgianna Parkin, State Director
227 Isenberg School of Management
University of Massachusetts
121 Presidents Drive
Amherst, MA 01001-9310
413-545-6301; Fax: 413-545-1273
e-mail: gep@msbdc.umass.edu
Web site: http://msbdc.som.umass.edu

Michigan SBDC
Carol Lopucki, State Director
510 W. Fulton Street
Grand Rapids, MI 49504
616-331-7480; Fax: 616-331-7389
e-mail: lopuckic@gvsu.edu
Web site: www.misbtdc.org

Minnesota SBDC
Michael Myhre, State Director
500 Metro Square
121 7th Place East
St. Paul, MN 55010-2146
651-297-5773; Fax: 651-296-1290
e-mail: michael.myhre@state.mn.us
Web site: http://www.mnsbdc.com

Mississippi SBDC
Walter Gurley, Jr., State Director
B-19 Jeanette Phillips Drive
P.O. Box 1848
University, MS 38677
662-915-5001; Fax: 662-915-5650
e-mail: wgurley@olemiss.edu
Web site:http://www.olemiss.edu/depts/mssbdc

Missouri SBDC
Max Summers, State Director
1205 University Avenue, Suite 300
Columbia, MO 65211
573-882-0344; Fax: 573-884-4297
e-mail: summersm@missouri.edu
Web site: http://www.mo-sbdc.org/index.shtml

Montana SBDC
Ann Desch, State Director
301 S. Park Avenue, Room 114
P.O. Box 200505
Helena, MT 59601
406-841-2747; Fax: 406-841-2728

e-mail: adesch@state.mt.us
Web site: http://commerce.state.mt.us/brd/
BRD_SBDC.html

Nebraska SBDC
Robert Bernier, State Director
60th & Dodge Street
CBA Room 407
Omaha, NE 68182
402-554-2521; Fax: 402-554-3473
e-mail: rbernier@unomaha.edu
Web site: http://nbdc.unomaha.edu/

Nevada SBDC
Sam Males, State Director
Reno College of Business Nazir Ansasri
Building 032, Room411
Reno, NV 89557-0100
775-784-1717; Fax: 775-784-4337
e-mail: males@unr.edu
Web site: http://www.nsbdc.org

New Hampshire SBDC
Mary Collins, State Director
108 McConnell Hall
Durham, NH 03824-3593
603-862-2200; Fax: 603-862-4876
e-mail: Mary.Collins@unh.edu
Web site: http://www.nhsbdc.org

New Jersey SBDC
Brenda Hopper, State Director
Rutgers–49 Bleeker Street
Newark, NJ 07102-1993
973-353-5950; Fax: 973-353-1110
e-mail: bhopper@andromeda.rutgers.edu
Web site: http://www.njsbdc.com/home/

New Mexico SBDC
Roy Miller, State Director

6401 Richards Avenue
Santa Fe, NM 87505
505-428-1362; Fax: 505-428-1469
e-mail: rmiller@santa-fe.cc.nm.us
Web site: http://www.nmsbdc.org

New York SBDC
Jim King, State Director
SUNY—State State University Plaza
41 State Street
Albany, NY 12246
518-443-5398; Fax: 518-443-5275
e-mail: Kingjl@nyssbdc.org
Web site: http://www.nyssbdc.org

North Carolina SBDC
Scott Daugherty, State Director
5 West Hargett Street
Suite 600
Raleigh, NC 27601
919-715-7272; Fax: 919-715-7777
e-mail: sdaugherty@sbtdc.org
Web site: http://www.sbtdc.org

North Dakota SBDC
Christine Martin, State Director
UND—118 Gamble Hall, UND
Box 7308
Grand Forks, ND 58202
701-777-3700; Fax: 701-777-3225
e-mail: christine.martin@und.nodak.edu
Web site: http://www.ndsbdc.org

Ohio SBDC
Holly Schick, State Director
77 South High Street
Columbus, OH 43215-6108
614-466-2711; Fax: 614-466-0829
e-mail: hschick@odod.state.oh.us
Web site: http://www.ohiosbdc.org

Oklahoma SBDC
Grady Pennington, State Director
517 University, Box 2584, Station A
Durant, OK 74701
580-745-7577; Fax: 580-745-7471
e-mail: gpennington@sosu.edu
Web site: http://www.osbdc.org

Oregon SBDC
William Carter, State Director
44 West Broadway, Suite 203
Eugene, OR 97401-3021
541-726-2250; Fax: 541-345-6006
e-mail: carterb@lanecc.edu
Web site: http://www.bizcenter.org

Pacific Islands SBDC
Casey Jeszenka, State Director
Pacific Islands SBDC
P.O. Box 5061—U.O.G. Station
Mangilao, GU 96923
671-735-2590; Fax: 671-734-2002
e-mail: cjeszenka@hotmail.com
Web site: http://www.uog.edu/sbdc
*For Guam time, add 15 hours to EST.

Pennsylvania SBDC
Gregory Higgins, State Director
Upenn-/Vance Hall, 4th Floor
3733 Spruce Street
Philadelphia, PA 19104-6374
215-898-1219; Fax: 215-573-2135
e-mail: ghiggins@wharton.upenn.edu
Web site: http://pasbdc.org

Puerto Rico SBDC
Carmen Marti, Executive Director
Union Plaza Building
Suite 701
416 Ponce de Leon Avenue

Hato Rey, PR 00918
787-763-6811; Fax: 787-763-6875
e-mail: cmarti@prsbdc.org
Web site: http://www.prsbdc.org

Rhode Island SBDC
Robert Hamlin, State Director
Bryant College
1150 Douglas Pike
Smithfield, RI 02917
401-232-6111; Fax: 401-232-6933
e-mail: rhamlin@bryant.edu
Web site: http://www.risbdc.org

South Carolina SBDC
John Lenti, State Director
USC—Darla Moore School of Business
Hipp Building
Columbia, SC 29208
803-777-4907; Fax: 803-777-4403
e-mail: lenti@darla.badm.sc.edu
Web site: http://scsbdc.moore.sc.edu

South Dakota SBDC
Wade Druin, State Director
414 East Clark Street
Vermillion, SD 57069
605-677-5287; Fax: 605-677-5427
e-mail: wdruin@usd.edu
Web site: http://www.sdsbdc.org

Tennessee SBDC
Albert Laabs, State Director
1415 Murfreesboro Road
Suite 350
Nashville, TN 36217
615-366-3900; Fax: 615-366-3939
e-mail: alaabs@tbr.state.tn.us
Web site: http://www.tsbdc.org

Texas SBDC
Mike Young, State Director
2302 Fannin, Suite 200
Houston, TX 77002
713-752-8444; Fax: 713-756-1500
e-mail: fyoung@uh.edu
Web site: http://sbdcnetwork.uh.edu

Texas-North SBDC
Liz Klimback, State Director
Bill J. Priest Institute for Economic Dev.
1402 Corinth Street
Dallas, TX 75215
214-860-5831; Fax: 214-860-5813
e-mail: emk9402@dcccd.edu
Web site: http://www.ntsbdc.org/

Texas-NW SBDC
Craig Bean, State Director
2579 South Loop 289, Suite 114
Lubbock, TX 79423
806-745-3973; Fax: 806-745-6207
e-mail: c.bean@nwtsbdc.org
Web site: http://www.nwtsbdc.org

South-West Texas Border Region SBDC
Robert McKinley, State Director
145 Duncan Drive, Suite 200
San Antonio, TX 78226-1816
210-458-2450; Fax: 210-458-2464
e-mail: rmckinley@utsa.edu
Web site: http://www.iedtexas.org

Utah SBDC
Greg Panichello, State Director
9750 S. 300 E. MCPC 201
Sandy, UT 84070
801-957-3483; Fax: 801-957-3488
e-mail: Greg.Panichello@slcc.edu

Vermont SBDC
Donald Kelpinski, State Director
Vermont Technical College
Maine Street
Randolph Center, VT 05061-0188
802-728-9101; Fax: 802-728-3026
e-mail: Dkelpins@vtc.vsc.edu
Web site: http://www.vtsbdc.org

Virgin Islands SBDC
Warren Bush, State Director
8000 Nisky Center
Suite 202
Charlotte Amalie, VI 00802-5804
340-776-3206; Fax: 340-775-3756
e-mail: wbush@webmail.uvi.edu
Web site: http://rps.uvi.edu/SBDC

Virginia SBDC
Ms. Jody Keenan, Director
Small Business Development Center
George Mason University
4031 University Drive, Suite 200
Fairfax, VA 22030-3409
703-277-7727; Fax: 703-277-7730
e-mail: jkeenan@GMU.edu
Web site: http://www.virginiasbdc.org

Washington SBDC
Dr. Carolyn Clark, State Director
534 E. Trent #201
P.O. Box 1495
Spokane, WA 99210-1495
509-358-7765; Fax: 509-358-7764
e-mail: clrk@wsu.edu
Web site: http://www.wsbdc.org

West Virginia SBDC
Conley Salyer, State Director

1900 Kanawha Boulevard Building
Suite 600
Charleston, WV 25301
304-558-2960; Fax: 304-558-0127
e-mail: csalyer@wvsbdc.org
Web site: http://www.wvsbdc.org

Wisconsin SBDC
Erica Kauten, State Director
432 North Lake Street
Room 423
Madison, WI 53706
608-263-7794; Fax: 608-263-7830
e-mail: erica.kauten@uwex.edu
Web site: http://www.wisconsinsbdc.org

Wyoming SBDC
Diane Wolverton, State Director
University of Wyoming
Wyoming Hall
Room 414
Laramie, WY 82071-3922
307-766-3505; Fax: 307-766-3406
e-mail: DDW@uwyo.edu
Web site: http://www.uwyo.edu/sbdc

U.S. Department of Commerce
14th and Constitution Avenue
Washington, DC 20230
202-377-2000
Web site: http://www.osec.doc.gov/

You can forget about any substantive marketing assistance from this department. Food marketing (domestic and international) is not conducted by the DOC. Check instead with the Department of Agriculture and its Foreign Agricultural Service.

U.S. Food and Drug Administration
International Activities Branch
Center for Food Safety and Applied
Nutrition FDA (HFS–585)
200 C Street, SW
Washington, DC 20204
Web site: http://fda.gov

Request a free copy of information on how
to start a food business. The Web site contains a lot of information, including a *Food
Labeling Guide.*

FDA State Offices
Web site: http://www.fda.gov/oca/sthealth.htm

The Web site will get you to a complete listing of all state departments of health. These
include food safety sections.

Specialty Food Market Profile

The following is a close look at current trends in the gourmet and specialty food market written by A. Elizabeth Sloan, Ph.D., Contributing Editor of *Food Technology*. Dr. Sloan is also President of Sloan Trends & Solutions, Inc., in Escondido, California. She can be reached via e-mail: sloantrend@attglobal.net. This article is reprinted from *Food Technology*, July 2004, copyright Institute of Food Technologists. Please see http://www.specialty foodresource.com for updates.

Gourmet and Specialty Food Trends

Some of the most lucrative and sustainable mass-market food trends debuted in gourmet and specialty markets. For example, energy beverages, nutrition bars, and sports drinks originated in the sports performance segment. Refrigerated salad dressings and pre-cut and bagged salads first appeared in natural food markets. Bottled water came from health and natural food stores; imported, artisan, and high-end natural cheeses from gourmet delicatessens; and fortified yogurt smoothies from health food stores and natural juice bars. While not all specialty market success stories will translate to the mass market, the potential is greater than ever.

Energy beverages were the fastest-growing supermarket category in 2003, nutrition bars were 4th (up 17 percent last year), and sports drinks were seventh (up 19 percent). Refrigerated salad dressings were second (up 26 percent), and pre-cut and bagged salads topped $2 billion in supermarkets alone. Bottled water was up 17 percent in grocery stores; imported, artisan, and high-end natural cheeses were up 7 percent; and fortified yogurt smoothies were up 68 percent (IRI, 2004, 2003).

Many foods consumers want fresh prepared convenience foods, higher-quality, additive-/pesticide-free foods, and environmentally, agriculturally, and animal-friendly products—are also beginning to cross over from premium markets to the mass market. In 2003, for example, *better-quality products* emerged as an important reason why one-third of supermarket shoppers regularly shopped for foods at other locations, right behind *convenience* and *price*. In 2004, 26 percent of grocery shoppers said they shopped other channels for higher-quality products, up from 18 percent in 2003. *Variety* was another important reason (FMI, 2004).

Just over four out of ten adults say they will choose products and services that are environmentally friendly and that they will make purchase decisions with an understanding of the effect they will have on the health and sustainability of the world, its environment, and people. According to NMI (2004a, b), 39 percent of adults say it is important for their store to have food from farms with a commitment to sustainable agriculture; 46 percent completely agree that they care about socially responsible business; and 38 percent will usually purchase products from companies whose values are most like their own. Moreover, as Americans continue to widen their culinary sphere, accelerate their interest in health, and position convenient high-quality natural foods as one of the "little luxuries of life," the opportunity for crossover products will continue to grow. Continued spending at restaurants and growth in the high-end, full-service "white-tablecloth" segment will also fuel the demand for premium foods.

The National Restaurant Association forecasts that restaurant-industry sales will continue to rise throughout 2004, reaching a record $440 billion and marking the 13th consecutive real sales growth for the industry—full-service restaurant sales are expected to reach $157 billion in 2004, for a growth rate of 4.6 percent, while quick-service restaurants (QSRs) are projected to grow 3.9 percent (NRA, 2004a). Traditionally, the demographics of the prime gourmet/specialty store shopper coincided with those of the Baby Boom generation—in their peak earning and spending years—with consumers age 45 and over having the highest propensity to purchase specialty foods. However, perhaps most important is the role that America's young adults—more culinary and health-aware than any other generation in history—are likely to play in ensuring the long-term opportunity for specialty foods.

Nearly one-third of young adults age 15–24 eat their evening meal at a restaurant three or more times per week—almost double the frequency of any other population segment (FMI, 2004). This age group uses ethnic foods more frequently, with more than seven out of ten young adults buying ethnic foods in a supermarket at least once per month. Use decreases with age to 4 in 10 shoppers over age 65. In a Wharf Research study (Wharf, 2003), 87 percent of those age 15–21 years were familiar with quesadillas, compared to 73 percent of those age 55–74; 86 percent with sushi vs. 72 percent of the older groups. Six out of ten young adults were aware of spring rolls, 48 percent pot stickers, 45 percent pesto, and 16 percent samosas.

According to Packaged Facts (2004a), those age 18–24 are the most likely to say they like to eat gourmet whenever they can, closely followed by those 25–34. These two age groups also index the highest among those consumers who like to try new foods. But in terms of younger folks and food, fresh, simple, and sophisticated it will be! This group does not "prefer" foods prepared as an "art form"—common at so many high-end restaurants—and indexes among the lowest for those with a preference for spicier foods, quite contrary to popular belief. Those aged 15–24 are also more likely than the general population to shop at ethnic specialty stores (24 percent vs. 10 percent, respectively) and natural/organic stores (11 percent vs. 10 percent, respectively)—posing a serious question for the industry as to the direction shoppers will take in the future (FMI, 2004). Surprisingly, conventional supermarket gourmet aisles lead the market for gourmet foods and beverages, ringing up almost 45 percent of total retail dollar sales, followed by gourmet/specialty stores (34 percent) and warehouse clubs (5 percent), according to a Packaged Facts (2004a) report. The report projects that retail sales of all gourmet foods/beverages will reach $35.3 billion in 2004 and $43.5 billion by 2007. Gourmet beverages and confectionery, the largest segment, accounts for 49 percent of retail sales, followed by foods and ready-to-eat meals (33.4 percent) and condiments/ cheese (18 percent). At the same time, natural product sales in all channels reached $42.8 billion in 2003, an 8.1

percent increase over 2002 (Spencer and Rea, 2004). Natural product retailers saw their sales rise to $20.5 billion, a 9.9 percent increase over 2002. Mass-market sales rose 7.8 percent—higher than last year but still less than their natural counterparts. Organic food sales reached $10.3 billion in 2003 (up 20 percent), with 44 percent of sales occurring in the mass market. The remainder of this article will explore trends likely to cross over from the gourmet/specialty, natural/organic, gourmet deli, and high-end restaurant markets.

Specialty Foods

Condiments, with sales of $1.82 billion last year (up 7 percent), have long dominated the $22.9-billion specialty foods market and are more than double the sales of their closest followers: tea, cheese, coffee, snacks, cookies/bars, and cooking oils (Mintel, 2004). As customers search for new and trendy items, new-product introductions have kept pace, rising to 3,250 in 2003. New "meal" products jumped 538 percent, dairy products 101 percent, snacks 93 percent, soups 35 percent, and pet food 22 percent. In the past two years, sales of specialty milk, cream, and half-and-half climbed 48 percent as more small dairies came to market. Free-range, exotic, and high-nutrient-content eggs rose 43 percent, frozen fruits/vegetables 40 percent, puddings 34 percent, cold/ hot cereals 31 percent, conserves/jams/nut butters 28 percent, juices/functional beverages 29 percent, cheese 25 percent, and nuts, seeds, dried/fruits and trail mixes 25 percent.

Pesto, laced with some of America's favorite ingredients—basil, garlic, and Parmesan cheese—and its newfound generation of roasted red pepper and sun-dried tomato sauces, will find a new role in sandwiches, salads, and sauces. Flavor-laden spreads such as Peace Works' *Meditalia's Mediterranean Spreads,* including *Green Olive* and *Tuscan Eggplant Spread*, will also be in high demand.

Flavored vinaigrettes are moving from salads to sauces, showing up on sandwiches and grilled foods and as garnishes at the center of the plate. Gourmet mustards and horseradish, now commonly mixed into mayonnaise or yogurt, are key ingredients in crusts on fish and meats. Aioli, the garlic–mayonnaise Mediterranean basic now paired with ethnic flavors and ingredients, will find a plethora of new uses, from sandwiches to dipping sauces. Wildwood Harvest Foods' *Wildwood Organic Aioli Spread Mayonnaise Alternative* is egg- and dairy-free and comes in garlic, lemon-dill, and creamy chipotle flavors.

From olive oil flavored with truffle and lemon to toasted and organic sesame oils, flavored oils are bringing unusual mild flavors to foods, whether used as a bread-dipping first course or for adding a sizzling finish to hot, cooked foods. While extra-virgin olive oils are being smoked, pressed with Meyer lemons, or mixed with vanilla flavors, other oils like Soofer Co.'s *Sadaf Pure Grapeseed Oil*—high in antioxidants—are finding mainstream appeal. Oils from avocado, nuts such as almond and peanut, rice bran, and tea are being touted for their health properties. Pistachio oil offers an intense nut flavor and a distinct emerald green color for topping salads or ice cream. Macadamia nut oil and rice bran oil—commonly used in Japanese cooking—can withstand high heat. Pumpkin seed oil is best used as a dressing. Golden West Specialty Co.'s *Tophe Rice Bran Oil* is made in the U.S. from rice grown by American farmers.

Hot on the heels of the healthy oil trend is the move to healthier and gourmet butters as flavored alternatives to peanut butter or traditional spreads. Nut butters, which soared 26 percent in the natural channel last year—such as NSpired Natural Foods' *Almond, Cashew,* and *Macadamia Nut Butters* with no *trans* fats, hydrogenated oils, sugar, artificial flavors, colors or preservatives—will have strong mass market appeal. Peanut Better, Inc.'s *Peanut Better* comes in *Deep Chocolate* and *Vanilla Cranberry* sweet flavors and *Thai Ginger & Red Pepper* and *Hickory Smoked* savory flavors. European butters—such as Keller's Creamery's *Plugra European Style Butter,* which is richer and creamier than American butters, are also developing a strong following.

Chutney—any spicy, relish-like condiment that contains fruit or sometimes a vegetable, vinegar, sugar, and spices—is likely to rival salsa, not just as a dip, a topping for meat or fish, or an accompaniment to cheese, but also as a sweet-and-sour flavor enhancer for many foods. Savory jams and marmalades, now laced with everything from roasted garlic to jalapeños, are not only becoming the next generation of "toast toppers" for those shunning anything sweet, but are also frequently mixed into dressings, vinaigrettes, marinades, glazes, and cream sauces as a common recipe element.

And when it comes to salsa, take a taste of Riba Foods', Arriba!'s *California-style Berry Mango Salsa* and *Mandarin Avocado Fire Roasted Salsa*. And guacamole lovers will surely go for Cedar Run Farms' all-natural, low-carb *Chunky Asparagus Salsa* or *Zesty Asparagus Guacamole*!

As tea drinkers upgrade to finer, more indulgent teas and the media tout tea's antioxidant and potential weight-loss properties, a new generation of health-directed tea aficionados is emerging. Tea sales in 2003 jumped 12.2 percent in specialty stores, reaching $838 million (Mintel, 2004) and 20.9 percent in natural food stores (SPINS, 2004). More exotic teas, such as Yogi Tea's *African Redbush Peach, Egyptian Licorice Mint,* and *Andes Yerba Mate,* are capturing adventuresome drinkers. White teas, which are made from the tender young buds that have not fully developed, are among the most popular new entries. Organic and "after-dinner" dessert-flavored teas such as Hain Celestial Group's *Celestial Seasonings' English Toffee* and *Vanilla Hazelnut* teas are fast gaining in popularity, as are its fruit teas.

Tazo Tea's *Juiced Iced Teas* in *Plum Delicious* and *Wild Orange* flavors have created a new niche in the iced tea market, along with Tazo's *Organic Iced Green Tea* and *Lemon Ginger Iced Tea.* Traditional Indian Chai—a savory mixture of tea, milk, sugar, ginger, cardamom, and other spices—continues to gain in popularity in hot and cold forms. Rooibos gives Yogi Tea's *Redbush Chai* an unusual distinction, in comparison to its traditional *Black Chai* and *Green Chai.* Yogi also offers creamy *Tea Latte* concentrates in *Classic India Spice* and *Vanilla Hazelnut.* Oregon Chai's ready-to-drink *Chai Tea Lattés* and iced tea concentrates in *Expresso, Honey, Almond,* and *Organic* varieties are another cutting-edge trend.

Healing and herbal formulas such as Yogi Tea's *Women's, Bedtime, Calming,* and *Stomach Ease* teas continue to provide natural remedies for a variety of ailments. Estate teas—which identify the estate or farm on which they are grown—are also commanding unprecedented attention.

Tea for kids is another hot item. Khoisan Tea from South Africa is targeting children with its latest flavored rooibos teas, which include *Bubbly Gum* and *Vanilla Gorilla.* And Whitward of Chelsea, a popular

UK tea and coffee retailer, has launched a new chain of teashops in the United States.

Celestial Seasonings—the number one brand in the tea category—has added a new *Natural Cider* mix line in flavors such as *Apple Caramel Kiss* and *Honey Vanilla Apple*.

Sales of specialty coffee, coffee substitutes, and cocoa in 2003 jumped 11.1 percent in gourmet stores, reaching $811 million, and a whopping 42.9 percent in natural food stores (Mintel, 2004). Artisan roasters, who hand-roast daily in small batches and ship within 24 hours to ensure freshness, are setting the pace—*Peet's Coffee & Tea* is the number-one coffee brand in the natural channel. New and exciting exotic sources and blends continue to demand attention. Currently in vogue are coffees sourced in the Pacific, especially those from Sumatra and New Guinea; American coffees from Costa Rica, Guatemala, and Panama; and African and Arabian coffees, including those from Kenya and Ethiopia. "Fair-trade" coffee and cocoa—whose aim is to guarantee farmers a respectable wage and use responsible agricultural techniques—is moving mainstream. Also grabbing customer attention are organic, Kosher, non-GMO, and shade-grown coffee. *Mount Hagen Instant Coffee,* the category leader in natural food stores, was the first freeze-dried, certified organic regular, and decaffeinated instant coffee. Skylar Haley's *Achieve One* is a high protein, low-carb, fortified, ready-to-drink, single-serve coffee. And *Caffé Botanica* has introduced coffee beans infused with herbs and minerals.

Sweetener sales increased 3.9 percent, reaching $555 million in 2003 in the specialty markets and 35.2 percent in natural food markets (Mintel, 2004; SPINS, 2004). Pure maple syrup and gourmet honeys, such as manuka, orange blossom, and clover, can add excitement to any food. Florida Crystals mills its cane, organic, and demerara sugars right on the farm. Wholesome Sweeteners offers all-natural demerara, brown muscovado, and dark brown molasses sugars.

Fancy chocolates continue to gain appeal as carb counters look for a better way to cheat. Chocolate-covered pretzels, cherries, and strawberries are just a few of the bestselling items. Quickly attracting new customers are smaller-portions sizes and packaging of decadent items in single-unit premium packages. Premium truffles, fudge, and almond toffee remain key players. Artisan and hand-made or hand-dipped chocolates appear to be immune to the low-carb and sugar-free trends. In-store bar markets that may feature up to 500 different individual bars are also grabbing customer attention.

The demand for organic candy and fruit leathers remains particularly strong for kids. Fair-trade candy is a growing trend, as are chocolate products that benefit the rain forests. Diet candy jumped 90 percent across all channels, and 3 percent of all candy was sugar-free or low-carb last year (NCA, 2004). Low-carb, no-sugar-added premium options like Seattle Chocolates' *Skinny Truffles'* line are right on target, and so are the company's sophisticated truffle bars in flavors like *Seville Orange, Black Forest Cherry,* and *Lemon Mousse.* Harbor Sweets' whimsical chocolate *Sea Creatures* are also available sugar-free.

Natural Foods

As the desire for food purity gains momentum, the natural channel will continue to grow. NMI (2004a) reports that 63 percent of consumers use natural foods/beverages and 40 percent use organic; 53 percent think it is important for their store to have foods grown without pesticides; 49 percent favors foods that are natural; and 35 percent seek foods that are free of GMOs; and 18 percent use only natural sugars like honey and turbinado sugar. Also playing an increasingly important role in food purchases is avoiding antibiotics, hormones, and additives.

Led by Whole Foods Markets and Wild Oats Markets, food sales in natural product stores reached $11.4 billion in 2003 (Spencer and Rae, 2004). Packaged groceries topped $2 billion in 2003 (up 12 percent), produce $1.8 billion (16 percent), nutrition bars $1 billion (25 percent), dairy $934 million (11 percent), frozen/refrigerated $935 million (11 percent), bulk packaged $927 million (8 percent), and foodservice, deli, restaurant, and juice bars $805 million (9 percent). Natural product stores averaged 9.9 percent growth last year, ranging from 8 percent in the Mountain Region to 6 percent back East.

With $4.4 billion in 2003 sales (up 17 percent last year), organic foods are a dominant force in the natural channel (Spencer and Rae, 2004). In terms of category sales, produce, led by Earthbound Farms, remains the largest segment ($1.5 billion, with 86 percent of all produce sold classified as organic), followed by packaged grocery ($779 million, 38 percent organic), dairy ($626 million, 64 percent organic), nondairy ($380 million, 80 percent organic), and nonalcoholic beverages ($236 million, 64 percent organic). While still a relatively small category, organic fresh meat and seafood enjoyed the highest growth rate (51 percent), followed by nutrition bars and beer/wine, both at 48 percent. Other categories also enjoying significant growth were produce (19 percent), dairy (18 percent), packaged grocery (17 percent), and frozen/ refrigerated prepared items (16 percent).

Attitudes about the "meat case" are changing, too. NMI (2004a) reports that half of consumers are more interested in organic beef products, and 42 percent in natural beef, than they used to be, and 35 percent are now more concerned about the safety of the meat supply. Claims of "certified humane," "free-range," "grass-fed," "no antibiotics or hormones," "Kosher," "halal," and "ground today, sold today" are everywhere.

Organic and all-natural meats are now cutting across all varieties and forms, from lamb to buffalo. Maverick Ranch Natural Meats offers a full complement of pork, buffalo, lamb, beef, and air-chilled free-range chickens, which have an 85 percent lower bacteria count than water-chilled poultry. Laura's Lean competes in the natural, low-fat category and now offers a precooked pot roast and barbecue. Wellshire Farms offers *All-Natural Shredded Pork in BBQ Sauce, All-Natural Polska Kielbasa,* and other all-natural products. Other major players are Applegate Farms, which offers antibiotic-free, no-nitrate cold cuts, cheese, and deli items, and Coleman Natural Products, which offers all-natural, uncured beef hot dogs and more than 500 SKUs of beef cuts.

Marketers are also touting quality by certifying the breed, such as Meyer Natural Angus's *Quality Angus Beef,* "raised naturally to taste best." A "Certified Hereford" program is also underway. Japanese Kobe Beef—astonishingly tender, finely marbled, and richly flavored—is now being sold in premium stores; the cattle are massaged with sake and fed a daily diet that never includes ordinary grains and grass. Premium Obe Organic Beef, raised naturally in Australia by OBE Beef Pty. Ltd., is another super-premium meat. Shelton's

Premium Poultry's *Shelton's Naturally Delicious* frozen dinners feature *Turkey Meatloaf* and other favorites made with all-natural, free-range poultry, with no antibiotics, growth hormones, or preservatives.

Dave's *Hook and Line Caught Gourmet Albacore* "no salt added" tuna and Natural Sea's *Wild Premium Alaskan Pink Salmon*—"no salt added, sustainably harvested and rich in heart-healthy Omega 3s"—are also grabbing customer attention. And right on target for the low-carb movement is Pecan Wells Jerky Co.'s *Natural Turkey, Pork,* and *Beef Jerky* with "no erythorbate, no nitrite, no MSG, minimally processed and raised without hormones."

All-natural and organic convenience entrées and meals are another explosive category. Fairfield Farms' *Organic Classics* line offers home-style entrées, such as *Organic Chicken Tetrazzini,* and organic vegetarian entrées, such as *Southwest Cornbread & Red Beans* under the *Moosewood* label. Fantastic Foods' shelf-stable vegetarian meals include popular *Risotto, Spanish Paella,* and *Mushroom Stroganoff.* Convenience foods that support sustainable practices are also finding a receptive audience; examples include Natural Sea's *Tuna Noodle Casserole* and Ian's Natural Foods' all-natural frozen *Kids' Fish Sticks, Chicken Nuggets,* and *Alphatots* potatoes.

Prepared Indian and Asian meals are two of the natural channel's fastest-growing prepared-meal segments. Ethnic Gourmet Foods' all-natural *Ethnic Gourmet Bowls* range from *Pad Thai with Shrimp* to *Szechwan Vegetarian Chicken.* Amy's new Indian frozen meals include *Samosa Wraps, Mattar Paneer,* and others. Arch Foods' *Curry Classics* range from *Chicken Curry* to *Chicken Tandoori with Spinach* and other authentic flavors. Among the most popular Asian brands are Thai Kitchen's extensive line of products, including *Noodle Cart Rice Noodles, Thai Peanut Mixes* for sauces and baking, *Thai Kitchen Organic Coconut Milk,* and Simply Asia's *Rice Noodle Soup Bowls,* sauces, and *Instant Rice Noodle Soups.*

Other gourmet convenience items, such as Rice Expressions' organic rice mixes that cook in just three minutes, rival any mainstream convenience product. Organic frozen breads such as French Meadow Bakery & Café's *100 percent Spelt Garlic Texas Toast* and Fresh Gourmet's *Organic Seasoned Premium Croutons* are other natural crossover items.

Frozen fruits and vegetables are another skyrocketing category, rising 23 percent in 2003 (SPINS, 2004). The number-one brand is Cascadian Farms, which markets 100 percent organic frozen fruits, such as sliced gourmet-quality peaches, cherries, and blackberries; vegetables, such as *California, Thai Stir-Fry,* and *Garden Blends*; and upscale frozen side dishes such as *Szechuan Green Beans* and *Vegetarian Skillet Meals.*

Alexia Foods, which offers a wide range of gourmet frozen potato products, also enjoyed significant growth in 2003. The company's all-natural, *trans*-free, organic *Oven Crinkles* come in *Onion & Garlic* and other flavors. Its *Oven Reds* are made from Columbia Basin red potatoes blended with 100 percent pure olive oil and upscale seasonings such as *Sun-Dried Tomatoes & Pesto.*

Baking mixes, supplies, and flours, many of them directed at a low-carb lifestyle, comprised another fast-emerging category last year, up 34 percent (SPINS, 2004). CarbSense Foods unveiled an extensive line of low-carb dry baking mixes, ranging from pancake, pizza crust, and bread SKUs to brownie, cake, and biscuit, although Atkins Nutritionals' *Baking Mixes* and *Low Carb Flour* posted the most dramatic growth in the category. Category leader Arrowhead Mills, which packages its *100 percent Certified Organic* whole-grain flours in sturdy, recyclable paper bags with protective UV lining, offers 18 diverse flours, including millet, amaranth, spelt, unbleached white flour, and other flours. The company also offers a range of organic baking ingredients, mixes, and breakfast cereals.

Bob's Red Mill, which also enjoyed significant growth, provides a wide variety of stone-ground exotic flours made from 100 percent organic grains, such as *Bean & Pea & Lentil Flour, Potato Flour, Sweet Rice Flour,* and *10 Grain Flour,* as well as mixes, such as *Irish Soda Bread,* many of which are gluten-free.

Three categories continue to sell more product in the natural channel than in the mainstream—organic baked goods (65 percent of total baked goods sold), organic soup (60 percent), and organic yogurt and kefir (59 percent) (SPINS, 2004). All-natural and/ or organic gourmet soup—single-serve or family-sized, fresh, refrigerated, and frozen—is one of the many categories helping to drive traffic in natural stores.

Restaurant supplier Kettle Cuisine's *Fresh Soup for One* line of fully cooked and ready-to-heat gourmet soups—ranging from *Organic Carrot Ginger* to *Hungarian Mushroom*—are also color-coded by the type of stock. All of Heartland's *100 percent Natural* refrigerated ready-to-serve-soups are under 220 calories per serving. Fairfield Farms' *Moosewood* brand offers a wide range of organic refrigerated soups, chowders, stews, and sauces, including *Broccoli Parmesan Sauce.* Natural Sea's *Clam Chowder* and *Lobster Bisque* are cooked in small kettles and made from sustainably harvested shellfish.

Although the soyfoods market is starting to show signs of maturity in several categories, total retail sales increased 10 percent in 2003, hitting the $4-billion mark (Soyatech/SPINS, 2004). Soy-based energy bars (up 12 percent), soymilks (11 percent), and soy yogurts (24 percent) continued to show strong growth. The advent of fortified soymilks like Silk's *Soymilk Enhanced* with Omega-3 and other antioxidants, cultured/ probiotic soymilks like WholeSoy Company's *Cultured Soy Drink,* and new positionings like Kikkoman's *Pearl Soymilk* (great with cereal) or WholeSoy's low-carb and low-sugar *Lite Soy Smoothies,* should help to broaden the appeal.

Up-and-coming soy categories include chips/snacks, like GeniSoy's *Low Carb Tortilla Chips* and *Low Carb Crunch Bars,* cookies/snack bars, shelf-stable juices, and functional beverages with soy—like Leading Brand Inc.'s *Soy2O.* All grew by more than 100 percent in 2003. Tofu sales, spurred by a number of prepared products, including Soga's *Grilled & Marinated Tofu in Tomato Basil,* were up 4.5 percent. Cold cereals, hot cereals, meal replacements, and soynuts were among the year's losers.

Soyatech confirms that new meat alternatives, frozen entrées, nondairy foods, private-label products, and low-carb foods with soy will fuel the category. Nutrition Kitchen's *Soybean Pastas* and El Burrito Mexican Food Products' *Soyrizo, SoyTaco, Meatless Taco Filling,* and *Breakfast Soy Sausages* are among the products to watch.

And while not necessarily soy-based, the number of new vegan products commands attention, as does the increasing incidence of gluten-free products. Deep Foods, Inc.'s *Green Guru* line of frozen Indian, Thai, and Chinese dinners, Alberto Natural Foods, Inc.'s *100 percent*

Organic Vegan Pastas, and Vegan Eats' *Soy Jerky* are some cutting-edge additions.

Spurred by the success of Cascadian Farms' organic ready-to-eat breakfast cereals and Kashi's diverse cereal line—including *Heart to Heart, Good Friends,* and *Seven in the Morning*—sales of organic ready-to-eat cereals continue to soar across all channels! Recent additions in the natural channel have focused on two categories: exotic grains and young children.

Organic eggs, a favorite of low-carb natural consumers, also posted impressive sales, led by Giving Nature Organic Eggs and Chino Valley Ranchers, and made even more healthful by Gold Circle Farms' high-vitamin-E, DHA eggs.

Undoubtedly most important is the impact of low-carb foods. With NMI (2004a) reporting that 67.6 percent of consumers used high-protein foods in 2003 (up 10.1 percent over 2002) and 66.0 percent used low-carb foods (up 7.5 percent), it's not surprising that low-carb sales—excluding products such as produce, meat, and coffee/tea—reached $485 million in the natural channel in 2003 (Spencer and Rae, 2004). Large health food stores sold the largest share of low-carb foods, $137 million, or 17 percent of sales. Whole Foods reported 4 percent of sales coming from low-carb products, while Wild Oats reported 8 percent. Literally hundreds of low-carb products are being introduced every month, all of them worth watching. Especially interesting are DeBoles' *Carb Fit Spaghetti,* Todd's Health & Fitness Products' *2-Carb Pizzas, Bagels,* and *3-Carb Breads,* and Southwest Foods' *LeCarb Dairy Drink* and other "milks" from companies that use membrane technology to remove the lactose from regular whole milk, leaving wholesome ingredients like milk proteins and calcium behind.

Gourmet Deli Foods

Low-carb diets have encouraged customers to indulge in high-protein foods like meat, cheese, quiche, and other gourmet deli favorites such as smoked fish, sausage, pâté, mousse, and olives. More than ever, Americans are looking to high-end delis for more sophisticated take-home meals—like Cooper Farms' *Apple and Cranberry Stuffed*

Turkey Breast Roast—as well as quick snacks/mini-meals, upscale foods for home entertaining, and, recently, foods that meet their dietary agenda.

Half (51 percent) of adults say they would buy more from the deli if the food was guaranteed fresh, 43 percent if meals were healthier, 42 percent if items were prepared to order, 39 percent if sampling was permitted, and 37 percent if a fixed-priced meal was available (IDDBA, 2004). Salads, followed by sandwiches, are now the most popular deli items, up 20 percent in the past five years.

All-natural, organic, nitrite/preservative-free, and breed-certified meats are also becoming an important trend. Orders of turkey— which 45 percent now purchase weekly—chicken, and fried chicken are at their highest levels ever. While boldly flavored varieties remain popular, watch for more-savory/less-sweet, uniquely wood-smoked, and lighter flavors like basil and tarragon to come on strong.

Across the board, Asian and Hispanic influences continue to appeal in the deli meat case. Exotic fowl, including various breeds of duck, Guinea hen, pheasant, quail, and ostrich; darker meat portions; and smaller birds like Cornish hens represent a new gourmet niche. At the same time, suppliers like Farmland Foods have developed a portfolio of low-carb meat and poultry items—the top-ranking weekly dinner among carb watchers—to help deli operators create low-carb menu options and special deli sections.

With ham remaining the number-one sandwich for more than 20 years, it's not surprising that French bistro, Serrano, and other traditional cured, smoked, and country hams are enjoying renewed popularity, including Smithfield's Virginia, Bavarian, and Canadian Brand Maple hams. Italian cured meats— Cappola, Mortadella, Coppa, and Pancetta—are another explosive trend. Ethnic salami and sausages of all kinds, especially Hispanic varieties like chorizo, bolita, and andouille, and classic German sausages such as Braunschweiger, are fast gaining attention. Highly flavored retro premium meats like pastrami and corned beef are also enjoying a triumphant return, as are slow-roasted pork, brisket, and authentic barbecue items, especially with a twist. Old World items will continue to add excitement as customers discover the regions of Spain, Greece, Germany, and South America, too.

With Boomers' growing preference for fish and seafood over meat, deli operators are adding more marinated seafood items—prepared clams, oysters, and muscles; sushi, sashimi, and ceviche; smoked delicacies, including salmon, sturgeon, trout, and a wide range of domestic and imported caviar; pickled products; and gefilte fish. Signature seafood salads, skewered ocean tidbits, and bisques/chowders are helping to draw upscale customers.

Cheese sales—which jumped 12 percent in specialty stores and 21 percent in natural stores in 2003—are an integral part of deli operations (Mintel, 2004; SPINS, 2004). Swiss, Parmesan, Provolone, Muenster, Italian blends, Feta, and Queso Fresco and (other Hispanic cheeses) top the list in terms of total retail sales—Queso Fresco up 21 percent from 2002–03, and all other Hispanic cheeses up 18.2 percent. However, it's the specialty cheeses that are getting the attention. Crema Mexicana was the fastest grower in the specialty cheese aisle, up 141 percent in the last two years, followed by fresh Mozzarella 41 percent, Cheshire 36 percent, Manchego 30 percent, Queso Blanco 27 percent, Mascarpone 22 percent, Butterkase 22 percent, yogurt cheese 22 percent, and Gloucester/Cotswold 22 percent (Wisconsin, 2004).

America's artisan and farmstead cheeses have ignited a worldwide cheese war. Mozzarella Fresca produces world-class, 100 percent-natural California Mozzarella, Mascarpone, and Ricotta cheeses, and Wisconsin's Belgioioso Cheese, Inc. produces Auribella, Asiago, Gorgonzola, Pepato, and Kasseri. American artisan sheep and goat cheeses are another new direction. Firefly Farms offers organic *Fresh Mountain Blue* and *Buche Noir* goat cheeses, the latter coated in French vegetable ash and aged for several weeks. American goat cheeses now range from Brie to washed-rind, triple creams, and hard aged cheeses. Domestically produced Latin American cheeses such as Queso Fresco, Cotija, and Panela are also finding a welcoming market. Strong-flavored European washed-rind cheeses such as Epoisses, Munster Taleggio, and Reblochon are also finding favor, along with Liederkranz and Limburger.

At the same time, the influx of imported cheeses continues to excite customers. Classics like Jarlsberg and English Cheddar are now joined by a variety of German cheeses such as Käserei Champignon's Knoblauch, Rougette, Montagnolo, and Cambozola. Spanish cheeses such as

Tronchon, Iberico, and Tetilla have strong gourmet appeal. Gourmet quiches, fondues, and Mozzarella salads— such as Cantare Foods' *Fresh Italian Antipasto Salad* and *Mediterranean Salads*—and dessert goat cheeses such as Woolwich Dairy's *Madame-Chevre Elite* cranberry and port or red pepper-topped chevre are also flying off the shelves.

The demand for premium items such as pâté continues to grow. Fowl, mildly spiced and liquor-enhanced pâtés, and spreadable mousses such as Alexian Foods' *VerMousse*—duck and pork liver with sage and vermouth—are gaining in popularity. The addition of olives, nuts, and even fruit—such as orange or port to duck pâté—is another recent trend, as are venison, rabbit, and veal pâtés. Gourmet crackers—such as Cape Cod Potato Chips' new *Late July Organic Round Saltines,* or Back to Nature's *White Cheddar Rice Thins* are also important deli staples.

Sales of appetizers in delis—such as Sevan Bakery's *Mediterranean Thin Crust Pizzas* and *Turnovers*—jumped 22 percent in 2003 (IDDBA, 2004). Like specialty and low-carb breads, spreads and sauces are key players on deli shelves. Sun-dried tomato pesto spreads, olive tapenade, Creole relish, fresh gourmet pasta—such as Putney Pasta's *Butternut Squash* or *Black Bean & Habanero Ravioli with Green Chili Sauce*—are other popular items. Dips and salsas are other important offerings, including G&G Specialty Foods' authentic Greek skordalia or melitzanes dips, Lundberg's *Pico de Gallo Bean & Rice Chips,* and Cedar's inventive *Hommus Scoopers.*

Gourmet snacks such as Mama Mellace's *Cinnamon, Butter Rum, and Cranberry Pecans* and PeaNotz's *Roasted Soy Notz Crunch Mixes* are also enjoying brisk sales. Sticky Fingers' all-natural English scones, jams, and curds come in a variety of upscale flavors. Controlled Carb Gourmet offers "outrageously delicious" brownies and cookies; La Paloma offers *Concha, Polvoron,* and *Orejas* cookies; and the Cannoli Factory offers cannoli and tiramisu.

Fine Dining

With nine out of ten consumers agreeing that they like lots of choices on menus so they can decide exactly what they want to eat (NRA, 2003), monitoring restaurants to determine up-and-coming food trends is a better barometer than ever. Although white-tablecloth restaurants still inspire most culinary trends, casual-dining and chain restaurants are also increasingly affecting taste trends.

NRA's Tableservice Operators Survey (NRA, 2004b) asked operators what foods customers were ordering more of compared to two years ago. In fine-dining establishments, seafood entrées topped the list—64 percent of operators reported that their customers ordered more seafood entrées—followed by salad entrées 56 percent, vegetarian entrées 39 percent, take-out items 36 percent, appetizers 35 percent, pork entrées 34 percent, beef entrées 30 percent, specialty coffee 29 percent, and spicy dishes 27 percent. Only 19 percent ordered more chicken, 19 percent more pasta, and 4 percent more turkey entrées than in the past.

In the casual-dining segment, salad entrées topped the list— 56 percent of operators indicated an increase in salad entrée orders— followed by seafood entrées 53 percent, take-out items 52 percent, vegetarian entrées 48 percent, chicken entrées/appetizers 36 percent, spicy entrées 31 percent, beef entrées 30 percent, and pork entrées 29 percent. Interestingly, nearly twice as many casual-dining patrons as fine-dining patrons ordered a pasta entrée.

Analysis of the "Top 100" chain restaurant menus (Technomic, 2004) reveals that Asian was again the largest-growing menu category in terms of U.S. sales in 2003, up 27.2 percent, followed by donuts 20.5 percent, Italian 14.3 percent, BBQ 13.3 percent, varied menu 9.0 percent, steak 7.3 percent, limited-service Mexican 7.3 percent, sandwich 6.5 percent, burger 5.3 percent, and seafood and chicken 3.4 percent each. Pizza fell 1.3 percent, and casual Mexican dropped 17.9 percent.

Food Beat (2004) observes that there are significant differences in the protein component of appetizer menus of the Top 200 chains and their finer-dining counterparts, as monitored by its *Trendspotter* service. With the low-carb craze so prominent, this is an important observation. Shellfish topped the fine-dining protein appetizer list at 43 percent, followed by cheese 20 percent, fish 19 percent, pork 7 percent, and chicken 3 percent. Conversely, cheese topped the protein appetizer list in the Top 200 chains at 37 percent, chicken 19 percent, shellfish 18 percent, pork 6 percent, and fish 4 percent. Other trends include the continued popularity of small bites, samplers, and trios of items. Food Beat has also observed more fruit in salads, a strong jump in flavored mayonnaise, and Amuse Bouche—bite-sized treats served before the meal. Another major trend in fine dining is the move to smaller portion sizes, especially for gourmet desserts, like those from Galaxy Foods, which also has a low-carb line.

Last, with the popularity of the Food Channel, cooking magazines, and celebrity chefs, analyzing media coverage can also provide an important clue to future trends. According to Packaged Facts (2004b), Italian remains the ethnic cuisine most covered by the media, nearly double the coverage of French cuisine, which falls into second place, with Asian a not-too-distant third. In 2003, Spanish cuisines received slightly more coverage than Mexican, and nearly double any other "trendy" cuisines, including Caribbean, Latin, Thai and Indian!

References

FMI. 2004. Trends 2004 in the United States: Consumer attitudes and the supermarket. Food Mktg. Inst., Washington, DC, http://www.fmi.org.

Food Beat. 2004. Chain Account Menu Survey Reports. Food Beat Inc., Wheaton, IL, http://www.foodbeat.com.

IDDBA. 2004. What's in store 2005 report. International Dairy Deli Bakery Assn., Madison, WI, http://www.iddba.org.

IRI. 2003. Convenience vs. healthier eating—Who's winning? *Times & Trends Newsletter*, pp. 4-15. Information Resources, Inc., Chicago, IL, http://www.infores.com.

IRI. 2004. Low-carb product trends analysis. Presented at Intl. Dairy Foods Assn. meeting, New Orleans, March 17, Information Resources, Inc., Chicago, IL, http://www.infores.com.

Mintel. 2004. Specialty foods: State of the industry report. Mintel International Group in conjunction with the Natl. Assn. of Specialty Food Retailers and SPINS, San Francisco, CA, http://www.Mintel.com.

NCA. 2004. Candy statistics compiled in cooperation with Information Resources, Inc. Natl. Confectioners Assn. http://www.ecandy.com.

NMI. 2004a. Health & Wellness Trends Database. Natural Mktg. Inst., Harleysville, PA, http://www.nmisolutions.com.

NMI. 2004b. The LODAS Consumer Trends Database. Natural Mktg. Inst., Harleysville, PA, http://www.nmisolutions.com.

NRA. 2003. 2003 consumer survey. National Restaurant Association, Washington, DC, http://www.restaurant.org.

NRA. 2004a. 2004 Restaurant industry forecast: Executive summary. Natl. Restaurant Assn., Washington, DC, http://www.restaurant.org.

NRA. 2004b. Tableservice restaurant trends 2004. Natl. Restaurant Assn., Washington, DC, http://www.restaurant.org.

Packaged Facts. 2004a. The U.S. market for gourmet and specialty foods and beverages, Oct. 2003, Packaged Facts, Div. of Market research.com, New York, NY, http://www.packagedfacts.com.

Packaged Facts. 2004b. Market trends: Food flavor and ingredient outlook 2004. Packaged Facts, Div. of Marketresearch.com, New York, NY, http://www.packagedfacts.com.

Soyatech/SPINS. 2004. Soyfoods: The U.S. market 2004. Soyatech, Bar Harbor, ME, http://www.soyatech.com, in conjuction with SPINS, San Francisco, CA, wwwspinscom.

Spencer, M. and Rae, P. 2004. Natural product sales top $42 billion. Natural Foods Merchandiser 25(6): 1.

SPINS. 2004. Natural food product sales trends, SPINSscan full year 2003. SPINS Market Research, San Francisco, CA. http://www.spins.com.

Technomic. 2004. The 2004 Technomic top 100. Update and analysis of the 100 largest U.S. chain restaurant companies. Technomic, Inc., Chicago, IL, http://www.technomic.com.

Wharf. 2003. Tweens take a liking to ethnic foods survey. Familiarity with individual foods. Wharf Research, San Francisco, CA, http://www.wharfresearch.com.

Wisconsin. 2004. Analysis of Information Resources, Inc./Fresh Marketing Group retail data. Wisconsin Milk Marketing Board, Inc., Madison, WI, http://www.wislink.org.

Specialty Food Trends Resource List

Please see http://www.specialtyfoodresource.com for updates.

Analyzing and predicting trends in any market is a multilayered task. Trends affecting the food industry as a whole can usually be seen in each specific market, as in the case of convenience and better-for-you foods in the specialty trade. Trends also have a tendency to feed and play off of one another as well, with each lasting a varied amount of time before either falling off the consumer's radar or becoming a staple.

Trends in the marketplace influence every consumer's behavior. Trends affect the food industry on a zillion levels, from specific food choices to changing meal patterns. Not all trends are the same. Some are pervasive, influencing the whole social landscape; others are really just fads. Trends have a life cycle, and the particular stage of a trend is critical in determining its connection to a particular product or service.

Trends can exist on many levels. For instance, we can talk about a growing penchant for "hot" foods or dining at home. If both are trends, might one explain the other? Does an understanding of one general sociological trend help explain a specific food trend?

How Do Trends Relate to Food Marketing?

Successful businesses are market-driven when they design their products and services to fulfill consumer needs. They can define the marketplace through demographics (identifiable, measurable characteristics such as age, economic status, ethnic background, etc.), and psychographics (lifestyle or attitude characteristics).

Knowledge of today's trends can help you develop products and promotions for the future. The world is changing at an accelerated pace. Not much looks as it did 50 years ago. Like every other industry, the food industry has had to adapt to consumer demands driven by changing lifestyles.

How to Find Out about Underlying Forces and Changing Trends

Good sources of trend information appear in the media. This includes the Internet, which is being used with increasing frequency as a communication means. Several resources look at what's going on in the marketplace. Targeted to varying audiences, they each have their own focus and format. What they have to say is extremely valuable for developing staying power in the food world. Make your job easier by learning what the experts are saying. In addition to the professional trade journals listed in Appendix A, the following may be useful in developing a deeper understanding of consumer trends and their impact on specialty food marketing.

Publications

ACNielsen
This global market research company provides sales data and analysis of mainly supermarket product activity.
770 Broadway
New York, NY 10003
646-654-5000
Fax: 646-654-5002
Web site: http://www.acnielsen.com

American Demographics Magazine of Consumer Trends
American Demographics
c/o Customer Service
P.O. Box 2042
Marion, OH 43306-8142
800-529-7502
Web site: http://demographics.com

American Demographics is a tool for marketing strategists. Readers gain vital insight into the connections between age, education, geography, income, wealth, lifestyles, and spending. They find clues as to what consumers want now and what they're likely to want tomorrow. Every issue includes cutting-edge marketing techniques, helpful diagrams, and usually exclusive data that help readers to maximize opportunities in key market segments. Subscriptions for U.S. subscribers are $58 annually (ten issues).

Forecast

Forecast is a twice-a-month newsletter dedicated to delivering in-depth news and analysis of the Census 2000 statistics to help marketers understand what the information means and what it may portend for the future. Each issue analyzes the latest Census 2000 information to provide insight into consumer behavior, attitudes, and demographics at every level. There is analysis of where Americans are living, how their households are changing, how industries are responding, and trends that project what the future America will look like. A one-year subscription to *Forecast* costs $269.

e-mail: subscriptions@mediacentral.com.

The Food Channel Newsletter

Strategic Foods Resources
Division of Noble Associates
Springfield, MO and Chicago, IL
417-875-5129; Fax: 417-875-5051
Editor: Chris Wolf, e-mail: chris.wolf@noble.net
Web site: http://www.foodchannel.com

Formerly the *Food Channel HotBytes newsletter*, *The Food Channel TrendWire* newsletter has been the food industry's source for food trends since November 1988. It's published 52 times a year and distributed electronically to subscribers. Individual e-letter subscriptions are $195 per year. Corporate subscriptions are $895. For subscription inquiries, contact Debbie Merritt.

Foodwatch

Eleanor Hanson and Linda Smithson, co-Editors/Publishers
125 Thatcher Avenue

River Forest, IL 60305-2020
708-366-4599
Web site: http://www.foodwatchtrends.com

Foodwatch reports consumer food trends, tracking, analysis, and insights drawn from its review of newspapers from ten major U.S. cities and nineteen popular consumer magazines. Published monthly in electronic and hardcopy formats. Subscriptions are $60 per year.

Mintel's Global New Products Database (GNPD)

Web site: http://www.gnpd.com

Providing the world's premier editorial coverage of new-product development, Mintel's GNPD is a comprehensive database that monitors worldwide product innovation in consumer packaged goods. Mintel's GNPD offers unrivaled coverage of new-product activity for monitoring competitors and generating new product ideas.

Comment: This may or may not be of value to the specialty foods marketer. Mintel notes: *"New Product News* used to be part of Mintel, but it is no longer a separate publication. As for pricing for GNPD, we do not publish those rates."

Export Assistance

The following organizations work with the U.S. Department of Agriculture's Foreign Agriculture Service, and are involved actively in the overseas promotion of value-added food products. Please see http://www.specialtyfoodresource.com for updates.

National Association of State Departments of Agriculture (NASDA)
1156 15th Street, NW, Suite 1020
Washington, DC 20005
202-296-9680; Fax: 202-296-9686
e-mail: nasda@nasda.org

NASDA sponsors The U.S. Food Export Showcase that is supported in part by Foreign Agricultural Service (FAS) market development funds. It is held each year at Chicago's McCormick Place in conjunction with the Food Marketing Institute's Supermarket Industry Exposition, which attracts supermarket industry executives from around the world. The 2005 show will feature five events at one location—The FMI (Food Marketing Institute) Show, Fancy Food Show, U.S. Food Export Showcase, United Produce Expo and Conference, and All Things Organic.

U.S. Department of Agriculture (USDA)
Foreign Agricultural Service (FAS)
AG Export Services
Washington, DC 20250-1000
202-690-3576; Fax: 202-690-0193
Web site: http://www.fas.usda.gov

The Foreign Agricultural Service (FAS) maintains a global network of agricultural counselors, attachés, and officers covering more than 100 countries, to help build markets overseas and gather and assess information on world agricultural production and trade. Its traditional focus has been on agricultural commodities, but it has recently developed a sensitivity to the market potential and longer profits associated with high-value, retail-packaged food products.

Food Export USA—Northeast
150 S. Independence Mall West, Suite 1036

Philadelphia, PA 19106
215-829-9111
Web site: http://www.foodexportusa.org

Food Export USA—Northeast is a nonprofit organization that promotes the export of food and agricultural products from the northeast region of the United States. The organization has been helping exporters of northeast food and agricultural products sell their goods overseas since 1973, when it was first created as a cooperative effort between ten northeastern state agricultural promotion agencies and the United States Department of Agriculture's Foreign Agricultural Service (FAS). Food Export USA, in conjunction with its member states, provides a wide range of services to facilitate trade between local food companies and importers around the world. These services include: export promotion, customized export assistance, and a cost-share funding program.

Food Export USA member states include Connecticut, Delaware, Maine, Massachusetts, New Hampshire, New Jersey, New York, Pennsylvania, Rhode Island, and Vermont.

Connecticut Department of Agriculture
165 Capital Avenue
Hartford, CT 06106
860-566-4845; Fax: 860-566-6094

Delaware Department of Agriculture
2320 S. DuPont Highway
Dover, DE 19901
302-698-4500; Fax: 302-697-6287
Web site: http://www.state.de.us/deptagci

Massachusetts Department of Agricultural Resources
251 Causeway Street
Room 500
Boston, MA 02114
617-626-1700; Fax: 617-626-1850
Web site: http://www.mass.gov.agr

Maine Department of Agriculture
28 State House Station
Augusta, ME 04333
207-287-3871
Web site: http://www.state.me.us/agriculture

New Hampshire Department of Agriculture
P.O. Box 2042
Concord, NH 03302-2042
603-271-3551; Fax: 603-271-1109
Web site: http://www.agriculture.nh.gov

New Jersey Department of Agriculture
P.O. Box 330
Trenton, NJ 08625
609-984-2279; Fax: 609-984-5367
Web site: http://www.state.nj.us/agriculture

New York Department of Agriculture and Markets
108 Airline Drive
Albany, NY 12235
518-457-7076; Fax: 518-457-2716
Web site: http://www.agmkt.state.us

Pennsylvania Department of Agriculture
2301 N. Cameron Street
Harrisburg, PA 17110
717-787-4737
e-mail: aginfo@state.pa.us
Web site: http://www.agriculture.state.pa.us

Rhode Island Division of Agriculture
235 Promenade Street
Providence, RI 02908
401-222-2781; Fax: 401-222-6047
Web site: http://www.state.ri.us/dem/index

Vermont Department of Agriculture
116 State Street
Montpelier, VT 05602
802-828-2416; Fax: 802-828-3831
Web site: http://www.vermontagriculture.com

Western USA Trade Association (WUSATA)
4601 NE 77th Avenue, Suite 200
Vancouver, WA 98662
360-693-3373; Fax: 360-693-3464
Web site: http://www.wusata.org/body.html

WUSATA Members
Alaska Department of Natural Resources
P.O. Box 949
Palmer, AK 99645-0949
907-745-7200; Fax: 907-745-7112

Arizona Department of Agriculture
1688 West Adams Street
Phoenix, AZ 85007
602-542-0982; Fax: 602-542-0969

California Department of Food & Agriculture
1220 N Street, Room A280
Sacramento, CA 95814
916-654-0389; Fax: 916-653-2604
e-mail: 74404.273@compuserve.com

Colorado Department of Agriculture
700 Kipling Street, #4000
Lakewood, CO 80215-5894
303-239-4114; Fax: 303-239-4125
e-mail: CdaJimR@aol.com

Hawaii Department of Agriculture
P.O. Box 22159
1428 S. King Street
Honolulu, HI 96823-2159
808-973-9564; Fax: 808-973-9590
e-mail: CAOLIVE@PIXICOM

Idaho Department of Agriculture
P.O. Box 790
Boise, ID 83701
208-332-8530; Fax: 208-334-2879
e-mail: lhobbs@agri.state.id.us

Montana Department of Agriculture
Capitol Station
Helena, MT 59620
406-444-2402; Fax: 406-444-5409
e-mail: ck0331%zip004@mt.gov

New Mexico Department of Agriculture
Box 5600
Las Cruces, NM 88003
505-646-4929; Fax: 505-646-3303

Oregon Department of Agriculture
121 S.W. Salmon Street, #240
Portland, OR 97204-2987
503-229-6734; Fax: 503-229-6113
e-mail: kvainess@oda.state.or.us

Utah Department of Agriculture
P.O. Box 146500
Salt Lake City, UT 84114-6500
801-538-7108; Fax: 801-538-7126

Washington Department of Agriculture
P.O. Box 42560
Olympia, WA 98504-2560
360-902-1933; Fax: 360-902-2089
e-mail: 74323.2112@compuserve.com

Wyoming Department of Agriculture
2219 Carey Avenue
Cheyenne, WY 820020100
307-777-7321; Fax: 307-777-6593

**Middle America International
Agri-Trade Council (MIATCO)**
309 W Washington Street
Suite 600
Chicago, IL 60606
312-334-9200; Fax: 312-334-9230
Web site: http://www.miatco.org/trade.html

MIATCO Members
Illinois Department of Agriculture
P.O. Box 19281
Springfield, IL 62794-9281
217-782-6675; Fax: 217-524-5960

**Indiana Office of the Commissioner
of Agriculture**
One North Capitol, Suite 700
Indianapolis, IN 46204
317-233-4459; Fax: 317-232-4146

**Iowa Department of Agriculture & Land
Stewardship**
Henry A. Wallace Bldg.
Des Moines, IA 50319
515-2426238; Fax: 515-2425015

Kansas State Board of Agriculture
901 S. Kansas Avenue, Room 103
Topeka, KS 66612-1282
913-296-3736; Fax: 913-296-2247

Michigan Department of Agriculture
P.O. Box 30017
Lansing, MI 48909
517-373-1058; Fax: 517-335-7071

Minnesota Trade Office
1000 World Trade Center
30 East 7th Street
St. Paul, MN 55101
612-297-4222; Fax: 612-296-3555

Missouri Department of Agriculture
P.O. Box 630
Jefferson City, MO 65102
314-751-4338; Fax: 314-751-2868

Nebraska Department of Agriculture
P.O. Box 94947
Lincoln, NE 68509
402-471-4876; Fax: 402-471-2759

North Dakota Department of Agriculture
600 East Boulevard
Bismark, ND 58505
701-328-2231; Fax: 701-328-4567

Ohio Department of Agriculture
International Trade Program
65 South Front Street, Room 608
Columbus, OH 43215-4193
614-752-9815; Fax: 614-644-5017

South Dakota Department of Agriculture
523 East Capitol Avenue
Pierre, SD 57501-3182
605-773-3375; Fax: 605-773-3481
e-mail: agmail@state.sd.us

Wisconsin Department of Agriculture
P.O. Box 8911
Madison, WI 53708
608-224-5112; Fax: 608-224-5111

**Southern United States Trade Association
(SUSTA)**
World Trade Center, Suite 1540

2 Canal Street
New Orleans, LA 70130-1408
504-568-5986
Web site: http://www.susta.org

SUSTA Members
Arkansas
Reference SUSTA listing, above.

Florida Department of Agriculture &
Consumer Services
Box A, Room 411, Mayo Building
Tallahassee, FL 32339-0800
904-488-4366; Fax: 904-922-0374

Georgia Department of Agriculture
Capitol Square
Atlanta, GA 30334-4201
404-656-3740; Fax: 404-656-9390

Kentucky Department of Agriculture
500 Mero Street, 7th Floor
Frankfort, KY 40601
502-564-4696; Fax: 502-564-6527

Louisiana Department of Agriculture &
Forestry
P.O. Box 3334
Baton Rouge, LA 70821-3334
504-922-1280; Fax: 504-922-1289

Maryland Department of Agriculture
50 Harry S. Truman Parkway
Annapolis, MD 21401
410-841-5880

Mississippi Department of Agriculture and
Commerce
P.O. Box 1609
Jackson, MS 39215
601-354-7097; Fax: 601-354-6001

North Carolina Department of Agriculture
P.O. Box 27647
Raleigh, NC 27611
919-733-7912; Fax: 919-733-0999

Oklahoma Department of Agriculture
2800 N. Lincoln Boulevard
Oklahoma City, OK 73105
800-580-6543 or 405-521-3864
Fax: 405-521-4912

South Carolina Department of Agriculture
Wade Hampton State Office Building
P.O. Box 11280
Columbia, SC 29211
803-734-2210; Fax: 803-734-2192

Tennessee Department of Agriculture
P.O. Box 40627
Nashville, TN 37204
615-360-0160; Fax: 615-360-0194

Virginia Department of Agriculture
P.O. Box 1163
Richmond, VA 23209
804-786-867

U.S. Department of Commerce (USDOC)
Industry and Trade Administration (ITA)
14th and Constitution Avenue, NW
Washington, DC 20230
202-377-2000
Web site: http://www.ita.doc.gov

Useful for economic and general marketing
data. No food-related assistance.

Small Business Administration (SBA)
1441 L Street, NW
Washington, DC 20416
800-368-5855 or 202-653-7561

Same as USDOC; generic small business
export assistance. Not foodspecific.

State Resources, Associations, and Agencies

This list is not all-inclusive nor meant to serve as an endorsement. Where only state departments of agriculture are listed, be prepared to receive limited assistance. Most such departments are devoted to commodity marketing, not retail-packaged, high value food products. In those instances where no state association is listed, you may wish to consult Appendix M: Sources of Export Assistance, for a listing of state departments of agriculture. Please see http://www.specialtyfoodresource.com for updates.

State Departments of Commerce

Every state has a department of commerce and business development, usually located at the state capital. Its sole purpose is to promote and develop business within the state and offer new businesses information on state regulations and any legal requirements that apply.

States with Specialty Food Marketing Associations

CONNECTICUT

Connecticut Specialty Food Association
195 Farmington Avenue, Suite 200
Farmington, CT 06032
860-677-8097; Fax: 860-677-8418
e-mail: info@ctfood.org

This association has published a directory of resources essential to food producers.

The book includes listings of glass manufacturers, box manufacturers, basket companies, packaging and bag businesses, printers, label designers, co-packers, truckers, food technologists, public relations agencies, etc.

Connecticut Department of Agriculture
Bureau of Agricultural Development and Resource Preservation
765 Asylum Avenue
Hartford, CT 06105
860-713-2538
e-mail: marketing.ctdeptag@po.state.ct.us

IDAHO

Marketing Idaho Food and Agriculture
Idaho State Department of Agriculture
P.O. Box 790
Boise, ID 83701-0790

208-332-8530; Fax: 208-334-2879
Web site: http://www.agri.state.id.us

Ask for a copy of their publication: "Starting a Specialty Food Business."

LOUISIANA
Louisiana Department of Agriculture and Forestry
P.O. Box 3334
Baton Rouge, LA 70821-3334
225-922-1280; Fax: 225-922-1289
Web site: http://www.ldaf.state.us

MASSACHUSETTS
Massachusetts Department of Food and Agriculture
Division of Agricultural Development
100 Cambridge Street, 21st Floor
Boston, MA 02202
617-727-3018, ext. 172

The department provides an array of marketing support services to both value-added specialty food and agricultural producers. Options for participation in Massachusetts pavilions at trade shows, special events, seminars, and referrals are provided. Ask for a copy of "The Massachusetts Food Processors Resource Manual."

Massachusetts Specialty Food Association
P.O. Box 551
Sudbury, MA 01776
800-813-5862
Web site: http://www.msfa.net

The association supports and strengthens specialty producers to enhance the Massachusetts economy and promotes the interest of food producers and processors in the state. It serves as an umbrella organization to assist its members in obtaining financial, scientific, management, marketing and technical assistance. The association has access to consultation in many fields, including research and development, business and financial management, marketing, and technical and scientific areas.

MINNESOTA
Minnesota Department of Agriculture
90 West Plato Boulevard
St. Paul, MN 55107
651-296-7945
Web site: http://www.mda.state.mn.us

NEW MEXICO
New Mexico Department of Agriculture
MSC 3189, Corner of Gregg and Espina
Box 30005
Las Cruces, NM 88003-88005
505-646-3007
Web site: http://www.nmdaweb.nmsu.edu

A producer-consumer service and regulatory department under the New Mexico State University (NMSU) Board of Regents. Its Marketing and Development Division assists in the development of new markets and expansion of existing markets, both domestic and international, for farm products and livestock produced or processed in the state. It also assists commodity commissions in organizing and implementing commodity promotions.

NORTH CAROLINA
North Carolina Department of Agriculture and Consumer Services
2 West Edenton Street
Raleigh, NC 27601
919-733-7125
Web site: http://www.ncagr.com

OHIO
Ohio Department of Agriculture
Ohio Proud
8995 East Main Street
Reynoldsburg, OH 43068
800-467-7683; Fax: 614-644-5017
e-mail: ohioproud@mail.agri.state.oh.us

SOUTH CAROLINA
South Carolina Specialty Food Products Association
Mary Ridgeway, Executive Director
P.O. Box 11280
Columbia, SC 29211
803-734-2200
e-mail: mridge@sc.gov
Web site: http://www.scsfa.org

TEXAS
Texas Department of Agriculture
"Go Texan"
P.O. Box 12847
Austin, TX 78711
512-475-1663; Fax: 512-463-9968
e-mail: SDUNN@AGR.STATE.TX.US
Web site: http://www.gotexan.org

This agency has access to a large database
called Texas Agriculture Marketing
Exchange (TAME).

VERMONT
Vermont Department of Agriculture, Food and Markets
116 State Street
Drawer 20
Montpelier, VT 05620-2901
802-828-2416; Fax: 802-828-2361

Ask for a copy of the very thorough
Vermont Specialty Food Resource Directory.

VIRGINIA
Virginia Department of Agriculture and Consumer Services
Division of Marketing
P.O. Box 1163
Richmond, VA 23209
804-786-4278; Fax: 804-371-6097

WASHINGTON
Washington Specialty Foods Association
P.O. Box 8226
Spokane, WA 99203
Web site: http://www.waspecialtyfoods.org

WISCONSIN
Wisconsin Cheese and Specialty Food Merchants Association
111 South Hamilton
Madison, WI 53703
608-255-0373; Fax: 608-255-6600

Wisconsin Specialty Cheese Institute
P.O. Box 1264
Madison, WI 53701
800-697-8861; Fax: 608-255-4434
Web site: http://www.wisspecialcheese.org

Something Special from Wisconsin Program
Wisconsin Department of Trade and
Consumer Protection
Division of Marketing
P.O. Box 8911
Madison, WI 53708-8911
608-224-5115; Fax: 608-224-5111
Web site: http://www.datcp.state.wi.us

Sample Forms

Forms Listing

Sample Application for Credit

Sample Price List/Order Form

Sample Invoice

Sample Broker Statement

Sample Statement of Account

Sample Dunning Letter 1

Sample Dunning Letter 2

Sample Dunning Letter 3

Sample Application for Credit

Application for Credit

Date: _____

Company Name: _____

Business Address: _____

_____

Mailing Address: _____

City, State, Zip: _____

Phones: _____ Web site: _____ E-mail: _____

Type of business: _____

Year business started: _____ Years at present location: _____

Type ☐ Private Corporation ☐ Partnership

☐ Public Corporation ☐ Individual

Officers — Name	Position	Home Address	Phone

Banking References

1st Bank: _____

2nd Bank: _____

Trade References

1st Firm: _____

2nd Firm: _____

3rd Firm: _____

Credit Limit Requested: $ _____

In making this application for credit, the customer agrees to pay all invoices within 30 days from date of invoice and to pay a service charge of 1-1/2% per month, which is an annual percentage rate of 18% on all overdue balances. In the event a suit is necessary to collect any amount, the customer agrees to pay the seller's reasonable attorney fees and costs including attorneys fees for appeal.

Signature: _____ Title: _____ Date: _____

Sample Price List

Product or Company Name

Address • City, State, Zip

Phone • Web site • E-mail

Sales Message/Testimonial

Retailer Price List and Order Form   Date:

Cases Ordered	Description	Case Pack	Case Lbs. Shipping Wt.	Unit Price	Case Price
_____	New Gourmet Condiment	12/8 Oz. Jar	9	$ 3.75	$ 45.00
_____	New Gourmet Condiment	12/12 Oz. Jar	14	7.00	84.00

Bill To: _____   Ship To: _____

Address: _____   Address: _____

City: _____ State: ____ Zip: _____   City: _____ State: ____ Zip: _____

Special Handling Instructions: _____

Customer Order Number: _____   Your Company Number: _____

Terms: C.O.D. Until Credit Approved, then Net 30 days, F.O.B. my warehouse
      Prices subject to change without notice.

Thank You For Your Order

If available, this space should be used for more product and promotional data

My Company Name, Address, Telephone, Fax, Etc.

Sample Invoice

Your Company Name
Address
City, State, Zip
Telephone:
Web site:

Date:
No. :
Your Order No. :
Fax:
E-mail:

Sold To:
*
*
*

Shipped To:
*
*
*

Our No.	Salesperson	Terms	FOB	Ship Date	Shipped Via

Ordered	Shipped	Description	Unit Price	Amount

–THANK YOU FOR YOUR ORDER–
(prices subject to change without notice)

FREIGHT

TOTAL DUE | $

Sample Broker Statement

Your Company Name
Broker Commission Statement

Web site: E-mail:

Broker Name: Period From: To:

	Date	Order	Account	Invoice Amount	Rate	Amount
1						
2						
3						
4						
5						
6						
7						
8						
9						
10						

TOTAL >>>

Comments: _____

Total Commission:
Less Advance/Credit:
Commission Payable:

Sample Statement

Your Company Name
Address • City, State, Zip
Phone • Web site • E-mail

To:

STATEMENT

Number:	
Statement Date:	
Terms:	
Customer No.:	

Item	Date	Description	Charge	Credit	Balance
		Previous Balance Brought Forward			

Thank You for Your Business   Please pay this amount

Sample Dunning Letter (at the 33rd day)

Your Company Name
Address
Telephone Number

Date:
To:
Reference: Invoice number ——————— of ————— (date)
Subject: Friendly reminder

To whom it may concern:

Our records indicate that the above referenced invoice remains unpaid.
Please comply with our terms and remit $ ————————————— to us immediately.

Let us know if your records do not concur with ours, and thank you for
your attention.

Sincerely,

Sample Dunning Letter (at the 45th day)

Your Company Name
Address
Telephone Number

Date:
To:
Reference: Invoice number _____ of _____ (date)
Subject: Second notice

To whom it may concern:

We still show an amount due of $ _____ for the referenced invoice.
Please contact us immediately if you feel there has been an error.
Otherwise we expect your remittance now.

Sincerely,

Sample Dunning Letter (at the 60th day)

Your Company Name
Address
Telephone Number

Date:
To:
Reference: Invoice number _____ of _____ (date)
Subject: Final Notice

To whom it may concern:

We have yet to receive payment of the referenced invoice. Since the amount due is now 60 days late, and in violation of our terms, we have no other recourse except to place your account into collection which we would rather not do. To avoid this unpleasant action, please remit $ _____ now!

Sincerely,

Miscellaneous Resources

The following list is not all-inclusive, nor is it meant to serve as an endorsement. Please see http://www.specialtyfoodresource.com for updates.

Business Development

FastTrac National Headquarters
4747 Troost
Kansas City, MO 64110
800-689-1740; Fax: 816-235-6216
For orders/customer service: 877-450-9800
e-mail: info@fasttrac.org

FastTrac is a comprehensive entrepreneur-ship-educational program that provides entrepreneurs with business insights, leadership skills and professional networking connections so they are prepared to create a new business or expand an existing enterprise. The nine FastTrac programs include practical, hands-on business development programs and workshops for existing entrepreneurs, aspiring entrepreneurs, as well as entrepreneurship curriculum for college students. FastTrac is designed to help entrepreneurs hone the skills needed to create, manage and/or grow successful businesses.

Food Marketing and Economics Group
129 C Street
Davis, CA 95616
530-753-1632; Fax: 530-753-6113
e-mail: foodmarketing@mindspring.com

Primary focus: Market research and marketing program development for small food companies. Product experience includes energy drinks, energy bars, specialty sugars, seafood, wild rice, chili peppers, rice mixes, olives, beans, and fruit juices. Contact: Dr. Shermain Hardesty.

Green Harbor Associates
4 Calypso Lane
Marshfield, MA 02050
781-837-1664; Fax: 781-837-8304
e-mail: greenharbor@adelphia.net

Primary focus: The firm offers a marketing-consulting service to manufacturers of specialty foods, from assisting in label design to picking a distribution channel to implementing an extensive marketing strategy. In addition, the firm handles all aspects of trade advertising and public relations. Interested parties are invited to contact the firm's principal, Ronald M. Cardoos.

Northeast Center for Food Entrepreneurship (NECFE)
Cornell University
New York State Food Venture Center
Cornell University
NYS Agricultural Experiment Station
630 West North Street
Geneva, NY 14456
Call Cornell direct at 315-787-2274
e-mail NECFE at: necfe@nysaes.cornell.edu

The Resource Center provides access to information about:

✧ Available facilities

✧ Equipment for the food processing business

✧ Business and marketing basics

✧ Terms and definitions common in the food processing industry

✧ Regulatory information

✧ Links to trade groups and agencies associated with the food production industry

✧ NECFE business and marketing services

✧ NECFE product processing development services

NXLevel Training Network
800-873-9378

e-mail: info@nxlevel.org
Web site: http://www.nxlevel.org/

The NxLeveL Entrepreneurial Training Programs are practical, hands-on business development courses designed to help entrepreneurs advance their skills in starting growing and managing their business. NxLeveL classes are offered throughout the United States through the NxLeveL Training Network. The NxLeveL Training Network® is a group of organizations engaged in entrepreneurial training, the purpose of which is to develop the best training curriculums possible, and to share best practices among network partners, including effective operational, funding and management strategies.

Pennsylvania State University
Web site: http://foodsafety.cas.psu.edu/processor/resources.htm

This resource offers an extensive listing of links that can answer your questions about starting a food processing business.

Business Lists

Info USA, Inc.
5711 South 86th Circle
Omaha, NE 68127
402-331-7169
Web site: http://www.infousa.com

Business listings compiled from nationwide Yellow Pages.

Gourmet News
P.O. Box 1056
Yarmouth, ME 04096

207-846-0800
Web site: http://www.gourmetnews.com

Rents its extensive listing of specialty food decision makers.

Mail Order

Catalog Solutions
972-907-1464
e-mail: tony@catalogsolutions.net
Web site: http://www.Catalogsolutions.net

Catalog Solutions serves as an outsourced mail order and online marketing department for specialty food companies. "The 7 Habits of the Highly Ineffective Cataloger," available online. Subscribe to their Food by Mail Industry Updates via e-mail.

Nutritional Analysis

Lawrence-Allen Group NutriLABEL
2031 Fairmont Drive
San Mateo, CA 94402-3925
800-609-2909 or 650-345-2909
Fax: 650-345-9723
e-mail: info@nutrilabel.com
Web site: http://www.nutrilabel.com

Primary focus: Provides fast, low-cost services, including food-product nutritional analysis, camera-ready nutrition-facts panel art, FDA labeling compliance assistance, ingredient statement preparation, trademark research, and new specialty food product development and consulting services. This is a confidential service with more than 50 years' experience. Contact Larry Imes.

Strasburger & Seigel, Inc.
1229 National Drive
Hanover, MD 21076
800-875-6532 or 410-712-7373
Fax: 410-712-7378
Web site: http://www.sas-labs.com

Strasburger and Siegel is just one of many laboratories that offer competitively-priced analytical services, including microbiological and microanalytical services, consulting services (project design, product stability, and shelf-life evaluation, thermal process engineering, etc.), and customized product development services.

Produce Marketing

Sell What You Sow! The Grower's Guide to Successful Produce Marketing
New World Publishing
3085 Sheridan Street
Placerville, CA 95667
916-622-2248

Sell What You Sow! by Eric Gibson, is a guide to profitable produce marketing that covers marketing plans, research, crop selection, and selling through farmers' markets, restaurants, roadside markets, pick-your-own operations, and retail outlets. It is a comprehensive how-to book of high-value produce marketing.

Quality Issues

A couple of good sources for improving your knowledge of quality and productivity are:

The Deming Route to Quality and Productivity
by William W. Scherkenbach

CEEPress Books
George Washington University, 1992

The Memory Jogger II
by Michael Brassard and Diane Ritter
GOAL/QPC, 1994
800-643-4316
Web site: http://www.goalqpc.org

This is a pocket guide of tools for continuous improvement and effective planning.

Uniform Product Code

Uniform Code Council, Inc.
8163 Old Yankee Road, Suite J
Dayton, OH 45458
513-435-3870
Web site: http://www.uc-council.org
Contact: Harold P. Juckett, Executive Vice President

The Uniform Code Council is the central management and information center for manufacturers and retailers participating in the system. Current cost of registration is $300.

Women in the Food Industry

Office of Women's Business Ownership (OWBO)
1110 Vermont Street, NW
Washington, DC 20416
202-606-4000, 800-827-5722
Web site: http://www.sba.gov/womenin business

The Office of Women's Business Ownership is the primary advocate for the interests of women business owners and provides current and potential women business owners access to the following services and programs:

✧ Technical, financial, and management information

✧ Information about selling to the federal government

✧ Access to capital

✧ Women's Prequalification Loan Program

Online Women's Business Center
Web site: http://www.onlinewbc.gov

With over 60 centers nationwide, the Women's Business Centers program provides long-term training, counseling, networking, and mentoring to all types of potential and existing women entrepreneurs.

Other Government Organizations

Office of Minority Enterprise Development
202-205-6410
Web site: http://www.sba.gov/8abd

The main objective of this office is to foster business ownership by individuals who are socially and economically disadvantaged and to promote the competitive viability of such firms. The SBA has combined its efforts with those of private industry, banks, local communities, and other government agencies to meet these goals.

The following programs or services are offered:

✧ Management and technical assistance

✧ Section 8(a) Business Development Program certification

✧ Federal procurement opportunities

✧ Bonding

Council for Entrepreneurial Development
919-549-7500
Web site: http://www.cednc.org

CED provides educational courses, networking opportunities, mentoring, and capital formation resources for new and existing entrepreneurs.

Count Me In for Women's Economic Independence (Women and Money)
e-mail: Info@count-me-in.org
Web site: http://www.count-me-in.org

Count Me In for Women's Economic Independence is a national nonprofit organization that will raise money from women to be lent to women. Count Me In is a lending and learning organization dedicated to strengthening women's position in the economy. The concept is straightforward: millions of women across America will be asked—and inspired—to contribute a minimum of $5 to Count Me In to create a national loan fund for women. The money will be redistributed to qualifying women in the form of small business loans ranging from $500 to $10,000, and scholarships for business training and technical assistance.

Index

FREE SUPPLIER CD

A Complete Listing of Key Suppliers and Vendors to the Specialty Food Industry

To receive your free supplier CD, please go to our web site: http://www.specialtyfoodresource.com. Use the password: SUCCESS

Included are the following categories, plus much more:

- Specialty food trade associations
- Specialty food trade show sponsors/managers
- Co-packers
- Labeling materials
- Packaging materials
- Packing materials
- Transport (UPS, FedEx, USPS, etc.)
- Public relations agencies
- Advertising agencies
- Promotional materials preparers (catalog sheets, etc.)
- Printing services
- Legal services
- Accounting services
- Small business services
- Telephone
- Cellphone
- Computers
- Software
- Internet services
- Web site design
- ASP's
- Educational institutions
- Importing agencies
- Small Business Development Centers, SCORE, Micro lending institutions
- Warehousing services

Contents

Vice President and Publisher: Cynthia A. Zigmund
Acquisitions Editor: Jonathan Malysiak
Senior Managing Editor: Jack Kiburz
Interior Design: Eliot House Productions
Cover Design: Studio Montage

Published by Kaplan Publishing,
a division of Kaplan, Inc.

Library of Congress Cataloging-in-Publication Data
Hall, Stephen F.
   From kitchen to market : selling your gourmet food specialty /
Stephen F. Hall.— 4th ed.
      p.   cm.
   Includes bibliographical references and index.
   ISBN 0-7931-9997-2 (pbk.)
   1. Food industry and trade—United States. 2. Food service—United
States. I. Title.
   HD9004.H25 2005
   664'.0068'8—dc22
                                          2004028756

For information about ordering Kaplan Publishing books at special quantity discounts, please call 1-800-KAP-ITEM or write to Kaplan Publishing, 888 Seventh Avenue, 22nd floor, New York, NY 10106.

4th
Edition

from Kitchen to Market

Selling Your Gourmet Food Specialty

Stephen F. Hall

KAPLAN) PUBLISHING

through more specialized channels such as health food stores, C-stores, and nearby deli's and local grocery stores. In such cases you will absolutely need this book and find it saves you serious bucks and a lot of questions posed to distributors, health officials, and your suppliers. I know, because I spent months researching the options and not finding half the information that this book so succinctly provides. Note: I had so little success finding the information that I chose to team up with a businessman and I became vice president of Billy Bob's Pot Pies in Canby, Oregon. The ill-fated franchise attempt resulted in me returning to work in the Middle East so I could save enough bucks to start producing my meat pies for specialty markets."

—CHARLES W. ANDERSON

"Practical and strategic I use *From Kitchen to Market* as the text for a weekend class that I teach through University of California, Davis Extension, Getting Started in the Specialty Food Business. Hall's book is excellent; it is practical, not obtuse. He gets to the nitty-gritty of how to develop and launch a product. He also emphasizes the need to be market-oriented. You won't be guaranteed success just because you make a great-tasting product; Hall discusses how you need to package, market, and distribute your product effectively."

—SHERMAIN D. HARDESTY, PH.D., UNIVERSITY OF CALIFORNIA, DAVIS

Praise for Previous Editions

"How many of us have toyed with the idea of selling our favorite family recipes? The growing number of specialty food products on the market strongly suggests that people are doing more than just toying with the idea. Hall, a food industry consultant, has created a thorough guide to food marketing that is sure to help food entrepreneurs at all levels, from the rank beginner to the most experienced. Hall clearly points out possible pitfalls and concerns as he takes the reader step by step through the entire marketing process, offering guidelines on market research, packaging, pricing, and advertising. Interesting vignettes on actual successes and failures allow a realistic view of possible scenarios. The appendixes, which make up a good portion of the book and list trade shows, journals, associations, sample forms, and so forth, are a terrific quick resource that significantly enhance this already strong and well-written guide. Strongly recommended for public and academic libraries."

—LIBRARY JOURNAL, MARGARET B. BARTLETT, ROCHESTER INSTITUTE OF TECHNOLOGY, NY.
COPYRIGHT 1992 REED BUSINESS INFORMATION, INC.

"An absolute must for aspiring food wholesalers! Having owned a specialty-food store, and having developed a unique food product that distributors were interested in marketing through convenience and other specialty food stores (including McDonald's Express), I can attest to the accuracy of most of this book. If you are already producing a great-tasting product in a restaurant or deli and making a living, you probably are wise to concentrate on expanding your retail business. If, however, you are tiring of the daily grind of running a small retail business, but wish to concentrate on producing your product rather than serving it to the public, then you probably have considered wholesaling. Your wholesaling options are numerous. For marketing through supermarkets I advise you to thoroughly read Packaged Facts' book, *How to Get Your Product into Supermarkets*. First, though, you should try marketing

Praise for Previous Editions

"I think you've got the definitive book on the industry."

—MARTHA FURST, TERRAPIN RIDGE

"I was struck by so many positives: the clarity of your writing; the wisdom of your advice; and the practical tools you offer. So many times I am involved in a conversation that starts something like this: "My wife is a great cook, and we'd like to market her specialties!" Now I'll have your book at my fingertips to more comprehensively be a guide."

—MARY LOU BESSETTE, DIRECTOR, BUSINESS OWNER ON CAMPUS, ARIZONA STATE UNIVERSITY COLLEGE OF BUSINESS

"Stephen F. Hall's *From Kitchen to Market* is an exceptional title that tells exactly how aspiring cooks can turn an original product into a moneymaker."

—JAMES A. COX, EDITOR-IN-CHIEF, THE MIDWEST BOOK REVIEW

"*From Kitchen to Market* makes it easy to get a wealth of information in the way it is presented."

—LISA BOSTWICK, CHOCOLATE MANUFACTURER

"Regarding the 'demo' advice in your book—I have been to a couple of herb shows, and by demos, I sold more than I ever dreamed!"

—DONITA CHRIS, SAVORY SPECIALTIES

"Learn the secrets of successfully launching a gourmet food product in the $30 billion specialty food marketplace. *From Kitchen to Market* delivers proven strategies for successful packaging, pricing, positioning, and promotion. You'll get 'inside' industry tips to maximize product exposure and profits."

—INGRAM BOOK COMPANY